THE GENERALL HISTORIE

of

Virgina, New England, & The Summer Isles

Together with

The True Travels, Adventures, and Obſervations of CAPTAINE JOHN SMITH

VOLUME II

THE GENERALL HISTORIE

of

Virgina, New England, & The Summer Isles

Together with

The True Travels, Adventures, and Obſervations of CAPTAINE JOHN SMITH

VOLUME II

APPLEWOOD BOOKS
Bedford, Massachusetts

The Generall Historie of Virgina, New England, & The Summer Isles was originally printed in 1629.

The True Travels, Adventures, and Observations of Captaine John Smith was originally printed in 1630.

Thank you for purchasing an Applewood book. Applewood reprints America's lively classics–books from the past that are still of interest to modern readers. For a free copy of our current catalog, write to:

Applewood Books
PO Box 365
Bedford, MA 01730

ISBN 1-55709-363-6

THE TABLE

The Contents of the generall History—*Continued.*

THE SIXT BOOKE.

THE TABLE

The Contents of the generall History—*Continued.* PAGE

THE TABLE

The Contents of the generall History—*Continued.* PAGE

Its not his part that is the best Translator,
To render word for word to every Author.

CHAP. I.

CHAP. II.

CHAP. III.

THE TABLE

The Contents of the True Travels—*Continued.* PAGE

THE TABLE

The Contents of the True Travels—*Continued.* PAGE

THE TABLE

The Contents of the True Travels—*Continued.* PAGE

THE TABLE

The Contents of the True Travels—*Continued.* PAGE

THE TABLE

The Contents of 'A Sea Grammar'—*Continued.* PAGE

The Contents of 'A Sea Grammar'—*Continued.*

ILLUSTRATIONS

PANEGYRICK VERSES.

To his friend Captaine Smith, upon his description of New-England.

SIr; your Relations I have read: which shew,
Ther's reason I should honour them and you:
And if their meaning I have understood,
I dare to censure thus: Your Project's good;
And may (if follow'd) doubtlesse quit the paine,
With honour, pleasure and a trebble gaine;
Beside the benefit that shall arise
To make more happy our Posterities.
  For would we daigne to spare, though 'twere no more
Then what ore-fils, and surfets us in store,
To order Nature's fruitfulnesse a while
In that rude Garden, you New-England stile;
With present good, ther's hope in after-daies
Thence to repaire what Time and Pride decaies
In this rich Kingdome. And the spacious West
Being still more with English bloud possest,
The proud Iberians shall not rule those Seas,
To checke our ships from sailing where they please;
Nor future times make any forraine power
Become so great to force a bound to Our.
  Much good my minde foretels would follow hence
With little labour, and with lesse expence.
Thrive therefore thy Designe, who ere envy:
England may joy in England's Colony,

Virginia seeke her Virgin sisters good,
Be blessed in such happy neighbourhood:
  Or whatsoere Fate pleaseth to permit,
  Be thou still honour'd for first moving it.

George Wither, è societate Lincol.

To that worthy and generous Gentleman, my very good friend, Captaine Smith.

MAy Fate thy Project prosper, that thy name
May be eternized with living fame:
Though foule Detraction Honour would pervert,
And Envie ever waits upon desert:
In spight of Pelias, when his hate lies cold,
Returne as Jason with a fleece of gold.
  Then after-ages shall record thy praise,
  That a New-England to this Ile didst raise:
And when thou di'st (as all that live must die)
Thy fame live here; thou, with Eternity.

R. Gunnell.

To his worthy Captaine, the Author.

OFt thou hast led, when I brought up the Rere
In bloudy wars, where thousands have beene slaine.
Then give me leave in this some part to beare;
And as thy servant, here to reade my name.
  Tis true, long time thou hast my Captaine beene
In the fierce warres of Transilvania:
  Long ere that thou America hadst seene,
Or led wast captiv'd in Virginia;
  Thou that to passe the worlds foure parts dost deeme
No more, then t'were to goe to bed, or drinke,
  And all thou yet hast done, thou dost esteeme
As nothing. This doth cause me thinke
  That thou I'ave seene so oft approv'd in dangers,

(And thrice captiv'd, thy valour still hath freed)
  Art yet preserved, to convert those strangers:
By God thy guide I trust it is decreed.
    For me: I not commend but much admire
    Thy England yet unknowne to passers by-her.
    For it will praise it selfe in spight of me;
    Thou it, it thou, to all posterity.

Your true friend and souldier, Ed. Robinson.

To my honest Captaine, the Author.

MAlignant Times! What can be said or done,
  But shall be censur'd and traduc't by some!
  This worthy Worke, which thou hast bought so deare,
  Ne thou, nor it, Detractors need to feare.
Thy words by deeds so long thou hast approv'd,
Of thousands know thee not thou art belov'd.
  And this great Plot will make thee ten times more
  Knowne and belov'd, than ere thou wert before.
I never knew a Warrier yet, but thee,
From wine, Tobacco, debts, dice, oaths, so free.
  I call thee Warrier: and I make the bolder;
  For, many a Captaine now, was never Souldier.
Some such may swell at this: but (to their praise)
When they have done like thee, my Muse shall raise
  Their due deserts to Worthies yet to come,
  To live like thine (admir'd) till day of Doome.

Your true friend, sometimes your souldier,
Tho. Carlton.

THE SECOND VOLUME

CONTAINING

The Sixth Booke of the Generall Historie of Virginia, New England, and The Summer Isles ; together with the True Travels, Adventures and Observations, and A Sea Grammar

The Generall Historie of New-England.

Concerning this History you are to understand the Letters-Patents granted by his Majesty in 1606. for the limitation of Virginia, did extend from 34. to 44. which was divided in two parts; namely, the first Colony and the second: the first was to the honourable City of London, and such as would adventure with them to discover and take their choice where they would, betwixt the degrees of 34. and 41. The second was appropriated to the Cities of Bristol, Exeter and Plimoth, &c. and the West parts of England, and all those that would adventure and joine with them, and they might make their choise any where betwixt the degrees of 38. and 44. provided there should bee at least 100. miles distance betwixt these 2 Colonies, each of which had lawes, privileges and authoritie, for the government and advancing their severall Plantations alike. Now this part of America hath formerly beene called Norumbega, Virginia, Nuskoncus, Penaquida, Cannada, and such other names as those that ranged the Coast pleased. But because it was so mountainous, rocky and full of Iles, few have adventured much to trouble it, but as is formerly related; notwithstanding, that honourable Patron of vertue, Sir John Popham, Lord chiefe Justice of England, in the yeere 1606. procured meanes and men to possesse it, and sent Captaine George Popham for President, Captaine Rawley Gilbert for Admirall, Captaine Edward Harlow master of the Ordnance, Captaine Robert Davis Sargeant-Major, Captaine Elis Best Marshall, Master Seaman Secretary, Captaine James Davis to be Captaine of the Fort, Master Gome Carew chiefe Searcher: all those were of the Councell, who with some hundred more were to stay in the Country: they set saile from Plimoth the last of May, and fell with Monahigan the eleventh of August. At Sagadahock 9. or 10. leagues southward, they planted themselves at the mouth of a faire navigable River, but the coast all thereabouts most extreme stony and rocky: that extreme frozen Winter was so cold they could not range nor search the Country, and their provision so small, they were glad to send all but 45. of their company backe againe: their noble President Captaine Popham died, and not long after arrived two ships well provided of all necessaries to supply them, and some small time after another, by whom under-

Sir Francis Popham Treasurer.

[VI. 204.] standing of the death of the Lord chiefe Justice, and also of Sir John Gilbert, whose lands there the President Rawley Gilbert was to possesse according to the adventurers directions, finding nothing but extreme extremities, they all returned for England in the yeere 1608. and thus this Plantation was begunne and ended in one yeere, and the Country esteemed as a cold, barren, mountainous, rocky Desart.

Notwithstanding, the right Honourable Henry Earle of South-hampton and those of the Ile of Wight, imploied Captaine Edward Harlow to discover an Ile supposed about Cape Cod, but they found their plots had much abused them, for falling with Monahigan, they found onely Cape Cod no Ile but the maine, there they detained three Salvages aboord them; called Pechmo, Monopet and Pekenimne, but Pechmo leapt over board, and got away; and not long after with his consorts cut their Boat from their sterne, got her on shore, and so filled her with sand, and guarded her with Bowes and Arrowes the English lost her: not farre from thence they had three men sorely wounded with Arrowes. Anchoring at the Ile of Nohono, the Salvages in their Canowes assaulted the Ship till the English Guns made them retire, yet here they tooke Sakaweston, that after he had lived many yeeres in England went a Souldier to the warres of Bohemia. At Capawe they tooke Coneconam and Epenow, but the people at Agawom used them kindly, so with five Salvages they returned for England, yet Sir Francis Popham sent divers times one Captaine Williams to Monahigan onely to trade and make core fish, but for any Plantations there was no more speeches. For all this, as I liked Virginia well, though not their proceedings, so I desired also to see this country, and spend some time in trying what I could finde for all those ill rumors and disasters.

From the relations of Captaine Edward Harlow and divers others.

My first voyage to New England. 1614.

In the month of Aprill 1614. at the charge of Capt. Marmaduke Roydon, Capt. George Langam, Mr. John Buley and Mr. William Skelton, with two ships from London, I chanced to arrive at Monahigan an Ile of America, in 434. of Northerly latitude; our plot was there to take Whales, for which we had one Samuel Cramton and divers others expert in that faculty, & also to make trialls of a Mine of gold & copper; if those failed, Fish and Furs were then our refuge to make our selves savers howsoever: we found this Whale-fishing a costly conclusion, we saw many and spent much time in chasing them, but could not kill any. They being a kinde of Jubartes, and not the Whale that yeelds Fins and Oile as we expected; for our gold it was rather the Masters device to get a voyage that projected it, then any knowledge he had at all of any such matter; Fish and Furs were now our guard, & by our late arrivall and long lingring about the Whale, the prime of both those seasons were past ere wee perceived it, wee thinking that their seasons served at all times, but we found it otherwise, for by the middest of June the fishing failed, yet in July and August some were taken, but not sufficient to defray so great a charge as our stay required: of dry fish we made about forty thousand, of Cor-fish about seven thousand. Whilest the Sailers fished, my selfe with eight others of them might best bee spared, ranging the Coast in a small Boat, we got for trifles neere eleven thousand Bever skinnes, one hundred Martins, as many Otters, and the most of them within the distance of twenty leagues: we ranged the Coast both East and West much further, but Eastward our commodities were not esteemed, they were so neere the French who afforded them better, with whom the Salvages had such commerce that only by trade they made exceeding great voyages, though they were without the limits of our precincts; during the time we tried those conclusions, not knowing the coast, nor Salvages habitations: with these Furres, the traine Oile and Cor-fish, I returned for England in the Barke, where within six moneths after our departure from the Downes, wee safely arrived backe; the best of this fish was sold for 5. li. the hundred, the rest by ill usage betwixt three pounds and 50. shillings. The other ship stayed to fit her selfe for Spaine with the dry fish which was sold at Maligo at forty Rialls the Quintall, each hundred weighing two quintals and a halfe. But one Thomas Hunt the Master of this ship (when I was gone) thinking to prevent that intent I had to make there a Plantation, thereby to keepe this abounding Countrey still in obscuritie, that onely he and some few Merchants more might enjoy wholly the benefit of the Trade, and profit of this Countrey, betraied foure and twenty of those poore Salvages aboord his ship, and most dishonestly and inhumanely for their kinde usage of me and all our men, caried them with him to Maligo, and there for a little private gaine sold those silly Salvages

The commodities I got amounted to 1500. pounds.

[VI. 205.]

The trechery of Master Hunt.

for Rials of eight; but this vilde act kept him ever after from any more imploiment to those parts. Now because at this time I had taken a draught of the Coast, and called it New England, yet so long he and his Consorts drowned that name with the Eccho of Cannaday, and some other ships from other parts also, that upon this good returne the next yeere went thither, that at last I presented this Discourse with the Map, to our most gracious Prince Charles, humbly intreating his Highnesse hee would please to change their barbarous names for such English, as posteritie might say Prince Charles was their God-father, which for your better understanding both of this Discourse and the Map, peruse this Schedule, which will plainly shew you the correspondency of the old names to the new, as his Highnesse named them.

How Prince Charles called the most remarkable places in New England.

The old names.	The new names.
Cape Cod.	Cape James.
The Harbor at Cape Cod.	Milforth Haven.
Chawum.	Barwick.
Accomack.	Plimoth.
Sagoquas.	Oxford.
Massachusets Mount.	Chevit hills.
Massachusits River.	Charles River.
Totan.	Famouth.
A great bay by Cape Anne.	Bristow.
Cape Tragabigsanda.	Cape Anne.
Naembeck.	Bastable.
Aggawom.	Southampton.
Smiths Iles.	Smiths Iles.
Passataquack.	Hull.
Accominticus.	Boston.
Sassanows Mount.	Snowdon hill.
Sowocatuck.	Ipswich.
Bahanna.	Dartmouth.
A good Harbor within that Bay.	Sandwich.
Ancociscos Mount.	Shuters hill.
Ancocisco.	The Base.

The old names.	The new names.
Anmoughcawgen.	Cambridge.
Kenebecka.	Edenborow.
Sagadahock.	Leth.
Pemmayquid.	S. Johns towne.
Segocket.	Norwich.
Mecadacut.	Dunbarton.
Pennobscot.	Aberden.
Nusket.	Low mounds.

Those being omitted I named my selfe.

Monahigan.	Barties Iles.
Matinack.	Willowbies Iles.
Metinacus.	Haughtons Iles.

The rest of the names in the Map, are places that had no names we did know.

Aspersions against New England.

But to continue the History succeedingly as neere with the day and yeere as may bee. Returning in the Barke as is said; it was my ill chance to put in at Plimoth, where imparting those my purposes to divers I thought my friends, whom as I supposed were interested in the dead Patent of this unregarded Countrey, I was so encouraged and assured to have the managing their authoritie in those parts during my life, and such large promises, that I ingaged my selfe to undertake it for them. Arriving at London, though some malicious persons suggested there was no such matter to be had in that so bad abandoned Countrey, for if there had, other could have found it so well as I; therefore it was to be suspected I had robbed the French men in New France or Cannada, and the Merchants set me forth seemed not to regard it, yet I found so many promised me such assistance, that I entertained Michael Cooper the Master of the Barke, that returned with me and others of the Company: how he dealt with others, or others with him, I know not; but my publike proceeding gave such encouragement, that it became so well apprehended by some few of the Virginia Company, as those projects for fishing onely was so well liked, they furnished Couper with foure good ships to Sea, before they at Plimoth had made any provision at all for me; but onely a small Barke set out by them of the Ile of Wight. Some of Plimoth, and divers Gentlemen of the West Countrey, a little before I returned from New England, in search for a Mine of Gold about an Ile called Capawuck, Southwards from the Shoules of Cape James, as they were informed by a Salvage called Epenew; that having deluded them as it seems thus to get home, seeing they kept him as a prisoner in his owne Countrey, and before his friends, being a man of so great a stature, he was shewed up and downe London for money as a wonder, and it seemes of no lesse courage and authoritie, then of wit, strength, and proportion: for so well he had contrived his businesse, as many reported he intended to have surprised the ship; but seeing it could not be effected to his liking, before them all he leaped over-boord. Many shot they made at him, thinking they had slaine him, but so resolute they were to recover his body, the master of the ship was wounded, and many of his company; And thus they lost him, & not knowing more what to do, returned againe to England with nothing, which so had discouraged all your West Countrey men, they neither regarded much their promises, and as little either me or the Countrey, till they saw the London ships gone and me in Plimoth according to my promise, as hereafter shall be related. [VI. 206.]

Captaine Hobson his voiage to Capawuk.

I must confesse I was beholden to the setters forth of the foure ships that went with Couper, in that they offered me that imploiment if I would accept it; and I finde still my refusall incurred some of their displeasures, whose love and favour I exceedingly desired; and though they doe censure me opposite to their proceedings, they shall yet still in all my words and deeds finde, it is their error, not my fault that occasions their dislike: for having ingaged my selfe in this businesse to the West Countrey,

The Londoners send foure good ships to New England.

I had beene very dishonest to have broke my promise, nor will I spend more time in discovery or fishing, till I may goe with a Company for a Plantation; for I know my grounds, yet every one to whom I tell them, or that reads this Booke, cannot put it in practise, though it may helpe any that hath seene or not seene to know much of those parts: And though they endevour to worke me out of my owne designes, I will not much envy their fortunes: but I would be sorry their intruding ignorance should by their defailments bring those certainties to doubtfulnesse. So that the businesse prosper I have my desire, be it by whomsoever that are true subjects to our King and Countrey: the good of my Countrey is that I seeke, and there is more then enough for all, if they could be contented.

The situation of New England.

New England is that part of America in the Ocean Sea, opposite to Nova Albion in the South Sea, discovered by the most memorable Sir Francis Drake in his Voyage about the world, in regard whereof this is stiled New England, being in the same latitude New France of it is Northwards, Southwards is Virginia, and all the adjoyning continent with new Granado, new Spaine, new Andolosia, and the West-Indies. Now because I have beene so oft asked such strange questions of the goodnesse and greatnesse of those spatious Tracts of Land, how they can be thus long unknowne, or not possessed by the Spaniards, and many such like demands: I intreat your pardons if I chance to be too plaine or tedious in relating my knowledge for plaine mens satisfaction.

Notes of Florida.

Florida is the next adjoyning to the Indies, which unprosperously was attempted to be planted by the French, a Countrey farre bigger then England, Scotland, France and Ireland, yet little knowne to any Christian, but by the wonderfull endevours of Ferdinando de Soto, a valiant Spaniard, whose writings in this age is the best guide knowne to search those parts.

Notes of Virginia.

Virginia is no Ile as many doe imagine, but part of the Continent adjoyning to Florida, whose bounds may be stretched to the magnitude thereof, without offence to any Christian Inhabitant, for from the degrees of thirtie to forty eight, his Majesty hath now enlarged his Letters Patents. The Coast extending South-west and [VI. 207.] North-east about sixteene or seventeene hundred miles, but to follow it aboord the shore may well be three thousand miles at the least: of which twentie miles is the most gives entrance into the Bay of Chisapeacke, where is the London Plantation, within which is a Countrey, as you may perceive by the Map, of that little I discovered, may well suffice three hundred thousand people to inhabit: but of it, and the discoveries of Sir Ralph Laine and Master Heriot, Captaine Gosnold, and Captaine Waymouth, they have writ so largely, that posteritie may be bettered by the fruits of their labours. But for divers others that have ranged those parts since, especially this Countrey now called New England, within a kenning sometimes of the shore; some touching in one place, some in another; I must intreat them pardon me for omitting them, or if I offend in saying, that their true descriptions were concealed, or never were well observed, or died with the Authors, so that the Coast is yet still but even as a Coast unknowne and undiscovered. I have had six or seven severall plots of those Northerne parts, so unlike each to other, or resemblance of the Country, as they did me no more good then so much waste paper, though they cost me more, it may bee it was not my chance to see the best; but lest others may be deceived as I was, or through dangerous ignorance hazard themselves as I did, I have drawne a Map from point to point, Ile to Ile, and Harbour to Harbour, with the Soundings, Sands, Rocks, and Land-markes, as I passed close aboord the shore in a little Boat; although there bee many things to bee observed, which the haste of other affaires did cause me to omit: for being sent more to get present Commodities, then knowledge of any discoveries for any future good, I had not power to search as I would; yet it will serve to direct any shall goe that waies to safe Harbours and the Salvages habitations: what Merchandize and Commodities for their labours they may finde, this following discourse shall plainly demonstrate.

Observations for presumtuous ignorant directors.

Thus you may see of these three thousand miles, more then halfe is yet unknowne to any purpose, no not so much as the borders of the Sea are yet certainly discovered: as for the goodnesse and true substance of the Land, we are for most part yet altogether ignorant of them, unlesse it be those parts about the Bay of Chisapeack and Sagadahock, but onely here and there where we have touched or seene a little, the edges of those large Dominions which doe stretch themselves into the maine, God doth know how many thousand miles, whereof we can yet no more judge, then a stranger that saileth betwixt England and France, can describe the harbours and dangers by landing here or there in some River or Bay, tell thereby the goodnesse and substance of Spaine, Italy, Germany, Bohemia, Hungaria, and the rest; nay, there are many have lived fortie yeeres in London, and yet have scarce beene ten miles out of the Citie: so are there many have beene in Virginia many yeeres, and in New England many times, that doe know little more then the place they doe inhabit, or the Port where they fished, and when they come home, they will undertake they know all Virginia and New England, as if they were but two Parishes or little Ilands. By this you may perceive how much they erre, that thinke every one that hath beene in Virginia or New England, understandeth or knoweth what either of them are; Or that the Spaniards know one halfe quarter of those large Territories they possesse, no not so much as the true circumference of Terra incognita, whose large Dominions may equalize the goodnesse and greatnesse of America for any thing yet knowne. It is strange with what small power he doth range in the East-Indies, and few will understand the truth of his strength in America: where having so much to keepe with such a pampered force, they need not greatly feare his fury in Sommer Iles, Virginia, or New England, beyond whose bounds America doth stretch many thousand miles. Into the frozen parts whereof, one Master Hutson an English Mariner, did make the greatest discoverie of any Christian I know, where hee unfortunately was left by his cowardly Company, for his exceeding deserts, to end and die a most miserable death.

For Affrica, had not the industrious Portugals ranged [VI. 208.] her unknowne parts, who would have sought for wealth amongst those fried Regions of blacke brutish Negars, where notwithstanding all their wealth and admirable adventures and endevours more then one hundred and fortie yeeres, they know not one third part of those blacke habitations. But it is not a worke for every one to manage such an affaire, as make a discovery and plant a Colony, it requires all the best parts of art, judgement, courage, honesty, constancy, diligence, and industry, to doe but neere well; some are more proper for one thing then another, and therein best to be imploied: and nothing breeds more confusion then misplacing and misimploying men in their undertakings. Columbus, Courtes, Pitzara, Zoto, Magilanus, and the rest served more then a Prentiship, to learne how to begin their most memorable attempts in the West-Indies, which to the wonder of all ages successefully they effected, when many hundreds of others farre above them in the worlds opinion, being instructed but by relation, came to shame and confusion in actions of small moment, who doubtlesse in other matters were both wise, discreet, generous and couragious. I say not this to detract any thing from their incomparable merits, but to answer those questionlesse questions, that keepe us backe from imitating the worthinesse of their brave spirits, that advanced themselves from poore Souldiers to great Captaines, their posterity to great Lords, their King to be one of the greatest Potentates on earth, and the fruits of their labours his greatest power, glory and renowne.

The Description of New England.

THat part we call New England, is betwixt the degrees of fortie one and fortie five, the very meane betwixt the North pole and the line; but that part this Discourse speaketh of, stretcheth but from Penobscot to Cape Cod, some seventie five leagues by a right line distant each from other; within which bounds I have seene at least fortie severall habitations upon the Sea Coast, and sounded about five and twentie excellent good Harbours, in many whereof there is anchorage for five hundred saile of ships of any burden; in some of them for one thousand, and more then two hundred Iles over-growne with good Timber of divers sorts of wood, which doe make so many Harbours, as required a longer time then I had to be well observed.

The principall Countries or governments.

The principall habitation Northward we were at, was Pennobscot: Southward along the Coast and up the Rivers, we found Mecadacut, Segocket, Pemaquid, Nuscoucus, Sagadahock, Avmoughcowgen, and Kenebeke; and to those Countries belong the people of Segotago, Paghhuntanuck, Pecopassum, Taughtanakagnet, Warbigganus, Nassaque, Masherosqueck, Wawrigweck, Moshoquen, Wakcogo, Pasharanack, &c. To these are alied in confederacy, the Countries of Ancocisco, Accomynticus, Passataquack, Aggawom, and Naemkeck: All these for any thing I could perceive, differ little in language, fashion, or government, though most of them be Lords of themselves, yet they hold the Bashabes of Penobscot, the chiefe and greatest amongst them.

The next I can remember by name, are Mattahunts, two pleasant Iles of Groves, Gardens, and Corne fields a league in the Sea from the maine: Then Totant, Massachuset, Topent, Secassaw, Totheet, Nasrocomacack, Accomack, Chawum, Patuxet, Massasoyts, Pakanokick: then Cape Cod, by which is Pawmet and the Ile Nawset, of the language and aliance of them of Chawum; the others are called Massachusets, and differ somewhat in language, custome, and condition: for their Trade and Merchandize, to each of their principall families or habitations, they have divers Townes and people belonging, and by their relations and descriptions, more then twentie severall habitations and rivers that stretch themselves farre into the Countrey, even to the Borders of divers great Lakes, where they kill and take most of their Otters, from Pennobscot to Sagadahoc. This Coast is mountainous, [VI. 209.] and Iles of huge Rockes, but over-growne for most part, with most sorts of excellent good woods, for building Houses, Boats, Barks or Ships, with an incredible abundance of most sorts of Fish, much Fowle, and sundry sorts of good Fruits for mans use.

Betwixt Sagadahock, & Sowocatuck, there is but two or three Sandy Bayes, but betwixt that and Cape James very many: especially the Coast of the Massachusets is so indifferently mixed with high Clay or Sandy clifts in one place, and the tracts of large long ledges of divers sorts, and Quaries of stones in other places, so strangely divided with tinctured veines of divers colours: as Freestone for building, Slate for tyling, smooth stone to make Furnasses and Forges for Glasse and Iron, and Iron Ore sufficient conveniently to melt in them; but the most part so resembleth the Coast of Devonshire, I thinke most of the clifts would make such Lime-stone: if they bee not of these qualities, they are so like they may deceive a better judgement then mine: all which are so neere adjoyning to those other advantages I observed in these parts, that if the Ore prove as good Iron and Steele in those parts as I know it is within the bounds of the Countrey, I dare ingage my head (having but men skilfull to worke the Simples there growing) to have all things belonging to the building and rigging of ships of any proportion and good Merchandise for their fraught, within a square of ten or foureteene leagues, and it were no hard matter to prove it within a lesse limitation.

A proofe of an excellent clime.

And surely by reason of those sandy clifts, and clifts of rocks, both which we saw so planted with Gardens and Corne fields, and so well inhabited with a goodly, strong, and well proportioned people, besides the greatnesse of the Timber growing on them, the greatnesse of the Fish, and the moderate temper of the aire (for of five and forty not a man was sicke, but two that were many yeares diseased before they went, notwithstanding our bad lodging and accidentall diet) who can but approve this a most excellent place, both for health and fertilitie: and of all the foure parts of the world I have yet seene not inhabited, could I have but means to transport a Colony, I would rather live here then any where, and if it did not maintaine it selfe, were we but once indifferently well fitted, let us starve.

Staple Commodities present.

The maine staple from hence to bee extracted for the present, to produce the rest, is Fish, which howbeit may seeme a meane and a base Commoditie; yet who will but truly take the paines and consider the sequell, I thinke will allow it well worth the labour. It is strange to see, what great adventures the hopes of setting forth men of warre to rob the industrious innocent would procure, or such massie promises in grosse, though more are choaked then well fed with such hastie hopes. But who doth not know that the poore Hollanders chiefely by fishing at a great charge and labour in all weathers in the open Sea, are made a people so hardy and industrious, and by the venting this poore Commoditie to the Easterlings for as meane, which is Wood, Flax, Pitch, Tarre, Rozen, Cordage, and such like; which they exchange againe to the French, Spaniards, Portugals, and English, &c. for what they want, are made so mighty, strong, and rich, as no state but Venice of twice their magnitude is so well furnished, with so many faire Cities, goodly Townes, strong Fortresses, and that abundance of shipping, and all sorts of Merchandize, as well of Gold, Silver, Pearles, Diamonds, pretious Stones, Silkes, Velvets, and Cloth of Gold; as Fish, Pitch, Wood, or such grosse Commodities? What voiages and discoveries, East and West, North and South, yea about the world, make they? What an Army

Observations of the Hollanders.

by Sea and Land have they long maintained, in despight of one of the greatest Princes of the world, and never could the Spaniard with all his Mines of Gold and Silver, pay his debts, his friends, and Army, halfe so truly as the Hollanders still have done by this contemptible Trade of Fish. Divers (I know) may alleage many other assistances; but this is the chiefest Mine, and the Sea [VI. 210.] the source of those silver streames of all their vertue, which hath made them now the very miracle of industry, the onely paterne of perfection for these affaires: and the benefit of fishing is that Primum Mobile that turnes all their spheares to this height, of plentie, strength, honor, and exceeding great admiration.

Note. Herring, Cod, and Ling, is that triplicitie, that makes their wealth and shippings multiplicitie such as it is: and from which (few would thinke it) they should draw so many millions yeerely as they doe, as more in particular in the trials of New England you may see; and such an incredible number of ships, that breeds them so many Sailers, Mariners, Souldiers, and Merchants, never to be wrought out of that Trade, and fit for any other. I will not deny but others may gaine as well as they that will use it, though not so certainly, nor so much in quantitie, for want of experience: and this Herring they take upon the Coast of England and Scotland, their Cod and Ling upon the Coast of Izeland, and in the North seas, if wee consider what gaines the Hamburgans, the Biskinners, and French make by fishing; nay, but how many thousands this fiftie or sixty yeeres have beene maintained by New found land, where they take nothing but small Cod, where of the greatest they make Cor-fish, and the rest is hard dried, which we call Poore-John, would amaze a man with wonder. If then from all those parts such paines is taken for this poore gaines of Fish, especially by the Hollanders, that hath but little of their owne, for building of ships and setting them to sea; but at the second, third, fourth, or fift hand, drawne from so many parts of the world ere they come together to be used in those voiages:

If these (I say) can gaine, why should we more doubt then they; but doe much better, that may have most of all those things at our doores for taking and making, and here are no hard Landlords to racke us with high rents, or extorting fines, nor tedious pleas in Law to consume us with their many yeeres disputation for Justice; no multitudes to occasion such impediments to good orders as in popular States: so freely hath God and his Majestie bestowed those blessings, on them will attempt to obtaine them, as here every man may be master of his owne labour and land, or the greatest part (if his Majesties royall meaning be not abused) and if he have nothing but his hands, he may set up his Trade; and by industry quickly grow rich, spending but halfe that time well, which in England we abuse in idlenesse, worse, or as ill. Here is ground as good as any lieth in the height of forty one, forty two, forty three, &c. which is as temperate, and as fruitfull as any other parallel in the world.

Note.

Examples of the Altitude comparatively.

As for example, on this side the line, West of it in the South Sea, is Nova Albion, discovered as is said by Sir Francis Drake: East from it is the most temperate part of Portugall, the ancient Kingdomes of Galizia, Bisky, Navarre, Aragon, Cattilonia, Castillia the old, and the most moderatest of Castillia the new & Valentia, which is the greatest part of Spaine; which if the Histories be true, in the Romans time abounded no lesse with gold & silver Mines, then now the West-Indies, the Romans then using the Spaniards to worke in those Mines, as now the Spaniards doe the Indians. In France the Provinces of Gascony, Langadocke, Avignon, Province, Dolphine, Pyamont, and Turyne, are in the same parallel, which are the best and richest parts of France. In Italy the Provinces of Genua, Lumbardy, and Verona, with a great part of the most famous state of Venice, the Dukedomes of Bononia, Mantua, Ferrara, Ravenna, Bolognia, Florence, Pisa, Sienna, Urbine, Ancona, and the ancient Citie and Countrey of Rome, with a great part of the

In Spaine.

In France.

Kingdome of Naples. In Slavonia, Istria, and Dalmatia, with the Kingdomes of Albania. In Grecia those famous Kingdomes of Macedonia, Bullulgaria, Thessalia, Thracia, or Romania, where is seated the most pleasant and plentifull Citie in Europe, Constantinople. *In Greece.*

In Asia in the same latitude, are the temperatest parts of Natolia, Armenia, Persia, and China; besides divers other large Countries and Kingdomes in those most milde and temperate Regions of Asia. Southward in the same height is the richest of Gold Mines, Chily, and Baldinia, and the mouth of the great River of Plate, &c. for all the rest of the world in that height is yet unknowne. Besides these reasons, mine owne eies that have seene a great part of those Cities and their Kingdomes (as well as it) can finde no advantage they have in Nature but this, they are beautified by the long labour and diligence of industrious people and art; This is onely as God made it when hee created the world: Therefore I conclude, if the heart and intrailes of those Regions were sought, if their Land were cultured, planted, and manured by men of industry, judgement, and experience; what hope is there, or what need they doubt, having the advantages of the Sea, but it might equalize any of these famous Kingdomes in all commodities, pleasures, and conditions, seeing even the very hedges doe naturally affoord us such plentie, as no ship need returne away emptie, and onely use but the season of the Sea. Fish will returne an honest gaine, besides all other advantages, her treasures having yet never beene opened, nor her originals wasted, consumed, nor abused. *In Asia.* [VI. 211.] *Beyond the line.*

And whereas it is said the Hollanders serve the Easterlings themselves, and other parts that want with Herring, Ling, and wet Cod: The Easterlings, a great part of Europe, with Sturgion and Caviare, as the Blacke Sea doth Grecia, Podolia, Sagovia, Natolia, and the Hellespont. Cape Blanke, Spaine, Portugall, and the Levant, with Mulit and Puttargo. New found land, the most part of the chiefe Southerne Ports in Europe, with *The particular staple commodities that may be had by industry.*

a thin Poore-John, which hath beene so long, so much over-laied with Fishers, as the fishing decaieth, so that many oft times are constrained to returne with a small fraught. Norway and Poland affoords Pitch and Tarre, Masts and Yards. Sweathland and Russia, Iron and Ropes. France and Spaine, Canvase, Wine, Steele, Iron, and Oile. Italy and Greece, Silkes and Fruits. I dare boldly say, because I have seene naturally growing or breeding in those parts, the same materials that all these are made of, they may as well bee had here, or the most part of them within the distance of seventie leagues for some few ages, as from all those parts, using but the same meanes to have them that they doe; but surely in Virginia, their most tender and daintiest fruits or commodities, would be as perfit as theirs, by reason of the heat, if not in New England, and with all those advantages.

The nature of the ground approved.

First, the ground is so fertill, that questionlesse it is capable of producing any Graine, Fruits, or Seeds, you will sow or plant, growing in the Regions aforenamed: But it may be not to that perfection of delicacy, because the Summer is not so hot, and the Winter is more cold in those parts we have yet tried neere the Sea side, then wee finde in the same height in Europe or Asia: yet I made a Garden upon the top of a Rocky Ile in three and forty degrees and an halfe, foure leagues from the maine in May, that grew so well, as it served us for Sallets in June and July. All sorts of Cattle may here be bred and fed in the Iles or Peninsulaes securely for nothing. In the Interim, till they increase (if need be) observing the seasons, I durst undertake to have Corne enough from the Salvages for three hundred men, for a few trifles; and if they should be untowards, as it is most certaine they will, thirtie or fortie good men will be sufficient to bring them all in subjection, and make this provision, if they understand what to doe; two hundred whereof may eight or nine moneths in the yeere be imploied in helping the Fisher-men, till the rest provide other necessaries, fit to furnish us with other Commodities.

In March, Aprill, May, and halfe June, heere is Cod in abundance; In May, June, July, and August, Mullit and Sturgion, whose Roes doe make Caviare and Puttargo; Herring, if any desire them: I have taken many out of the bellies of Cods, some in nets; but the Salvages compare the store in the Sea with the haires of their heads: and surely there are an incredible abundance upon this Coast. In the end of August, September, October, [VI. 212.] and November, you may have Cod againe to make Core-fish or Poore-John: Hake you may have when the Cod failes in Summer, if you will fish in the night, which is better then Cod. Now each hundred you take here, is as good as two or three hundred in New found Land; so that halfe the labour in hooking, splitting and touring, is saved: And you may have your fish at what market you will, before they have any in New found land, where their fishing is chiefely but in June and July, where it is here in March, Aprill, May, September, October and November, as is said; so that by reason of this Plantation, the Merchants may have their fraught both out and home, which yeelds an advantage worth consideration. Your Core-fish you may in like manner transport as you see cause, to serve the Ports in Portugall, as Lisbone, Avera, Porta Port, and divers others, (or what market you please) before your Ilanders returne. They being tied to the season in the open Sea, and you having a double season, and fishing before your doores, may every night sleep quietly ashore with good cheere, and what fires you will, or when you please with your wives and family: they onely and their ships in the maine Ocean, that must carie and containe all they use, besides their fraught. The Mullits here are in that abundance, you may take them with nets sometimes by hundreds, where at Cape Blanke they hooke them; yet those are but a foot and a halfe in length; these two, three, or foure, as oft I have measured, which makes me suspect they are some other kinde of fish, though they seeme the same, both in fashion and goodnesse. Much Salmon some have found up the

The seasons for fishing approved.

Rivers as they have passed, and here the aire is so temperate, as all these at any time may be preserved. Now, young Boies and Girles Salvages, or any other bee they never such idlers, may turne, carie or returne a fish, without either shame or any great paine: He is very idle that is past twelve yeeres of age and cannot doe so much, and she is very old that cannot spin a threed to make Engins to catch a fish.

Imploiment for poore people and fatherlesse children.

The facilitie of the Plantation.

For their transportation, the ships that goe there to fish may transport the first: who for their passage will spare the charge of double manning their ships, which they must do in New found land to get their fraught; but one third part of that company are onely proper to serve a stage, carie a Barrow, and turne Poore-John; notwithstanding, they must have meat, drinke, clothes, & passage so well as the rest. Now all I desire is but this, That those that voluntarily will send shipping, should make here the best choice they can, or accept such as shall bee presented them to serve them at that rate: and their ships returning leave such with me, with the value of that they should receive comming home, in such provisions and necessarie tooles, armes, bedding, apparell, salt, nets, hookes, lines, and such like, as they spare of the remainings; who till the next returne may keepe their Boats, and doe them many other profitable offices. Provided, I have men of abilitie to teach them their functions, and a company fit for Souldiers to be ready upon any occasion, because of the abuses that have beene offered the poore Salvages, and the libertie that both French and English, or any that will, have to deale with them as they please; whose disorders will be hard to reforme, and the longer the worse: Now such order with facilitie might be taken, with every Port, Towne, or Citie, with free power to convert the benefit of their fraughts to what advantage they please, and increase their numbers as they see occasion, who ever as they are able to subsist of themselves, may begin the new Townes in New England, in memory of their old: which freedome being confined but to the necessitie of the generall good, the event (with Gods helpe) might produce an honest, a noble, and a profitable emulation.

Present Commodities. Salt upon Salt may assuredly be made, if not at the first in ponds, yet till they be provided this may be used: then the ships may transport Kine, Horse, Goats, course Cloth, and such Commodities as we want; by whose arrivall may be made that provision of fish to fraught the ships that they stay not; and then if the Sailers goe for wages it matters not, it is hard if this returne defray not the charge: but care must be had they arrive in the Spring, [VI. 213.] or else that provision be made for them against winter. *Kermes.* Of certaine red berries called Kermes, which is worth ten shillings the pound, but of these have beene sold for thirty or forty shillings the pound, may yeerely be gathered a good quantity. *Musquasses.* Of the Muskrat may be well raised gaines worth their labour, that will endevour to make triall of their goodnesse. *Bevers.* Of Bevers, Otters and Martins, blacke Foxes, and Furres of price, may yeerely be had six or seven thousand, and if the trade of the French were prevented, many more: 25000. this yeere were brought from those northerne parts into France, of which trade we may have as good part as the French if we take good courses. *Mines.* Of Mines of Gold and Silver, Copper, and probabilities of Lead, Crystall and Allum, I could say much if relations were good assurances; it is true indeed, I made many trialls according to the instructions I had, which doth perswade me I need not despaire but that there are metals in the Country: but I am no Alcumist, nor will promise more then I know: which is, who will undertake the rectifying of an iron Forge, if those that buy meat and drinke, coles, ore, and all necessaries at a deare rate, gaine, where all these things are to be had for taking up, in my opinion cannot lose.

Woods. Of woods, seeing there is such plenty of all sorts, if those that build ships and boats, buy wood at so great a price, as it is in England, Spaine, France and Holland, and all other provisions for the nourishment of mans life, live well by their trade; when labour is all required to take these necessaries without any other tax, what hazard will be here but to doe much better, and what commodity in Europe doth more decay then wood? for the goodnesse of the ground, let us take it fertill or barren, or as it is, seeing it is certaine it beares fruits to nourish and feed man & beast as well as England, and the Sea those severall sorts of fishes I have related: thus seeing all good things for mans sustenance may with this facility be had by a little extraordinary labour, till that transported be increased, & all necessaries for shipping onely for labour, to which may be added the assistance of the Salvages which may easily be had, if they be discreetly handled in their kinds, towards fishing, planting, and destroying woods, what gaines might be raised if this were followed (when there is but once men to fill your store houses dwelling there, you may serve all Europe better and farre cheaper then can the Iland Fishers, or the Hollanders, Cape-blanke, or Newfound land, who must be at much more charge then you) may easily be conjectured by this example.

An example of the gaines upon every yeere or six moneths returne.

Two thousand will fit out a ship of 200. tunnes, & one of 100. tuns, if of the dry fish they both make fraught, that of 200. and goe for Spaine, sell it but at ten shillings a quintall, but commonly it gives fifteene or twenty, especially when it commeth first, which amounts to 3. or 4000. pound, but say but ten, which is the lowest, allowing the rest for waste, it amounts at that rate to 2000. which is the whole charge of your two ships and the equipage, then the returne of the mony and the fraught of the ship for the vintage or any other voyage is cleere gaine, with your ship of one hundred tunnes of traine Oile and Corfish, besides the Bevers and other commodities, and that you may have at home within six moneths if God please to send but an ordinary passage; then saving halfe this charge by the not staying of your ships, your victuall, overplus of men and wages, with her fraught thither with necessaries for the Planters, the Salt being there made, as also may the nets and lines within a short time; if nothing may be expected but this, it might in time equalize your Hollanders gaines, if not exceede them, having their fraughts alwaies ready against the arrivall of the ships, this would so increase our shipping and sailers, and so incourage and imploy a great part of our Idlers and others that want imployment fitting their qualities at home, where they shame to doe that they would doe abroad, that could they but once taste the sweet fruits of their owne labours, doubtlesse many thousands would be advised by good discipline to take more pleasure in honest industry, then in their humors of dissolute idlenesse.

[VI. 214.]

A description of the Countrey in particular, and their situations.

But to returne a little more to the particulars of this Countrey, which I intermingle thus with my projects and reasons, not being so sufficiently yet acquainted in those parts, to write fully the estate of the Sea, the Aire, the Land, the Fruits, their Rocks, the People, the Government, Religion, Territories, Limitations, Friends and Foes: But as I gathered from their niggardly relations in a broken language, during the time I ranged those Countries, &c. the most Northerne part I was at, was the Bay of Pennobscot, which is East and West, North and South, more then ten leagues: but such were my occasions, I was constrained to be satisfied of them I found in the Bay, that the River ranne farre up into the Land, and was well inhabited with many people, but they were from their habitations, either fishing amongst the Iles, or hunting the Lakes and Woods for Deere and Bevers: the Bay is full of great Iles of one, two, six or eight miles in length, which divides it into many faire and excellent good Harbours. On the East of it are the Tarrentines, their mortall enemies, where inhabit the French, as they report, that live with those people as one Nation or Family: And Northwest of Pennobscot is Mecaddacut, at the foot of a high Mountaine, a kinde of fortresse against the Tarrentines, adjoyning to the high Mountaines of Pennobscot, against whose feet doth beat the Sea; but over all the Land, Iles, or other impediments, you may well see them foureteene or eighteene leagues from their situation.

Segocket is the next, then Nuskoucus, Pemmaquid, and Sagadahock: up this River, where was the Westerne Plantation, are Aumoughcawgen, Kinnebeke, and divers others, where are planted some Corne fields. Along this River thirtie or fortie miles, I saw nothing but great high clifts of barren Rocks overgrowne with Wood, but where the Salvages dwell there the ground is excellent salt, and fertill. Westward of this River is the Country of Aucocisco, in the bottome of a large deepe Bay, full of many great Iles, which divides it into many good Harbours. Sawocotuck is the next, in the edge of a large Sandy Bay, which hath many Rockes and Iles, but few good Harbours, but for Barkes I yet know; but all this Coast to Pennobscot, and as farre as I could see Eastward of it is nothing, but such high craggy clifty Rockes and stony Iles, that I wonder such great Trees could grow upon so hard foundations. It is a Countrey rather to affright then delight one, and how to describe a more plaine spectacle of desolation, or more barren, I know not, yet are those rocky Iles so furnished with good Woods, Springs, Fruits, Fish and Fowle, and the Sea the strangest Fish-pond I ever saw, that it makes me thinke, though the coast be rocky and thus affrightable, the Vallies and Plaines and interior parts may well notwithstanding be very fertill. But there is no Country so fertill hath not some part barren, and New-England is great enough to make many Kingdomes and Countries, were it all inhabited. As you passe the coast still westward, Accominticus and Passataquack are two convenient Harbours for small Barkes; and a good Country within their craggy clifts. Augoan is the next: this place might content a right curious judgement, but there are many sands at the entrance of the Harbour, and the worst is, it is imbayed too farre from the deepe Sea; here are many rising hils, and on their tops and descents are many corne fields and delightfull groves: On the East is an Ile of two or three leagues in length, the one halfe plaine marish ground, fit for pasture or salt Ponds, with many faire high groves of Mulbery trees and Gardens; there is also Okes, Pines, Walnuts, and other wood to make this place an excellent habitation, being a good and safe Harbour.

Naiemkeck, though it be more rocky ground, for Augoan is sandy, not much inferiour neither for the harbour, nor any thing I could perceive but the multitude of people: from hence doth stretch into the Sea the faire headland Tragabigzanda, now called Cape An, fronted with the three Iles wee called the three Turkes heads; to the north of this doth enter a great Bay, where we found some habitations and Corne fields, they report a faire River and at least 30 habitations doth possesse this Country. But [VI. 215.] because the French had got their trade, I had no leisure to discover it: the Iles of Mattahunts are on the west side of this Bay, where are many Iles and some Rocks that appeare a great height above the water like the Pyramides in Ægypt, and amongst them many good Harbours, and then the country of the Massachusits, which is the Paradice of all those parts, for here are many Iles planted with Corne, Groves, Mulberies, salvage Gardens and good Harbours, the Coast is for the most part high clayie sandy clifts, the sea Coast as you passe shewes you all along large Corne fields, and great troupes of well proportioned people: but the French having remained here neere six weekes, left nothing for us to take occasion to examine the Inhabitants relations, viz. if there be three thousand people upon those Iles, and that the River doth pierce many daies journey the entrailes of that Country: we found the people in those parts very kinde, but in their fury no lesse valiant, for upon a quarrell we fought with forty or fifty of them, till they had spent all their Arrowes, and then we tooke six or seven of their Canowes, which towards the evening they ransomed for Bever skinnes, and at Quonahasit falling out there but with one of them, he with three others crossed the Harbour in a Canow to certaine rockes whereby wee must passe, and there let flie their Arrowes for our shot, till we were out of danger, yet one of them was slaine, and another shot through his thigh.

An Indian slaine, another shot.

Then come you to Accomacke an excellent good Harbour, good land, and no want of any thing but industrious people: after much kindnesse, wee fought also with them, though some were hurt, some slaine, yet within an houre after they became friends. Cape Cod is the next presents it selfe, which is onely a headland of high hils, over-growne with shrubby Pines, hurts and such trash, but an excellent harbour for all weathers. This Cape is made by the maine Sea on the one side, and a great Bay on the other in forme of a Sickell, on it doth inhabit the people of Pawmet, and in the bottome of the Bay them of Chawum: towards the South and South-west of this Cape, is found a long and dangerous shoule of rocks and sand, but so farre as I incercled it, I found thirty fathome water and a strong currant, which makes mee thinke there is a chanell about this Shoule, where is the best and greatest fish to be had winter and summer in all the Country; but the Salvages say there is no Chanell, but that the Shoales beginne from the maine at Pawmet to the Ile of Nawset, and so extends beyond their knowledge into the Sea. The next to this is Capawucke, and those abounding Countries of Copper, Corne, People and Mineralls, which I went to discover this last yeere, but because I miscarried by the way I will leave them till God please I have better acquaintance with them.

The Massachusets they report sometimes have warres with the Bashabes of Pennobscot, & are not alwaies friends with them of Chawum and their alliance; but now they are all friends, and have each trade with other so farre as they have society on each others frontiers, for they make no such voyages as from Pennobscot to Cape Cod, seldome to Massachuset. In the North as I have said they have begun to plant Corne, whereof the south part hath such plenty as they have what they will from them of the North, and in the Winter much more plenty of fish and fowle, but both Winter & Summer hath it in one part or other all the yeere, being the meane, and most indifferent temper betwixt heat and cold, of all the Regions betwixt the Line and the Pole, but the Furs Northward are much better, and in much more plenty then Southward.

The land Markes. The remarkablest Iles and Mountaines for land Markes are these: the highest Ile is Sorico in the Bay of Pennobscot, but the three Iles, and the Iles of Matinack are much further in the Sea: Metynacus is also three plaine Iles, but many great Rocks: Monahigan is a round high Ile, and close by it Monanis, betwixt which is a small Harbour where we rid; in Damerils Iles is such another, Sagadahocke is knowne by Satquin, and foure or five Iles in their mouth. Smiths Iles are a heape together, none neere [VI. 216.] them against Accomintycus: the three Turkes heads, are three Iles, seene farre to Sea-ward in regard of the Head-land. The chiefe Head-lands, are onely Cape Tragabigzanda, and Cape Cod, now called Cape James, and Cape Anne.

The chiefe Mountaines, them of Pennobscot, the twinkling Mountaine of Acocisco, the great Mountaine of Sassanow, and the high Mountaine of Massachuset. Each of which you shall finde in the Map, their places, forme, and altitudes. The waters are most pure, proceeding from the intrailes of rocky Mountaines: the Herbs *Herbs and Fruits.* and Fruits are of many sorts and kinds, as Alkermes, Currans, Mulberies, Vines, Respises, Gooseberies, Plums, Wall-nuts, Chesse-nuts, Small-nuts, Pumpions, Gourds, Strawberies, Beanes, Pease, and Maize; a kinde or two of Flax, wherewith they make Nets, Lines, and Ropes, both small and great, very strong for their quantities.

Woods. Oake is the chiefe wood, of which there is great difference, in regard of the soyle where it groweth, Firre, Pine, Wall-nut, Chesse-nut, Birtch, Ash, Elme, Cipris, Cedar, Mulbery, Plum tree, Hazell, Saxefras, and many other sorts.

Birds. Eagles, Grips, divers sorts of Hawkes, Craines, Geese, Brants, Cormorants, Ducks, Cranes, Swannes, Sheldrakes, Teale, Meawes, Gulls, Turkies, Divedoppers, and many other sorts whose names I know not.

Fishes. Whales, Grompus, Porkpisces, Turbut, Sturgion, Cod,

Hake, Haddocke, Cole, Cuske or small Ling, Sharke, Mackarell, Herring, Mullit, Base, Pinnacks, Cunners, Pearch, Eeles, Crabs, Lobsters, Mustels, Wilks, Oisters, Clamps, Periwinkels, and divers others, &c.

Beasts. Moos, a beast bigger than a Stag, Deare red and fallow, Bevers, Wolves, Foxes both blacke and other, Aroughcunds, wilde Cats, Beares, Otters, Martins, Fitches, Musquassus, and divers other sorts of Vermin whose names I know not: all these and divers other good things doe here for want of use still increase and decrease with little diminution, whereby they grow to that abundance, you shall scarce finde any bay, shallow shore or Cove of sand, where you may not take many clamps or Lobsters, or both at your pleasure, and in many places load your Boat if you please, nor Iles where you finde not Fruits, Birds, Crabs and Mustels, or all of them; for taking at a low water Cod, Cuske, Hollibut, Scate, Turbut, Mackarell, or such like are taken plentifully in divers sandy Bayes, store of Mullit, Bases, and divers other sorts of such excellent fish as many as their Net can hold: no River where there is not plenty of Sturgion, or Salmon, or both, all which are to be had in abundance observing but their seasons: but if a man will goe at Christmas to gather Cherries in Kent, though there be plenty in Summer, he may be deceived; so here these plenties have each their seasons, as I have expressed; we for the most part had little but bread and Vinegar, and though the most part of July when the fishing decayed, they wrought all day, lay abroad in the Iles all night, and lived on what they found, yet were not sicke: But I would wish none long put himselfe to such plunges, except necessity constraine it: yet worthy is that person to starve that here cannot live if he have sense, strength and health, for there is no such penury of these blessings in any place but that one hundred men may in two or three houres make their provisions for a day, and he that hath experience to manage these affaires, with forty or thirty honest industrious men, might well undertake (if they dwell in these parts) to subject the Salvages, and feed daily two or three hundred men, with as good Corne, Fish, and Flesh as the earth hath of those kinds, and yet make that labour but their pleasure: provided that they have Engines that be proper for their purposes. Who can desire more content that hath small meanes, or but onely his merit to advance his fortunes, then to tread and plant that ground he hath purchased by the hazard of his life; if hee have but the taste of vertue and magnanimity, what to such a minde can bee more pleasant then planting and building a foundation for his posterity, got from the rude earth by Gods blessing and his owne industry without prejudice to any, if hee have any graine of faith or zeale in Religion, what can he doe lesse hurtfull to any, or more agreeable to God, then to seeke to convert those poore Salvages to know Christ and humanity, whose labours with discretion will triple requite thy charge and paine; what so truly sutes with honour and honesty, as the discovering things unknowne, erecting Townes, peopling Countries, informing the ignorant, reforming things unjust, teaching vertue and gaine to our native mother Country; a Kingdome to attend her, finde imploiment for those that are idle, because they know not what to doe: so farre from wronging any, as to cause posterity to remember thee, and remembring thee, ever honour that remembrance with praise. Consider what were the beginnings and endings of the Monarchies of the Chaldeans, the Syrians, the Grecians and Romans, but this one rule; what was it they would not doe for the good of their common weale, or their mother City? For example: Rome, what made her such a Monarchesse, but onely the adventures of her youth, not in riots at home, but in dangers abroad, and the justice and judgement out of their experiences when they grew aged; what was their ruine and hurt but this, the excesse of idlenesse, the fondnesse of parents, the want of experience in Majestrates, the admiration of their undeserved honours, the contempt of true merit, their unjust jealousies, their

A note for men that have great spirits and small meanes.

[VI. 217.]

politike incredulities, their hypocriticall seeming goodnesse and their deeds of secret lewdnesse; finally in fine, growing onely formall temporists, all that their Predecessors got in many yeeres they lost in a few daies: those by their paines and vertues became Lords of the world, they by their ease and vices became slaves to their servants; this is the difference betwixt the use of armes in the field, and on the monuments of stones, the golden age and the leaden age, prosperity and misery, justice and corruption, substance and shadowes, words and deeds, experience and imagination, making common weales, and marring common weales, the fruits of vertue, and the conclusions of vice.

Then who would live at home idly, or thinke in himselfe any worth to live, onely to eat, drinke and sleepe, and so die; or by consuming that carelesly, his friends got worthily, or by using that miserably that maintained vertue honestly, or for being descended nobly, and pine with the vaine vaunt of great kindred in penury, or to maintaine a silly shew of bravery, toile out thy heart, soule and time basely; by shifts, tricks, Cards and Dice, or by relating newes of other mens actions, sharke here and there for a dinner or supper, deceive thy friends by faire promises and dissimulation, in borrowing where thou never meanest to pay, offend the Lawes, surfet with excesse, burthen thy Countrie, abuse thy selfe, despaire in want, and then cousen thy Kindred, yea even thy owne brother, and wish thy Parents death (I will not say damnation) to have their estates, though thou seest what honours and rewards the world yet hath for them, that will seeke them and worthily deserve them.

I would bee sorry to offend, or that any should mistake my honest meaning; for I wish good to all, hurt to none: but rich men for the most part are growne to that dotage through their pride in their wealth, as though there were no accident could end it or their life.

And what hellish care doe such take to make it their owne misery and their Countries spoile, especially when there is most need of their imploiment, drawing by all manner of inventions from the Prince and his honest Subjects, even the vitall spirits of their powers and estates: as if their baggs or brags were so powerfull a defence, the malicious could not assault them, when they are the onely bait to cause us not onely to bee assaulted, but betrayed and murthered in our owne security ere wee will perceive it.

[VI. 218.] *An example of secure covetousnesse.*

May not the miserable ruine of Constantinople, their impregnable walls, riches and pleasures last taken by the Turke, which were then but a bit in comparison of their mightinesse now, remember us of the effects of private covetousnesse, at which time the good Emperour held himselfe rich enough, to have such rich subjects, so formall in all excesse of vanity, all kinde of delicacy and prodigality: his poverty when the Turke besieged the Citizens (whose merchandizing thoughts were onely to get wealth) little conceiving the desperat resolution of a valiant expert enemy, left the Emperour so long to his conclusions, having spent all he had to pay his young raw discontented Souldiers, that suddenly he, they, and their City were all a prey to the devouring Turke, and what they would not spare for the maintenance of them who adventured their lives to defend them, did serve onely their enemies to torment them, their friends and Country, and all Christendome to this present day. Let this lamentable example remember you that are rich (seeing there are such great theeves in the world to rob you) not grudge to lend some proportion to breed them that have little, yet willing to learne how to defend you, for it is too late when the deed is doing.

The Romans estate hath beene worse then this, for the meere covetousnesse and extortion of a few of them so moved the rest, that not having any imploiment but contemplation, their great judgements grew to so great malice, as themselves were sufficient to destroy themselves by faction; let this move you to imbrace imployment, for those whose educations, spirits and judgements want but your purses, not only to prevent such accustomed dangers, but also to gaine more thereby then you have; and you fathers that are either so foolishly fond, or so miserably covetous, or so wilfully ignorant, or so negligently carelesse, as that you will rather maintaine your children in idle wantonnesse till they grow your masters, or become so basely unkinde that they wish nothing but your deaths, so that both sorts grow dissolute, and although you would wish them any where to escape the Gallowes and ease your cares, though they spend you here one, two or three hundred pound a yeere, you would grudge to give halfe so much in adventure with them to obtaine an estate, which in a small time, but with a little assistance of your providence, might bee better then your owne; but if an Angell should tell you any place yet unknowne can affoord such fortunes, you would not beleeve it, no more then Columbus was beleeved there was any such land, as is now the well knowne abounding America, much lesse such large Regions as are yet unknowne, as well in America, as in Africa and Asia, and Terra incognita.

The Authors conditions.

I have not beene so ill bred but I have tasted of plenty and pleasure, as well as want and misery; nor doth necessity yet, or occasion of discontent force me to these endevours, nor am I ignorant what small thankes I shall have for my paines, or that many would have the world imagine them to bee of great judgement, that can but blemish these my designes, by their witty objections and detractions, yet (I hope) my reasons with my deeds will so prevaile with some, that I shall not want imploiment in these affaires, to make the most blinde see his owne senselesnesse and incredulity, hoping that gaine will make them affect that which Religion, Charity and the common good cannot. It were but a poore device in mee to deceive my selfe, much more the King and State, my Friends and Country with these inducements, which seeing his Majesty hath given permission, I wish all sorts of worthy honest industrious spirits would understand, and if they desire any further satisfaction, I will doe my best to give it, not to perswade them to goe onely, but goe with them; not leave them there, but live with them there: I will not say but by ill providing and undue managing, such courses may bee taken may make us miserable enough: but if I may have the execution of what I have projected, if they want to eat, let them eat or never digest mee; If I [VI. 219.] performe what I say, I desire but that reward out of the gaines may sute my paines, quality and condition, and if I abuse you with my tongue, take my head for satisfaction. If any dislike at the yeeres end, defraying their charge, by my consent they should freely returne; I feare not want of company sufficient, were it but knowne what I know of these Countries, and by the proofe of that wealth I hope yeerely to returne, if God please to blesse me from such accidents as are beyond my power in reason to prevent; for I am not so simple to thinke that ever any other motive then wealth will ever erect there a common wealth, or draw company from their ease and humors at home, to stay in New-England to effect my purposes.

The Planters pleasures and profit.

And lest any should thinke the toile might be insupportable, though these things may bee had by labour and diligence; I assure my selfe there are who delight extremely in vaine pleasure, that take much more paines in England to enjoy it, then I should doe here to gaine wealth sufficient, and yet I thinke they should not have halfe such sweet content: for our pleasure here is still gaines, in England charges and losse; here nature and liberty affoords us that freely which in England we want, or it costeth us deerely. What pleasure can bee more then being tired with any occasion a shore, in planting Vines, Fruits, or Herbes, in contriving their owne grounds to the pleasure of their owne minds, their Fields, Gardens, Orchards, Buildings, Ships, and other workes, &c. to recreate themselves before their owne doores in their owne Boats upon the Sea, where man, woman and childe, with a small hooke and line, by angling may take divers sorts of excellent Fish at their pleasures; and is it not pretty sport to pull up two pence, six pence, and twelve pence, as fast as you can hale and vere a line; hee is a very bad Fisher cannot kill in one day with his hooke and line one, two, or three hundred Cods, which dressed and dryed, if they bee sold there for ten shillings a hundred, though in England they will give more then twenty, may not both servant, master and Merchant be well content with this gaine? if a man worke but three daies in seven, hee may get more then hee can spend unlesse hee will bee exceedingly excessive. Now that Carpenter, Mason, Gardiner, Tailer, Smith, Sailer, Forger, or what other, may they not make this a pretty recreation, though they fish but an houre in a day, to take more then they can eat in a weeke, or if they will not eat it, because there is so much better choise, yet sell it or change it with the Fisher-men or Merchants for any thing you want, and what sport doth yeeld a more pleasing content, and lesse hurt and charge then angling with a hooke, and crossing the sweet aire from Ile to Ile, over the silent streames of a calme Sea, wherein the most curious may finde profit, pleasure and content.

Thus though all men be not fishers, yet all men whatsoever may in other matters doe as well, for necessity doth in these cases so rule a common wealth, and each in their severall functions, as their labours in their qualities may be as profitable because there is a necessary mutuall use of all.

Imploiments for Gentlemen.

For Gentlemen, what exercise should more delight them then ranging daily these unknowne parts, using fowling and fishing for hunting and hawking, and yet you shall see the wilde Hawkes give you some pleasure in seeing them stoupe six or seven times after one another an houre or two together, at the skults of Fish in the faire Harbours, as those a shore at a fowle, and never trouble nor torment your selves with watching, mewing, feeding, and attending them, nor kill horse and man with running and crying, See you not a Hawke; for hunting also, the Woods, Lakes and Rivers affoord not onely chase sufficient for any that delights in that kinde of toile or pleasure, but such beasts to hunt, that besides the delicacie of their bodies for food, their skinnes are so rich, as they will recompence thy daily labour with a Captaines pay.

For Labourers, if those that sow Hempe, Rape, Turnups, Parsnips, Carrats, Cabidge, and such like; give twentie, thirtie, fortie, fiftie shillings yeerely for an Acre of Land, and meat, drinke, and wages to use it, and yet grow rich: when better, or at least as good ground may bee had and cost nothing but labour; it seemes strange to me any such should grow poore. [VI. 220.] *Imploiments for Labourers.*

My purpose is not to perswade children from their parents, men from their wives, nor servants from their masters; onely such as with free consent may bee spared: but that each Parish, or Village, in Citie, or Countrey, that will but apparell their fatherlesse children of thirteene or foureteene yeeres of age, or young maried people that have small wealth to live on, here by their labour may live exceeding well. Provided alwaies, that first there be a sufficient power to command them, houses to receive them, meanes to defend them, and meet provisions for them, for any place may be over-laine: and it is most necessary to have a fortresse (ere this grow to practise) and sufficient masters, of all necessarie, mecanicall qualities, to take ten or twelve of them for Apprentises; the Master by this may quickly grow rich, these may learne their trades themselves to doe the like, to a generall and an incredible benefit for King and Countrey, Master and Servant.

It would be a History of a large volume, to recite the adventures of the Spaniards and Portugals, their affronts and defeats, their dangers and miseries; which with such incomparable honor, and constant resolution, so farre beyond beleefe, they have attempted and indured in their discoveries and plantations, as may well condemne us of too much imbecillitie, sloth, and negligence; yet the Authors of these new inventions were held as ridiculous for a long time, as now are others that doe but seeke to imitate their unparalleld vertues, and though we see daily their mountaines of wealth (sprung from the Plants of *Examples of the Spaniards.*

The causes of our defailments.

their generous indevours) yet is our sensualitie and untowardnesse such, & so great, that we either ignorantly beleeve nothing, or so curiously contest, to prevent we know not what future events; that we either so neglect, or oppresse and discourage the present, as wee spoile all in the making, crop all in the blooming; and building upon faire Sand rather then upon rough Rocks, judge that we know not, governe that wee have not, feare that which is not; and for feare some should doe too well, force such against their wils to be idle, or as ill. And who is hee hath judgement, courage, and any industry or quality with understanding, will leave his Country, his hopes at home, his certaine estate, his friends, pleasures, libertie, and the preferment sweet England doth affoord to all degrees, were it not to advance his fortunes by enjoying his deserts, whose prosperitie once appearing, will encourage others: but it must be cherished as a childe, till it be able to goe and understand it selfe, and not corrected nor oppressed above its strength, ere it know wherefore. A childe can neither performe the office nor deeds of a man of strength, nor endure that affliction he is able: nor can an Apprentise at the first performe the part of a Master, and if twentie yeeres be required to make a childe a man, seven yeeres limited an Apprentise for his trade: if scarce an age be sufficient to make a wise man a States-man, and commonly a man dies ere he hath learned to be discreet; if perfection be so hard to be obtained, as of necessitie there must be Practice as well as Theoricke: Let no man then condemne this paradox opinion, to say that halfe seven yeres is scarce sufficient for a good capacitie to learne in these affaires how to carrie himselfe. And who ever shall try in these remote places the erecting of a Colony, shall finde at the end of seven yeeres occasion enough to use all his discretion: and in the Interim, all the content, rewards, gaines, and hopes, will be necessarily required, to be given to the beginning, till it be able to creepe, to stand, and goe, and to encourage desert by all possible meanes; yet time enough to keepe it from running, for there is no feare it will grow too fast, or ever to any thing, except libertie, profit, honor, and prosperitie there found, more binde the Planters of those affaires in devotion to effect it; then bondage, violence, tyrannie, ingratitude, and such double dealing, as bindes free men to become slaves, and honest [VI. 221.] men turne knaves; which hath ever beene the ruine of the most popular Common-weales, and is very unlikely ever well to begin anew.

The blisse of Spaine.

Who seeth not what is the greatest good of the Spaniard, but these new conclusions in searching those unknowne parts of this unknowne world; by which meanes he dives even into the very secrets of all his neighbours, and the most part of the world; and when the Portugals and Spaniards had found the East and West-Indies, how many did condemne themselves, that did not accept of that honest offer of Noble Columbus, who upon our neglect brought them to it, perswading our selves the world had no such places as they had found: and yet ever since we finde, they still (from time to time) have found new Lands, new Nations, and Trades, and still daily doe finde, both in Asia, Affrica, Terra incognita, and America, so that there is neither Souldier nor Mechanicke, from the Lord to the Begger, but those parts affoords them all imploiment, & discharges their native soile of so many thousands of all sorts, that else by their sloth, pride, and imperfections, would long ere this have troubled their neighbours, or have eaten the pride of Spaine it selfe.

Now hee knowes little that knowes not England may well spare many more people then Spaine, and is as well able to furnish them with all manner of necessaries; and seeing for all they have, they cease not still to search for that they have not, and know not; it is strange we should be so dull, as not maintaine that which we have, and pursue that we know: Surely, I am sure many would take it ill, to be abridged of the titles and honors of their predecessors; when if but truly they would judge themselves, looke how inferior they are to their Noble Vertues, so much they are unworthy of their honors and livings, which never were ordained for shewes and shadowes, to maintaine idlenesse and vice, but to make them more able to abound in honor, by Heroicall deeds of action, judgement, pietie, and vertue. What was it both in their purse and person they would not doe, for the good of their Common-wealth, which might move them presently to set out their spare children in these generous designes; Religion above all things should move us, especially the Clergie, if we are religious, to shew our faith by our works, in converting those poore Salvages to the knowledge of God, seeing what paines the Spaniards take to bring them to their adultered faith. Honor might move the Gentry, the valiant, and industrious, and the hope and assurance of wealth, all, if we were that we would seeme, and be accounted; or be we so farre inferior to other Nations, or our spirits so farre dejected from our ancient predecessors, or our mindes so upon spoile, piracy, and such villany, as to serve the Portugall, Spaniard, Dutch, French, or Turke, (as to the cost of Europe too many doe) rather then our God, our King, our Country, and our selves; excusing our idlenesse and our base complaints by want of imploiment, when here is such choice of all sorts, and for all degrees, in the planting and discovering these North parts of America.

My second voyage to New England.

My second Voiage to New England. 1615.

IN the yeere of our Lord 1615. I was imploied by many my friends of London, and Sir Ferdinando Gorges, a noble Knight, and a great favourer of those actions, who perswaded the reverend Deane of Exeter Doctor Sutliffe, and divers Merchants of the West, to entertaine this Plantation. Much labour I had taken to bring the Londoners and them to joyne together, because the Londoners have most Money, and the Westerne men are most proper for fishing; and it is neere as much trouble, but much more danger, to saile from London to Plimoth, then from Plimoth to New England, so that halfe the voiage would thus be saved, yet by no meanes I could prevaile, so desirous they were both to be Lords of this fishing. Now to make my words more apparant by my deeds, to begin a Plantation for a more ample triall of those conclusions, I was to have staied there but with sixteene men, whose names were; [VI. 222.]

Gent.

Tho. Dirmer.	Daniel Cage.
Edw. Stallings.	Francis Abbot.

Sould.

John Gosling.	David Cooper.
William Ingram.	John Partridge.

Were to learne to be Sailers.

Thomas Digby.	Adam Smith.
Daniel Baker.	Tho. Watson.
Walter Chisell.	Robert Miller.

And two Boyes.

I confesse I could have wished them as many thousands, had all other provisions beene in like proportion; nor would I have had so few, could I have had means for more: yet would God have pleased we had safely arrived, I doubted not but to have performed more then I promised, and that many thousands ere this would have bin there ere now. The maine assistance next God I had to this small number, was my acquaintance amongst the Salvages, especially with Dohoday, one of their greatest Lords, who had lived long in England, and another called Tantum, I caried with mee from England, and set on shore at Cape Cod; by the meanes of this proud Salvage, I did not doubt but quickly to have got that credit amongst the rest of the Salvages and their alliance, to have had as many of them as I desired in any designe I intended, and that trade also they had by such a kinde of exchange of their Countrey Commodities, which both with ease and securitie might then have beene used with him and divers others: I had concluded to inhabit and defend them against the Tarentines, with a better power then the

The ground and plot for our plantation.

French did them; whose tyrannie did inforce them to embrace my offer with no small devotion: and though many may think me more bold then wise, in regard of their power, dexteritie, treachery, and inconstancy, having so desperately assaulted, and betraied many others; I say but this (because with so many, I have many times done much more in Virginia then I intended here, when I wanted that experience Virginia taught mee) that to me it seemes no more danger then ordinary: and though I know my selfe the meanest of many thousands, whose apprehensive inspection can pierce beyond the bounds of my abilities, into the hidden things of Nature, Art, and Reason: yet I intreat such, give mee leave to excuse my selfe of so much imbecillitie, as to say, that in these eighteene yeeres which I have beene conversant with these affaires, I have not learned, there is a great difference betwixt the directions and judgement of experimentall knowledge, and the superficiall conjecture of variable relation: wherein rumour, humour, or misprision have such power, that oft times one is enough to beguile twentie, but twentie not sufficient to keepe one from being deceived. Therefore I know no reason but to beleeve my owne eies before any mans imagination, that is but wrested from the conceits of my owne projects and endevours, but I honor with all affection, the counsell and instructions of judiciall directions, or any other honest advertisement, so farre to observe, as they tie me, not to the crueltie of unknowne events. These are the inducements that thus drew me to neglect all other imploiments, and spend my time and best abilities in these adventures, wherein though I have had many discouragements, by the ingratitude of some, the malicious slanders of others, the falsenesse of friends, the treachery of cowards, and slownesse of Adventurers.

The meanes used to prevent it and me.

How I set saile and returned.

Now you are to remember, as I returned first from New England at Plimoth, I was promised foure good ships ready prepared to my hand the next Christmas, and what conditions and content I would desire, to put this businesse in practise, and arriving at London, foure more were offered me with the like courtesie. But to joyne the Londoners & them in one, was most impossible; so that in January with two hundred pound in Chash for adventure, and six Gentlemen well furnished, I went from London to the foure ships were promised me at Plimoth, but I found no such matter: and the most of those that had made such great promises, by the bad returne of the ship went for Gold, and their private emulations, were [VI. 223.] extinct and qualified. Notwithstanding at last, with a labyrinth of trouble, though the greatest of the burden lay on me, and a few of my particular friends, I was furnished with a ship of two hundred tunnes, and another of fiftie: But ere I had sailed one hundred and twentie leagues, she brake all her Masts, pumping each watch five or six thousand strokes; onely her spret-saile remained to spoone before the winde, till we had re-accommodated a Jury-mast to returne for Plimoth, or founder in the Seas.

My reimbarkement, encounter with Pirats, and imprisonment by the French.

My Vice-Admirall being lost, not knowing of this, proceeded her voyage; now with the remainder of those provisions, I got out againe in a small Barke of sixtie tuns with thirty men: for this of two hundred, and provision for seventie, which were the sixteene before named, and foureteene other Sailers for the ship; with those I set saile againe the foure and twentieth of June, where what befell me (because my actions and writings are so publike to the world) envy still seeking to scandalize my endevours, and seeing no power but death can stop the chat of ill tongues, nor imagination of mens minds, lest my owne relations of those hard events might by some constructors bee made doubtfull, I have thought it best to insert the examinations of those proceedings, taken by Sir Lewis Stukeley, a worthy Knight, and Vice-Admirall of Devonshire, which was as followeth.

[The Examination

The Examination of Daniel Baker, late Steward to Captaine John Smith, in the returne of Plimoth, taken before Sir Lewis Stukeley Knight, the eighth of December, 1615.

THe effect in briefe was this: being chased by one Fry an English Pirat, Edward Chambers the Master, John Minter his Mate, Thomas Digby the Pylot, and divers others importuned him to yeeld; much swaggering wee had with them, more then the Pirats, who agreed upon such faire conditions as we desired, which if they broke, he vowed to sinke rather then be abused. Strange they thought it, that a Barke of threescore tuns with foure guns should stand upon such termes, they being eightie expert Sea-men, in an excellent ship of one hundred and fortie tuns, and thirty six cast Peeces and Murderers: But when they knew our Captaine, so many of them had beene his Souldiers, and they but lately runne from Tunis, where they had stolne this ship, wanted victuall, and in combustion amongst themselves, would have yeelded all to his protection, or wafted us any whither: but those mutinies occasioned us to reject their offer, which afterward we all repented. For at Fiall we met two French Pirats, the one of two hundred tuns, the other thirty: no disgrace would cause our mutiners fight, till the Captaine offered to blow up the ship rather then yeeld, till hee had spent all his powder: so that together by the eares we went, and at last got cleere of them for all their shot. At Flowers we were againe chased with foure French men of warre, the Admirall one hundred and fortie tuns, and ninety men well armed; the rest good ships, and as well provided: much parly we had, but vowing they were Rochilers, and had a Commission from the King onely to secure true men, and take Portugals, Spaniards, and Pirats, and as they requested, our Captaine went to shew his Commission, which was under the broad Seale, but neither it nor their vowes they so much respected, but they kept him, rifled our ship, manned her with French men, and dispersed us amongst their Fleet: within five or six daies they were increased to eight or nine saile. At last they surrendred us our ship, and most of our provisions, the defects they promised the next day to supply, and did. Notwithstanding, there was no way but our mutiners would for England, though we were as neere New England, till the major part resolved with our Captaine to proceed. But the Admirall sending his Boat for our Captaine, they espying a Saile, presently gave chase, whereby our mutiners finding an opportunitie in the night ran away, and thus left our Captaine in his Cap, Bretches, and Wast-coat, alone among the French men: his clothes, armes, and what he had, our mutiners shared among them, and with a false excuse, faining for [VI. 224.] feare lest he should turne man of warre, they returned for Plimoth: fifteene of us being Land-men, not knowing what they did. Daniel Cage, Edward Stalings, Walter Chisell, David Cooper, Robert Miller, and John Partridge, upon oath affirmes this for truth before the Vice-Admirall.

A double treachery.

Now the cause why the French detained mee againe, was the suspition this Chambers and Minter gave them, that I would revenge my selfe upon the Banke, or in New found land, of all the French I could there encounter, and how I would have fired the ship, had they not overperswaded me: and that if I had but againe my Armes, I would rather sinke by them, then they should have from me but the value of a Bisket; and many other such like tales to catch but opportunitie in this manner to leave me, and thus they returned to Plimoth, and perforce with the French men I thus proceeded. Being a fleet of eight or nine saile, we watched for the West-Indies fleet, till ill weather separated us from the other eight: still wee spent our time about the Iles of the Assores, where to keepe my perplexed thoughts from too much meditation of my miserable estate, I writ this Discourse, thinking to have sent it to you of his Majesties Councell by some ship or other, for I saw their purpose was to take all they could. At last we were chased by one Captaine Barra,

A fleet of nine French men of war, and fights with the Spaniard.

an English Pirat in a small ship, with some twelve Peece of Ordnance, about thirty men, and neere all starved. They sought by courtesie releefe of us, who gave them such faire promises, as at last they betraied Captaine Wollistone his Lieutenant, and foure or five of his men aboord us, and then provided to take the rest perforce. Now my part was to be prisoner in the Gun-roome, and not to speake to any of them upon my life, yet had Barra knowledge what I was. Then Barra perceiving well those French intents, made ready to fight, and Wollistone as resolutely regarded not their threats, which caused us demurre upon the matter longer some sixteene houres, and then returned them againe Captaine Wollistone and all their Prisoners, and some victuall also upon a small composition: But whilest we were bartering thus with them; a Carvill before our faces got under the Castle of Gratiosa, from whence they beat us with their Ordnance.

A prise of Fish.

The next wee tooke was a small English man of Poole from New found land: the great Cabben at this present was my prison, from whence I could see them pillage these poore men of all that they had, and halfe their fish: when hee was gone, they sold his poore clothes at the maine Mast by an out-cry, which scarce gave each man seven pence a peece.

A Scotch prise.

Not long after we tooke a Scot fraught from Saint Michaels to Bristow, he had better fortune then the other; for having but taken a Boats loading of Sugar, Marmelade, Suckets, and such like, we descried foure saile, after whom we stood, who forling their maine Sailes attended us to fight, but our French spirits were content onely to perceive they were English red Crosses. Within a very small time after wee chased 4. Spanish ships that came from the Indies, we fought with them foure or five houres, tore their sailes and sides with many a shot betwixt wind and weather, yet not daring to boord them, lost them, for which all the Sailers ever after hated the Captaine as a professed coward.

A prise worth 36000 crownes.

A poore Carvill of Brasile was the next wee chased;

and after a small fight, thirteene or foureteene of her men being wounded, which was the better halfe, we tooke her with three hundred and seventy chests of Sugar, one hundred hides, and thirty thousand Rialls of eight.

The next was a ship of Holland, which had lost her Consorts in the Streights of Magilans, going for the South sea, she was put roomy, she also these French men with faire promises, cunningly betraied to come aboord them to shew their Commission, and so made prise of all: the most of the Dutch-men we tooke aboord the Admirall, and manned her with French-men, that within two or three nights after ran away with her for France, the wounded Spaniards we set on shore on the Ile of Tercera, the rest we kept to saile the Carvill.

A prise worth 200000 *crownes.*

[VI. 225.]

Within a day or two after, we met a West-Indies man of warre, of one hundred and sixtie tuns, a fore noone wee fought with her, and then tooke her with one thousand one hundred Hides, fiftie Chests of Cutchanele, foureteene Coffers of wedges of Silver, eight thousand Rialls of eight, and six Coffers of the King of Spaines Treasure, besides the good pillage and rich Coffers of many rich Passengers.

Two moneths they kept me in this manner to manage their fights against the Spaniards, and bee a Prisoner when they tooke any English. Now though the Captaine had oft broke his promise, which was to put me on shore the Iles, or the next ship he tooke; yet at the last he was contented I should goe in the Carvill of Sugar for France, himselfe seeming as resolved to keepe the Seas, but the next morning we all set saile for France, and that night we were separated from the Admirall and the rich prise by a storme. Within two daies after wee were hailed by two West-Indies men: but when they saw us waife them for the King of France, they gave us their broad sides, shot thorow our maine Mast, and so left us. Having lived now this Summer amongst those French men of warre, with much adoe we arrived at the Gulion, not farre from Rotchell: where in stead of the great promises they alwaies fed me with, of double satisfaction and full content, and tenne thousand Crownes was generally concluded I should have; they kept me five or six daies Prisoner in the Carvill, accusing me to be he that burnt their Colony in New France, to force me to give them a discharge before the Judge of the Admiraltie, and stand to their courtesies for satisfaction, or lie in prison, or a worse mischiefe: Indeed this was in the time of combustion, that the Prince of Cundy was with his Army in the field, and every poore Lord, or men in authoritie, as little Kings of themselves: For this injury was done me by them that set out this voyage (not by the Sailers) for they were cheated of all as well as I, by a few Officers aboord, and the owners on shore.

My escape from the French men.

But to prevent this choise, in the end of such a storme that beat them all under hatches, I watched my opportunitie to get a shore in their Boat, whereinto in the darke night I secretly got, and with a halfe Pike that lay by me, put a drift for Rat Ile: but the currant was so strong, and the Sea so great, I went a drift to Sea, till it pleased God the wind so turned with the tide, that although I was all this fearefull night of gusts and raine in the Sea the space of twelve houres, when many ships were driven ashore, and divers split: (and being with skulling and bayling the water tired, I expected each minute would sinke me) at last I arrived in an Oazy Ile by Charowne, where certaine Fowlers found me neere drowned, and halfe dead, with water, cold, and hunger. My Boat I pawned to finde meanes to get to Rotchell; where I understood our man of war & the rich prize, wherein was the Cap. called Mounsieur Poyrune, and the thirtie thousand Rialls of eight we tooke in the Carvill, was split, the Captaine drowned and halfe his Company the same night, within six or seven leagues of that place; from whence I escaped in the little Boat by the mercy of God, far beyond all mens reason or my expectation, arriving at Rotchell:

What law I had.

upon my complaint to the Judge of the Admiraltie, I found many good words and faire promises, and ere long many of them that escaped drowning, told me the newes they heard of my owne death: These I arresting, their severall examinations did so confirme my complaint, it was held proofe sufficient. All which being performed according to their order of justice, from under the Judges hand, I presented it to Sir Thomas Edmonds, then Ambassadour at Burdeaux, where it was my chance to see the arrivall of the Kings great mariage brought from Spaine.

Here it was my good fortune to meet my old friend Master Crampton, that no lesse grieved at my losse, then willingly to his power did supply my wants, and I must confesse, I was more beholden to the French men that escaped drowning in the man of warre, Madam Chanoyes at Rotchell, and the Lawyers of Burdeaux, then all the rest of my Country-men I met in France. Of the wracke of the rich prise, some three thousand six hundred crownes [VI. 226.] worth of goods came ashore, and was saved with the Carvill, which I did my best to arrest: the Judge promised I should have Justice, what will be the conclusion as yet I know not. But under the couler to take Pirats and the West-Indie men (because the Spaniards will not suffer the French to trade in the West-Indies) any goods from thence, though they take them upon the Coast of Spaine are lawfull prize, or from any of his Teritories out of the limits of Europe: and as they betraied me, though I had the broad-seale, so did they rob and pillage twentie saile of English men more, besides them I knew not of the same yeere.

My returne for England.

Leaving thus my businesse in France I returned to Plimoth, to finde them had thus buried me amongst the French; and not onely buried me, but with so much infamy as such treacherous cowards could suggest to excuse their villanies. The Chiefetaines of this mutiny that I could finde, I laid by the heeles, the rest like themselves confessed the truth, as you have heard. Now how I have or could prevent these accidents, having no more meanes, I rest at your censures; but to proceed to the matter; yet must I sigh and say, How oft hath Fortune in the world (thinke I) brought slavery, freedome, and turned all diversly. Newfoundland I have heard at the first, was held as desperate a fishing as this I project for New England, Placentia, and the Banke neare also as doubtfull to the French: But for all the disasters hapned me, the businesse is the same it was, and the five ships went from London, whereof one was reported more then three hundred tunnes, found fish so much, that neither Izeland man, nor Newfoundland man I could heare of hath bin there, will go any more to either place, if they may go thither. So that upon the good returne of my Vice-Admirall, this yeere are gone 4 or 5 saile from Plimoth, and from London as many, only to make voyages of profit: whereas if all the English had bin there till my returne, put all their returnes together, they would scarce make one a savour of neere a dozen I could nominate, except one sent by Sir Francis Popam; though there be fish sufficient, as I am perswaded, to fraught yeerely foure or five hundred Saile, or as many as will goe. For this fishing stretcheth along the Sea Coast from Cape James to Newfoundland, which is seven or eight hundred miles at the least, and hath his course in the deepes, and by the shore, all the yere long, keeping their hants and feedings, as the beasts of the field, and the birds of the aire. But all men are not such as they should be, that have undertaken those voyages: All the Romans were not Scipioes, nor Carthagenians Hanibals, nor all the Genweses Columbusses, nor all the Spaniards Courteses: had they dived no deeper in the secrets of their discoveries then we, or stopped at such doubts and poore accidentall chances, they had never beene remembred as they are, yet had they no such certainties to begin as we.

The successe of my Vice-Admirall.

But to conclude, Adam and Eve did first begin this innocent worke to plant the earth to remaine to posterity, but not without labour, trouble, and industry. Noe and his family began againe the second Plantation; and their seed as it still increased, hath still planted new Countries, and one Countrey another, and so the world to that estate it is: but not without much hazard, travell, mortalities, discontents, and many disasters. Had those worthy Fathers, and their memorable off-spring, not beene more diligent for us now in these ages, then we are to plant that yet is unplanted for the after livers. Had the seed of Abraham, our Saviour Christ, and his Apostles, exposed themselves to no more dangers to teach the Gospell then we, even wee our selves had at this present beene as salvage, and as miserable as the most barbarous Salvage, yet uncivilized. The Hebrewes and Lacedemonians, the Gothes, the Grecians, the Romanes, and the rest, what was it they would not undertake to inlarge their Teritories, enrich their subjects, resist their enemies. Those that were the founders of those great Monarchies and their vertues, were no silvered idle golden Pharises, but industrious Iron steeled Publicans: They regarded more provisions and necessaries for their people, then Jewels, [VI. 227.] riches, ease, or delight for themselves; Riches were their Servants, not their Masters. They ruled (as Fathers, not as Tirants) their people as Children, not as Slaves; there was no disaster could discourage them; and let none thinke they incountred not with all manner of incumbrances. And what hath ever beene the worke of the greatest Princes of the Earth, but planting of Countries, and civilizing barbarous and inhumane Nations to civilitie and humanitie, whose eternall actions fills our Histories.

Lastly, the Portugals and Spaniards, whose ever-living actions before our eies will testifie with them our idlenesse, and ingratitude to all posterities, and the neglect of our duties, in our pietie and religion. We owe our God, our King and Countrey, and want of Charitie to those poore Salvages, whose Countrey wee challenge, use and possesse; except wee be but made to use, and marre what our forefathers made, or but onely tell what they did, or esteeme our selves too good to take the like paines. Was it vertue in them to provide that doth maintaine us, and basenesse in us to doe the like for others? Surely no.

Then seeing we are not borne for our selves, but each to help other, and our abilities are much alike at the houre of our birth, and the minute of our death: seeing our good deeds or our bad by faith in Christs merits, is all we have, to carie our soules to heaven or hell. Seeing honor is our lives ambition, and our ambition after death to have an honorable memory of our life: and seeing by no meanes we would be abated of the dignities and glories of our predecessors, let us imitate their vertues to be worthily their successors: to conclude with Lucretius,

Its want of reason, or its reasons want
Which doubts the minde and judgement, so doth dant,
That those beginnings makes men not to grant.

John Smith writ this with his owne hand.

Here followeth a briefe Discourse of the trials of New England, with certaine Observations of the Hollanders use and gaine by fishing, and the present estate of that happy Plantation, begun but by sixtie weake men, in the yeere of our Lord 1620. and how to build a fleet of good ships to make a little Navy Royall, by the former Author.

HE saith, that it is more then foure and forty yeeres agoe, and it is more then fortie yeeres agoe since he writ it; that the Herring Busses out of the Low Countries under the King of Spaine, were five hundred, besides one hundred French men, and three or foure hundred saile of Flemings. The Coast of Wales and Lancashire was used by 300 Saile of Strangers. Ireland at Beltamore, fraughted yeerely three hundred saile of Spaniards, where King Edward the sixt intended to have made a strong Castle, because of the straight to have tribute for fishing. Black Rocke was yerely fished by three or foure hundred saile of Spaniards, Portugals, and Biskiners. *M. Dee his report.*

The Hollanders raise yeerely by Herring, Cod, and Ling, thirty thousand pounds: English and French, by Salt-fish, Poore-John, Salmons, and Pilchards, three hundred thousand pounds: Hambrough and the Sound, for Sturgion, Lobsters and Eeles, one hundred thousand pounds: Cape Blanke for Tunny and Mullit, by the Biskiners and Spaniards, thirty thousand pounds. *The benefit of fishing, as Mr. Gentleman and others report.*

That the Duke of Medina receiveth yeerely tribute of the Fishers, for Tunny, Mullit, and Porgos, more then ten thousand pounds. Lubecke hath seven hundred ships; Hambrough six hundred; Emden lately a Fisher towne, one thousand foure hundred, whose customes by fishing hath made them so powerfull as they be. Holland and Zeland not much greater then Yorkeshire, hath thirty walled Townes, foure hundred Villages, and twenty *The Records of Holland and other learned observers.* [VI. 228.]

thousand saile of Ships and Hoies; three thousand six hundred are Fisher-men, whereof one hundred are Doggers, seven hundred Pinkes and Well-Boats, seven hundred Fraud-boats, Britters, and Tode-boats, with thirteene hundred Busses, besides three hundred that yeerely fish about Yarmouth, where they sell their fish for Gold: and fifteene yeeres agoe they had more then an hundred and sixteene thousand Sea-faring men.

These fishing ships doe take yeerely two hundred thousand last of fish, twelve barrels to a last, which amounts to 300000. pounds by the fisher mens price, that 14. yeeres agoe did pay for their tenths three hundred thousand pound, which venting in Pumerland, Sprustia, Denmarke, Lefeland, Russia, Swethland, Germany, Netherlands, England, or else where, &c. makes their returnes in a yeere about threescore and ten hundred thousand pounds, which is seven millions; and yet in Holland there is neither matter to build ships nor merchandize to set them forth, yet by their industry they as much increase as other nations decay; but leaving these uncertainties as they are, of this I am certaine.

That the coast of England, Scotland and Ireland, the North Sea with Island and the Sound, Newfound-land and Cape Blanke, doe serve all Europe, as well the land townes as ports, and all the Christian shipping, with these sorts of staple fish, which is transported from whence it is taken many a thousand mile, viz. Herring, salt Fish, Poore-John, Sturgion, Mullit, Tunny, Porgos, Caviare, Buttargo.

Now seeing all these sorts of fish, or the most part of them may be had in a land more fertill, temperate and plentifull of all necessaries, for the building of ships, boats and houses, and the nourishment of man, the seasons are so proper, and the fishings so neere the habitations we may there make, that New-England hath much advantage of the most of those parts, to serve all Europe farre cheaper then they can, who at home have neither wood, salt, nor food, but at great rates, at Sea nothing but what they carry in their ships, an hundred or two hundred leagues from the habitation. But New-Englands fishings is neere land, where is helpe of Wood, Water, Fruits, Fowles, Corne or other refreshings needfull, and the Terceras, Mederas, Canaries, Spaine, Portugall, Prouaves, Savoy, Sicillia, and all Italy, as convenient markets for our dry fish, greene fish, Sturgion, Mullit, Caviare and Buttargo, as Norway, Swethland, Littuania or Germany for their Herring, which is heare also in abundance for taking; they returning but Wood, Pitch, Tar, Sope-ashes, Cordage, Flax, Wax, and such like commodities; wee Wines, Oiles, Sugars, Silkes, and such merchandize as the Straits affoord, whereby our profit may equalize theirs, besides the increase of shipping and Marriners: and for proofe hereof,

In the yeere of our Lord 1614. you have read how 1614.
I went from London: also the next yeere 1615. how 1615.
foure good ships went from London, and I with two more from Plimoth, with all our accidents, successes and
returnes: in the yeere 1616. ere I returned from France, 1616.
the Londoners for all their losse by the Turkes, sent foure ships more; foure more also went from Plimoth;
after I returned from France, I was perswaded againe to 1617.
goe to Plimoth with divers of my friends with one hundred pound for our adventures besides our charges, but wee found all things as untoward as before, and all their great promises nothing but aire: yet to prepare the voyage against the next yeere, having acquainted a great part of the Nobility with it, and ashamed to see the Prince his Highnesse till I had done some what worthy his Princely view; I spent that Summer in visiting the Cities and Townes of Bristoll, Exeter, Bastable, Bodnam, Perin, Foy, Milborow, Saltash, Dartmouth, Absom, Tattnesse, and the most of the Gentry in Cornewall and Devonshire, giving them Bookes and Maps, shewing how in six moneths the most of those ships had made their voyages, [VI. 229.] and some in lesse, and with what good successe; by which incitation they seemed so well contented, as they promised

My sute to the Country.

1617. twenty saile of ships should goe with mee next yeere, and in regard of my paines, charge, and former losses, the westerne Commissioners in behalfe of themselves and the rest of the Company, and them hereafter that should be joyned to them, contracted with me by articles indented under our hands, to be Admirall of that Country during my life, and in the renewing of their Letters-Patents so to be nominated. Halfe the fruits of our endevours to be theirs, the rest our owne; being thus ingaged, now the businesse is made plaine and likely to prosper, some of them would not onely forget me and their promises, but also obscure me, as if I had never beene acquainted in the businesse, but I am not the first they have deceived.

1618. There was foure good ships prepared at Plimoth, but by reason of their disagreement, the season so wasted, as onely two went forward, the one being of two hundred tunnes, returned well fraught to Plimoth, and her men in health, within five moneths; the other of fourescore tunnes went for Bilbow with drie fish and made a good returne. In this voyage Edward Rowcroft, alias Stallings, a valiant Souldier, that had beene with me in Virginia, and was with me also when I was betrayed by the French, was sent againe in those ships, and having some wrong offered him there by a French man, he tooke him, and as he writ to me, went with him to Virginia with fish, to trade with them for such commodities as they might spare: he had not past ten or twelve men, and knew both those countries well, yet he promised me the next spring to meet me in New-England, but the ship and he both perished in Virginia.

1619. This yeere againe, divers ships intending to goe from Plimoth, so disagreed, there went but one of two hundred tunnes, who stayed in the Country about six weeks, which with eight and thirty men and boies had her fraught, which she sold at the first penny for 2100 besides the Furres: so that every poore Sailer that had but a single share had his charges and sixteene pound ten shillings for his seven moneths worke. Master Thomas Dirmire an understanding and industrious Gentleman, that was also with me amongst the French men, having lived about a yeere in Newfoundland, returning to Plimoth, went for New-England in this ship, so much approved of this Country, that he staied there with five or six men in a little Boat, finding two or three French men amongst the Salvages who had lost their ship, augmented his company, with whom he ranged the Coast to Virginia, where he was kindly welcommed and well refreshed, thence returned to New-England againe, where having beene a yeere, in his backe returne to Virginia he was so wounded by the Salvages, he died upon it; let not men attribute these their great adventures, and untimely deaths to unfortunatenesse, but rather wonder how God did so long preserve them with so small meanes to doe so much, leaving the fruits of their labours to be an incouragement to those our poore undertakings, and as warnings for us not to undertake such great workes with such small meanes, and this for advantage as they writ unto me, that God had laid this Country open for us, and slaine the most part of the inhabitants by civill warres and a mortall disease, for where I had seene one hundred or two hundred Salvages, there is scarce ten to be found, and yet not any one of them touched with any sicknesse but one poore French man that died;

> They say this plague upon them thus sore fell,
> It was because they pleas'd not Tantum well.

From the West Country to make triall this yeere onely 1620.
to fish, is gone six or seven saile, three of which I am certainly informed made so good a voyage, that every Sailer that had a single share had twenty pound for his seven moneths work, which is more then in twenty moneths he should have gotten, had he gone for wages [VI. 230.]
any where. Now although these former ships have not made such good voiages as they expected, by sending opinionated unskilfull men, that had not experienced diligence to save that they tooke, nor take that there

was, which now patience and practice hath brought to a reasonable kinde of perfection; in despight of all detractors and calumniations the Country yet hath satisfied all, the defect hath beene in their using or abusing it, not in it selfe nor me: But,

Adue desert, for fortune makes provision
For Knaves and Fooles, and men of base condition.

My sute to the Citie. Now all these proofes and this relation I now called New-Englands triall. I caused two or three thousand of them to be printed, one thousand with a great many Maps both of Virginia and New-England. I presented to thirty of the chiefe Companies in London at their Halls, desiring either generally or particularly (them that would) to imbrace it, and by the use of a stocke of five thousand pound, to ease them of the superfluity of the most of their companies that had but strength and health to labour; neere a yeere I spent to understand their resolutions, which was to me a greater toile and torment, then to have beene in New-England about my businesse but with bread and water, and what I could get there by my labour; but in conclusion, seeing nothing would be effected, I was contented as well with this losse of time and charge as all the rest.

A Plantation in New-England.

1620. UPon these inducements some few well disposed Gentlemen, and Merchants of London and other places, provided two ships, the one of a hundred and threescore tunnes, the other of threescore and ten, they left the Coast of England the two and thirtieth of August, with about a hundred and twenty persons, but the next day the lesser ship sprung a leake, that forced their returne to Plimoth, where discharging her and twenty passengers; with the greater ship and one hundred passengers besides Sailers, they set saile againe the sixt of September, and the ninth of November fell with Cape James, but being pestred nine weekes in this leaking unwholsome ship, lying wet in their Cabins, most of them grew very weake and weary of the Sea; then for want of experience, ranging two and againe six weekes before they found a place they liked to dwell on, forced to lie on the bare ground without coverture, forty of them died, and threescore were left in very weake estate at the ships comming away, about the fifth of Aprill following, and arrived in England the sixth of May. Though the Harbour be good, the shore is so shallow, they were forced to wade a great way up to the knees in water, & used that that did them much hurt; & little fish they found but Whailes, and a great kinde of Mustell so fat, that few did eat of them that were not sicke: these miseries occasioned some discord, and gave some appearance of faction, but all was so reconciled, that they united themselves by common consent under their hands, to a kinde of combination of a body politike, by vertue whereof to inact and constitute lawes and ordinances, and Officers from time to time, as should bee thought most convenient for their generall good.

Their first journy by land.

Sixteene or seventeene daies they could doe little for want of their Shallop which was amending, yet Captaine Miles Standish, unto whom was joyned in Councell, William Bradfor, Stephen Hopkins and Edward Tilly, went well armed a shore, and by that time they had gone a mile, met five or six Indians that fled into the Woods: we traced them by the footing eight or ten miles, then the night approaching we made a fire, by which we lay that night, and the next morning followed the Salvages by their tract, thinking to finde their habitations, but by the way we found a Deere amongst many faire springs [VI. 231.] of water, where we refreshed our selves; then we went a shore and made a fire, that they at the ship might perceive where we were, and so marched to a place where we supposed was a River; by the way we saw many Vines, Saxefras, haunts of Deere & Fowle, and some fifty Acres of plaine ground had beene planted by the Indians, where were some of their graves; from thence we followed a path that brought us through three or foure fields that had bin planted that yeere; in one grave we digged, we found a basket or two of Indian Corne, so much as we could carry we tooke with us, the rest we buried as we found it, and so proceeded to the place we intended, but we found it not such a Harbour as we expected; and so we returned, till the night caused us take up our lodging under a tree, where it rained six or seven houres: the next morning as we wandred, we passed by a tree, where a young sprig was bowed downe over a bough, and some Acornes strewed under it, which was one of their Gins to catch a Deere, and as we were looking at it, Bradford was suddenly caught by the leg in a noosed Rope, made as artificially as ours; as we passed we see a lease of Bucks, sprung some Partriges, and great flocks of wilde Geese and Ducks, and so we returned well wearied to our ship.

Their first journy by Shallop.

Master Jones our Master with foure and thirty men, also went up and downe in the frost and snow, two or three daies in the extremity of the cold, but could finde no harbour; only among the old graves we got some ten bushels of Corne, some Beanes, and a bottle of Oile; and had we not thus haply found it, we had had no Corne for seede, so that place we ever called Corne-hill; the next day Master Jones with the Corne and our weakest men returned to the Ship, but eighteene of us quartered there that night, and in the morning following the paths, wee found in the Snow in a field a greater hill or grave then the rest, digging it wee found first a Mat, under that a boord three quarters long, painted and carved with three Tyns at the top like a Cronet, betweene the Mats also were Bowles, Traies and Dishes and such trash, at length we found a faire new Mat, and under that two bundles, the one biggar the other lesse; in the greater wee found a great quantity of fine red powder like a kinde of imbalmement, and yeelded a strong but no offensive smell, with the bones and skull of a man that had fine yellow haire still on it, and some of the flesh unconsumed, a Knife, a Pack-needle, and two or three old Iron things was bound up in a Sailers canvase Cassocke, also a paire of cloth Breeches; in the lesse bundle we found likewise of the same powder, and the bones and head of a little childe; about the legs and other parts of it was bound strings and braslets of white beades, there was also a little Bow, and some other odde knacks, the prettiest we tooke, and covered againe the corps as they were: not farre from thence were two of their houses, where were a great deale of their miserable houshold stuffe, which we left as wee found, and so returned to our Boat, and lay aboord that night.

Accidents.

Many arguments we had to make here our Plantation or not; in the Intrim, Mistris White was brought to bed of a young sonne, which was called Perigrine: and a Sailer shooting at a Whale, his peece flew in peeces stocke and all, yet he had no hurt. A foolish boy discharging his fathers peece hard by halfe a barrell of Powder, and many people by it, it pleased God it escaped firing, so that no hurt was done.

Their second journey by water to finde a place to plant in.

But to make a more certaine discovery where to seat our selves, Captaine Standish, Master Carver, William Branford, Edward Winsloe, John Tilly, Edward Tilly, with divers others to the number of seventeene, upon the sixt of December set saile, and having sailed six or seven leagues, we espied eight or ten Salvages about a dead Grampus: still following the shore we found two or three more cast up by the ill weather, many we see in the water, therefore we called it Grampus Bay: Ships may ride well in it, but all the shore is very shallow flats of sand; at last seven or eight of us went a shore, many fields we saw where the Salvages had inhabited, and a buriall place incompassed with a Palizado, so we returned to our Shallop, in the night we heard a hideous cry and [VI. 232.] howling of Wolves and Foxes; in the morning as we were ready to goe into our Shallop, one of our men being in the woods, came running crying, Indians, Indians, and with all their Arrowes flying amongst us, some of our men being in the boat, and their Armes a shore, so well it chanced, Captaine Standish with two or three more discharged their peeces till the rest were ready, one Salvage more stout then the rest kept under a tree, till he had shot three or foure Arrowes, and endured three or foure Musket shot, but at last they all fled, this was about breake of day in the morning when they saw us, and we not them.

Their first fight with the Salvages.

The description of their place to plant in.

Having the wind faire, we sailed along the coast 8. or 10. leagues, thinking to have got to a Harbour where one of our company had beene, within 8. leagues of Cape Cod, for neither cricke nor Harbour in this bay we could finde; and the wind so increased, our Rudder broke, and our Mast flew over-boord, that we were in danger to be cast away, but at last it pleased God we were in a harbor we knew not, thinking it one we were acquainted with, this we found to be an Ile where we rid that night, and having well viewed the land about it, and sounded the Bay to be a good Harbour for our ship, compassed with good land, and in it two faire Iles, where there is in their seasons innumerable store of all sorts of fish and fowle, good water, much plaine land, which hath beene planted; with this newes we returned to our ship, and with the next faire wind brought her thither, being but within the sight of Cape Cod; in the meane time Goodwife Alderton was delivered of a sonne, but dead borne. Upon the 28. of December, so many as could went to worke upon the hill, where we purposed to build our Platforme for our ordnance, which doth command all the Plaine and the Bay, and from whence wee may see far into the Sea, and be easily impailed, so in the afternoone we went to measure out the grounds, and divided our company into 19. families, alotting to every person halfe a poule in bredth and three in length, and so we cast lots where every man should lie, which we staked out, thinking this proportion enough at the first to impale for lodgings and gardens.

Another Boy borne in New-England.

Their first Plantation.

Francis Billington from the top of a tree seeing a great

water some three miles from us in the land, went with the Masters Mate, and found it two great Lakes of fresh water, the bigger five or six miles in circuit, and an Ile in it of a Cables length square; the other three miles in compasse, full of fish and fowle, and two brooks issuing from it, which will be an excellent helpe in time for us, where they saw seven or eight Indian houses, but no people. Foure being sent a mile or two from our plantation, two of them stragling into the woods was lost, for comming to a Lake of water they found a great Deere, having a mastive Bitch and a Spanell with them, they followed so farre they could not finde the way backe, that afternoone it rained, and did freeze and snow at night; their apparell was very thin, and had no weapons but two sickles, nor any victuals, nor could they finde any of the Salvages habitations; when the night came they were much perplexed that they had no other bed then the earth, nor coverture then the skies, but that they heard, as they thought, two Lions roaring a long time together very nigh them, so not knowing what to doe, they resolved to climbe up into a tree, though that would be an intollerable cold lodging, expecting their coming they stood at the trees root, and the bitch they held fast by the necke, for shee would have beene gone to the Lions or what they were, that as it chanced came not nigh them, so they watched the tree that extreme cold night, and in the morning travelling againe, passing by many lakes, brooks and woods, and in one place where the Salvages had burnt 4. or 5. miles in length, which is a fine champion Country, in the afternoone they discovered the two Iles in their Bay, and so that night neere famished they got to their Plantation, from whence they had sent out men every way to seeke them; that night the house they had built and thatched, where lay their armes, bedding, powder, &c. tooke fire and was burnt, the Coast is so shoule, the ship rides more then a mile from the Fort, but God be thanked no man was hurt though much was burnt.

Two faire Lakes.

Two men lost themselves in the woods.

[VI. 233.] *Their first conference with a Salvage.* All this time we could not have conference with a Salvage, though we had many times seene them and had many alarums, so that we drew a Councell, and appointed Captaine Standish to have the command of all martiall actions, but even in the time of consultation the Salvages gave an alarum: the next day also as wee were agreeing upon his orders, came a tall Salvage boldly amongst us, not fearing any thing, and kindly bad us welcome in English; he was a Sagamo, towards the North, where the ships use to fish, and did know the names of most of the Masters that used thither: such victuall as we had we gave him, being the first Salvage we yet could speake with, he told us this place where we were was called Patuxet, and that all the people three or foure yeeres agoe there died on the plague: in a day or two we could not be rid of him, then he returned to the Massasoyts from whence he came, where is some sixty people, but the Nawsits are 100. strong, which were they encountred our people at the first. *The second conference.* Two daies after this Samoset, for so was his name, came againe, and brought five or six of the Massasoyts with him, with certaine skinnes, and certaine tooles they had got that we had left in the woods at their alarums: much friendship they promised, and so departed, but Samoset would not leave us, but fained himselfe sicke, yet at last he went to entreat the Salvages come againe to confirme a peace: now the third time, as we were consulting of our Marshall orders, two Salvages appeared, but when we went to them they vanished: not long after came Samoset, & Squanto, a native of Patuxet where we dwell, and one of them carried into Spaine by Hunt, thence brought into England, where a good time he lived; and now here signified unto us, their great Sachem of Massasoyt, with Quadaquina his brother, and all their men, was there by to see us: not willing to send our Governour, we sent Edward Wollislo with presents to them both, to know their minds, making him to understand by his Interpreters how King James did salute him and was his friend; after a little conference with twenty of his men, he came over the brooke to our Plantation, where we set him upon a rug, and then brought our Governour to him with Drums and Trumpets; where after some circumstances, for they use few complements, we treated of peace with them to this effect.

Their conditions of peace.

That neither he nor any of his should injury or doe hurt to any of us; if they did, he should send us the offender, that we might punish him, and wee would doe the like to him: if any did unjustly warre against him, we would aid him, as he should us against our enemies, and to send to his neighbour confederats to certifie them of this, that they might likewise be comprised in these conditions, that when any of them came to us, they should leave their Bow and Arrowes behinde them, as we would our peeces when we came to them, all which the King seemed to like well of, and was applauded of his followers, in his person hee is a very lusty man, in his best yeeres, an able body, grave of countenance, and spare of speech: in his attire little differing from the rest; after all was done, the Governour conducted him to the brooke, but kept our hostage till our messengers returned: in like manner we used Quaddaquina, so all departed good friends.

Two of his people would have staied with us, but wee would not permit them, onely Samoset and Squanto wee entertained kindly; as yet wee have found they intend to keepe promise, for they have not hurt our men they have found stragling in the Woods, and are afraid of their powerfull Adversaries the Narrohiggansets, against whom hee hopes to make use of our helpe. The next day Squanto went a fishing for Eeles, and in an houre he did tread as many out of the Ose with his feet as he could lift with his hand, not having any other instrument.

A journey to Pakanoki.

But that we might know their habitations so well as they ours, Stephen Hopkins and Edward Winslo had Squantum for their guide and Interpreter; to Packanoki, the habitation of the King of Massasoyt, with a red horsemans coat for a present, to entreat him by reason

[VI. 234.] we had not victuall to entertaine them as we would, he would defend his people so much from visiting us; and if hee did send, he should alwaies send with the Messenger a copper Chaine they gave him, that they might know he came from him, and also give them some of his Corne for seede: that night they lodged at Namascet, some fifteene miles off: by the way we found ten or twelve women and children that still would pester us till we were weary of them, perceiving it is the manner of them, where victuall is to bee gotten with most ease, there they will live; but on that River of Namaschet have beene many habitations of the Salvages that are dead, and the land lies waste, and the River abounding with great plenty of fish, and hath beene much frequented by the French.

A great courage of two old Salvages.

The next day travelling with six or seven Indians, where we were to wade over the River, did dwell onely two old men of that Nation then living, that thinking us enemies, sought the best advantage they could to fight with us, with a wonderfull shew of courage, but when they knew us their friends they kindly welcommed us; after we came to a towne of the Massasoits, but at Pakanoki the King was not: towards night he arrived and was very proud, both of our message and presents, making a great oration to all his people, Was not he Massasoit, Commander of the country about him, was not such a towne his, and the people of it, and 20. townes more he named was his? and should they not bring their skins to us? to which they answered, they were his and they would; victual they had none, nor any lodging, but a poore planke or two, a foot high from the ground, wheron his wife and he lay at the one end, we at the other, but a thin Mat upon them, two more of his chiefe men pressed by and upon us, so that we were worse weary of our lodging then of our journey. Although there is such plenty of fish and fowle and wild beasts, yet are they so lasie they will not take paines to catch it till meere hunger constraine them, for in two or three daies we had scarce a meales

How the King used them.

meat, whereby we were so faint, we were glad to be at home: besides what for the fleas, and their howling and singing in the night in their houses, and the Musketas without doores, our heads were as light for want of sleepe, as our bellies empty for want of meat. The next voiage we made was in a Shallop with ten men to Nawsit, sixteene miles from us, to fetch a Boy was lost in the Woods we heard was there, whom Aspinet their King had bedecked like a salvage, but very kindly he brought him to us, and so returned well to Patuyet.

A voyage to Nawsit.

Immediatly after the arrival of the last ship, they sent another of five and fifty tuns to supply them; with seven and thirty persons they set saile in the beginning of July, but being crossed by westernly winds, it was the end of August ere they could passe Plimoth, and arrived in New-England at New-Plimoth, now so called the 11. of November, where they found all the people they left so ill, lusty and well for all their poverties, except six that died: a moneth they stayed ere they returned to England, loaded with Clap-boord, Wainscot and Wallnut, with about three hogs-heads of Bever skinnes the 13. of December: and drawing neere our coast was set on by a French man set out by the Marquesse of Cera, Governour of Ile Deu, where they kept the ship, imprisoned the Master and company, tooke from them to the value of 500 pound, and after 14. daies sent them home with a poore supply of victuall, their owne being devoured by the Marquesse and his hungry servants.

1621.

Now you are to understand this 37. brought nothing, but relied wholly on us to make us more miserable then before, which the Sachem Covanacus no sooner understood, but sent to Tusquantum our Interpreter, a bundle of new arrowes in a Snakes skinne; Tusquantum being absent, the Messenger departed, but when we understood it was a direct challenge, we returned the skin full of powder and shot, with an absolute defiance, which caused us finish our fortification with all expedition. Now betwixt our two Salvages, Tusquantum and Hobbamock,

grew such great emulation, we had much adoe to know which best to trust. In a journey we undertooke, in our way we met a Salvage of Tusquantums, that had cut his
[VI. 235.] face fresh bleeding, to assure us Massasoyt our supposed friend, had drawne his forces to Packanokick to assault us. Hobomak as confidently assured us it was false, and sent his wife as an espy to see; but when she perceived all was well, shee told the King Massasoyt how Tusquantum had abused him, divers Salvages also hee had caused to beleeve we would destroy them, but he would doe his best to appease us; this he did onely to make his Country-men beleeve what great power hee had with us to get bribes on both sides, to make peace or warre when he would, and the more to possesse them with feare, he perswaded many we had buried the plague in our store house, which wee could send when we listed whither wee would, but at last all his knavery being discovered, Massasowat sent his knife with Messengers for his head or him, being his subject; with much adoe we appeased the angry King and the rest of the Salvages, and freely forgave Tusquantum, because he speaking our language we could not well be without him.

A journey to the Towne of Namaschet, in defence of the King of Massasoyt, against the Narrohigganses, and the supposed death of Squantum.

A Great difference there was betwixt the Narrohigganses and the Massasoytes, that had alwaies a jealousie; Coubatant one of their petty Sachems was too conversant with the Narrohigganses, this Coubatant lived much at Namaschet, and much stormed at our peace with his King and others; also at Squantum, and Tokamahamon, and Hobomak our friends, and chiefe occasioners of our peace, for which he sought to murther Hobomak; yet Tokamahamon went to him upon a rumour he had taken Masasoyt prisoner, or forced him from his Country, but the other two would not, but in privat to see if they could heare what was become of their King; lodging at Namaschet they were discovered to Coubatant, who surprized the house and tooke Squantum, saying, if hee were dead the English had lost their tongue; Hobomak seeing that, and Coubatant held a knife at his brest, being a strong lusty fellow, brake from them and came to New-Plimoth, full of sorrow for Squantum, whom he thought was slaine.

They surprise the Salvages.

The next day we sent ten men with him armed to be revenged of Coubatant, who conducted us neere Namaschet, where we rested and refreshed our selves til midnight, and then we beset the house as we had resolved; those that entred the house demanded for Coubatant, but the Salvages were halfe dead with feare, we charged them not to stirre, for we came to hurt none but Coubatant, for killing Squantum, some of them seeking to escape was wounded, but at last perceiving our ends, they told us Coubatant was gone and all his men, and Squantum was yet living, & in the towne; in this hurly burly we discharged two peeces at randome, which much terrified all the inhabitants except Squantum and Tokamahamon, who though they knew not the end of our comming, yet assured themselves of our honesties, that we would not hurt them; the women and children hung about Hobomak, calling him friend, and when they saw we would hurt no women, the young youths cryed we are women; to be short, we kept them all, and whilest we were searching the house for Coubatant, Hobomak had got to the top, and called Squantum & Tokamahamon, which came unto us accompanied with others, some armed, others naked, those that had bowes we tooke them from them, promising them againe when it was day: the house wee tooke for our quarter that night and discharged the prisoners, and the next morning went to breakfast to Squantums house; thither came all them that loved us to welcome us, but all Coubatants faction was fled, then we made them plainly know the cause of our comming, & if their King Massasoyt were not well, we would be revenged upon the Narro-higgansets, or any that should doe injury to Hobomak,

Squantum, or any of their friends; as for those were wounded we were sorry for it, and offered our Surgion should heale them, of this offer a man and a woman [VI. 236.] accepted, that went home with us, accompanied with Squantum, and many other knowne friends, that offered us all the kindnesse they could.

From the West of England there is gone ten or twelve ships to fish, which were all well fraughted: those that came first at Bilbow, made seventeene pound a single share, besides Bevers, Otters, and Martins skinnes; but some of the rest that came to the same ports, that were all ready furnished, so glutted the market, that the price was abated, yet all returned so well contented, that they are a preparing to goe againe.

1622. There is gone from the West Countrey onely to fish, five and thirtie ships, and about the last of Aprill two more from London; the one of one hundred tunnes, the other of thirtie, with some sixtie Passengers to supply the Plantation. Now though the Turke and French hath beene somewhat too busie in taking our ships, would all the Christian Princes be truly at unitie, as his Royall Majestie our Soveraigne King James desireth, seventie Saile of good ships were sufficient to fire the most of his Coasts in the Levant, and make such a guard in the Straights of Hellespont, as would make the great Turke himselfe more affraid in Constantinople, then the smallest Red-Crosse that crosses the Seas would be, either of any French Pickaroun, or the Pirats of Algere.

An abstract of divers Relations sent from the Colony in New England, July 16. 1622.

Notes and observations. SInce the massacre in Virginia, though the Indians continue their wonted friendship, yet wee are more wary of them then before; for their hands hath beene imbrued in much English bloud, onely by too much confidence, but not by force, and we have had small supplies of any thing but men. Here I must intreat a little your favours to digresse, they did not kill the

English in Virginia, because they were Christians: but for their weapons and Copper, which were rare novelties; but now they feare we may beat them out of their dens, which Lions and Tigers will not admit but by force. But must this be an argument for an English man, and discourage any in Virginia or New England: No, for I have tried them both, as you may reade at large in the Historie of Virginia; notwithstanding since I came from thence, the Honourable Company hath beene humble suiters to his Majestie, to get vagabonds and condemned men to goe thither; nay, so the businesse hath beene so abused, that so much scorned was the name of Virginia, some did chuse to be hanged ere they would goe thither, and were: Yet for all the worst of spight, detraction, and discouragement, and this lamentable massacre, there is more honest men now suiters to goe, then ever hath beene constrained knaves. And it is not unknowne to most men of understanding, how happy many of those Collumners hath thought themselves that they might be admitted; and yet pay for their passage to goe now to Virginia, and I feare mee there goeth too many of those, that hath shifted heere till they could no longer; and they will use that qualitie there till they hazard all.

To range this Countrey of New England in like manner, I had but eight, as is said, and amongst their bruit conditions, I met many of their silly encounters, and I give God thankes, without any hurt at all to me, or any with mee. When your West-Countrey men were so wounded and tormented with the Salvages, though they had all the Politicke directions that had beene gathered from all the secret informations could be heard of, yet they found little, and returned with nothing. I speak not this out of vaine-glory, as it may be some gleaners, or some who were never there may censure me; but to let all men be assured by those examples, what those Salvages are, that thus strangely doe murder and betray our Countrymen: but to the purpose;

The Paragon with thirtie seven men sent to releeve

[VI. 237.] them, miscaried twice upon our English Coast, whereby they failed of their supplies. It is true, there hath beene taken one thousand Bases at a draught; and in one night twelve Hogsheads of Herrings: but when they wanted all necessaries both for fishing and sustinance, but what they could get with their naked industry, they indured most extreme wants, having beene now neere two yeeres without any supply to any purpose, it is a wonder how they should subsist, much lesse so to resist the Salvages, fortifie themselves, plant sixtie acres of Corne, besides their Gardens that were well replenished with many usuall fruits. But in the beginning of July came in two ships of Master Westons, though we much wanted our selves, yet we releeved them what we could: and to requite us, they destroied our Corne and Fruits then planted, and did what they could to have done the like to us. At last they were transported to Wichaguscusset at the Massachusets, where they abused the Salvages worse then us. We having neither Trade, nor scarce any thing remaining, God sent in one Master Jones, and a ship of Westons had beene at Monahigan amongst the Fisher-men, that for Bever skinnes and such Merchandize as wee had, very well refreshed us, though at deere rates. Weston left also his men a small Barke, and much good provision, and so set saile for England. Then wee joyned with them to trade to the Southward of Cape Cod, twice or thrice wee were forced to returne; first by the death of their Governor; then the sicknesse of Captaine Standish. At last our Governor Master Bradford undertooke it himselfe to have found the passage betwixt the Shoules and the Maine, then Tusquantum our Pilot died, so that we returned to the Massachusets, where we found the trade spoiled, and nothing but complaints betwixt the Salvages and the English. At Nawset we were kindly used and had good trade, though we lost our Barge, the Salvages carefully kept both her wracke, and some ten Hogsheads of Corne three moneths, and so we returned some by land, some in the ship.

They lived two yeeres without supply.

Westons Plantation.

The death of Tusquantum.

Captaine Standish being recovered, went to fetch them both, and traded at Namasket and Monomete, where the people had the plague, a place much frequented with Dutch and French. Here the Sachem put a man to death for killing his fellow at play, wherein they are so violent, they will play their coats from their backs, and also their wives, though many miles from them. But our provision decaying, Standish is sent to Mattachist, where they pretended their wonted love; yet it plainly appeared they intended to kill him. Escaping thence, wee went to Monomete, where we found nothing but bad countenances. Heare one Wittuwamat a notable villaine, would boast how many French and English hee had slaine: This Champion presenting a Dagger to the Sachem Canacum he had got from the English, occasioned us to understand how they had contrived to murder all the English in the Land, but having such a faire opportunitie, they would begin heere with us. Their scornfull usage made the Captaine so passionate to appease his anger and choler, their intent made many faire excuses for satisfaction: Scar a lusty Salvage, alwaies seeming the most to effect us, bestowed on us the best presents he had without any recompence, saying; Hee was rich enough to bestow such favours on his friends, yet had undertaken to kill the Captaine himselfe, but our vigilencies so prevented the advantage they expected, we safely returned, little suspecting in him any such treachery.

Tusquantum at his death desired the English to pray he might go dwell with the English mens God, for theirs was a good God.

They contrive to murder all the English.

During this time a Dutch ship was driven a shore at Massasowat, whose King lay very sicke, now because it is a generall custome then for all their friends to visit them: Master Winslow, and Master Hamden, with Habamok for their guide, were sent with such Cordialls as they had to salute him; by the way they so oft heard the King was dead, Habamok would breake forth in those words, My loving Sachem, my loving Sachem, many have I knowne, but never any like thee, nor shall ever see the like amongst the Salvages; for he was no lier, nor bloudy and cruell like other Indians, in anger soone reclaimed, he would be ruled

The sicknesse of King Massasowat.

by reason, not scorning the advice of meane men, and governed his men better with a few strokes, then others with many: truly loving where he loved, yea he feared wee
[VI. 238.] had not a faithfull friend left amongst all his Country-men, shewing how oft he had restrained their malice, much more with much passion he spoke to this purpose, till at last we arrived where we found the Dutchmen but newly gone, and the house so full we could hardly get in. By their charmes they distempered us that were well, much more him that was sicke, women rubbing him to keepe heat in him; but their charmes ended, understanding of us, though he had lost his sight, his understanding failed not; but taking Winslow by the hand, said, Art thou Winslow, Oh Winslow, I shall never see thee againe! Hobamock telling him what restauratives they had brought, he desired to taste them, with much adoe they got a little Confexion of many comfortable Conserves into his mouth, as it desolved he swallowed it, then desolving more of it in water, they scraped his tongue, which was al furred & swolne, and washed his mouth, and then gave him more of it to eat, and in his drinke, that wrought such an alteration in him in two or three houres, his eies opened to our great contents; with this and such brothes as they there provided for him, it pleased God he recovered: and thus the manner of his sicknesse and cure caused no small admiration amongst them.

His cure by the English.

The Kings thankfulnesse.

During the time of their stay to see his recovery, they had sent to New Plimoth for divers good things for him, which he tooke so kindly, that he fully revealed all the former conspiracies against us, to which he had oft beene moved; and how that all the people of Powmet, Nawset, Succonet, Mattachist, Manamet, Augawam, and Capawac, were joyned to murder us; therefore as we respected our lives, kill them of Massachuset that were the authors; for take away the principals and the plot wil cease, thus taking our leaves, & arriving at our fort, we found our brave liberall friend of Pamet drawing Standish to their Ambuscados, which being thus discovered, we sent him away, as though we knew nor suspected any thing. Them at the Massachusets, some were so vilde they served the Salvages for victuall, the rest sent us word the Salvages were so insolent, they would assault them though against their Commission, so fearefull they were to breake their Commission, so much time was spent in consultations, they all were famished, till Wassapinewat againe came and told them the day of their execution was at hand.

A bad example.

Then they appointed Standish with eight chosen men, under colour of Trade to catch them in their owne trap at Massachuset, & acquaint it with the English in the Towne, where arriving he found none in the Barke, and most of the rest without Armes, or scarce clothes, wandering abroad, all so sencelesly secure, he more then wondered they were not all slaine, with much adoe he got the most of them to their Towne. The Salvages suspecting their plots discovered, Pecksnot a great man, and of as great a spirit, came to Habamak, who was then amongst them, saying; Tell Standish we know he is come to kill us, but let him begin when he dare. Not long after many would come to the Fort and whet their Knives before him, with many braving speeches. One amongst the rest was by Wittawamat bragging he had a Knife, that on the handle had the picture of a womans face, but at home I have one hath killed both French & English, and that hath a mans face on it, and by and by these two must marrie: but this here, by and by shall see, and by and by eat, but not speake; Also Pecksnot being of a greater stature then the Captaine, told him, though he were a great Captaine he was but a little man, and I though no Sachem, yet I am of great strength and courage. These things Standish bare patiently for the present; but the next day seeing he could not get many of them together, but these two Roarers, and two more being in a convenient roome, and his company about him, Standish seased on Pecksnots Knife then hanging about his necke, wherewith he slew him, and the rest slew Wittuwamat and the other Salvage, but the youth they tooke, who

Captaine Standish sent to suppresse the Salvages.

Two desperate Salvages slaine.

being Brother to Wittuwamat, and as villanous as himselfe, was hanged. It is incredible how many wounds they indured, catching at their weapons without any feare or bruit, till the last gasp. Habamack stood by all this time very silent, but all ended, he said, Yesterday Pecksnot bragged of his strength and stature, but I see you are big enough to lay him on the ground.

[VI. 239.] *The Salvages overcommed.* The Towne he left to the guard of Westons people: three Salvages more were slaine; upon which rumour they all fled from their houses. The next day they met with a file of Salvages that let fly their Arrowes, shot for shot till Hobamack shewed himselfe, and then they fled. For all this, a Salvage Boy to shew his innocency, came boldly unto us and told us: Had the English Fugitives but finished the three Canowes they were a making, to have taken the ship, they would have done as much to all the English, which was onely the cause they had forborne so long. But now consulting and considering their estates, those that went in the Pinnace to Barty Iles to get passage for England, the rest to New Plimoth, where they were kindly entertained. The Sachem Obtakeest, & Powas, and divers other were guilty, the three fugitives in their fury there slew; but not long after so distracted were those poore scattered people, they left their habitations, living in swamps, where with cold and infinite diseases they endured much mortalitie, suing for peace, and crying the God of England is angry with them. Thus you see where God pleases, as some flourish, others perish.

1623. Now on all hands they prepare their ground, and about the middest of Aprill, in a faire season they begin to plant till the latter end of May; but so God pleased, that in six weekes after the latter setting there scarce fell any raine; so that the stalke was first set, began to eare ere it came to halfe growth, and the last not like to yeeld any thing at all. Our Beanes also seemed so withered, we judged all utterly dead, that now all our hopes were overthrowne, and our joy turned into mourning. And more to our sorrow, we heard of the twice returne of the

An extreme drought.

Paragon, that now the third time was sent us three moneths agoe, but no newes of her: onely the signes of a wracke we saw on the Coast which wee judged her. This caused not every of us to enter into a private consideration betwixt God and our consciences, but most solemnly to humble our selves before the Lord by fasting and praying, to releeve our dejected spirits by the comforts of his mercy. In the morning when wee assembled all together, the skies were as cleere, and the drought as like to continue as ever; yet our exercise continued eight or nine houres. Before our departure, the skies were all over-cast, and on the next morning distilled such soft, sweet, moderate showers, continuing foureteene daies, mixed with such seasonable weather, as it was hard to say, whether our withered Corne, or drooping affections were most quickned and revived; such was the bounty and mercy of God. Of this the Indians by the meanes of Hobamock tooke notice, who seeing us use this exercise in the midst of the weeke, said; It was but three daies since Sunday, and desired to know the reason; which when hee understood, he and all of them admired the goodnesse of God towards us, shewing the difference betwixt their conjurations and our praiers, and what stormes and dangers they oft receive thereby. To expresse our thankfulnesse, wee assembled together another day, as before, and either the next morning, or not long after, came in two ships to supply us, and all their Passengers well except one, and he presently recovered. For us, notwithstanding all these wants, there was not a sicke person amongst us. The greater ship we returned fraught; the other wee sent to the Southward, to trade under the command of Captaine Altom. So that God be thanked, we desire nothing, but what we will returne Commodities to the value.

A wonderfull blessing & signe of Gods love.

Thus all men finde our great God he,
That never wanted nature,
To teach his truth, that onely he
Of every thing is Author.

Forty saile sent to fish. For this yeere from England is gone about fortie saile of ships, only to fish, and as I am informed, have made a farre better voyage then ever.

[VI. 240.] Now some new great observers will have this an Iland, because I have writ it is the Continent: others report, that the people are so bruit, they have no religion, wherein surely they are deceived; for my part, I never heard of any Nation in the world which had not a Religion, deare, bowes and arrowes. *Their Religion.* They beleeve as doe the Virginians, of many divine powers, yet of one above all the rest, as the Southerne Virginians call their chiefe God Kewassa, and that wee now inhabit Oke, but both their Kings Werowance. The Masachusets call their great God Kiehtan, and their Kings there abouts Sachems: The Penobscotes their greatest power Tantum, and their Kings Sagomos. Those where is this Plantation, say Kiehtan made all the other Gods: also one man and one woman, and of them all mankinde, but how they became so dispersed they know not. They say, at first there was no King but Kiehtan that dwelleth farre westerly above the heavens, whither all good men goe when they die, and have plentie of all things. The bad men goe thither also and knocke at the doore, but he bids them goe wander in endlesse want and miserie, for they shall not stay there. They never saw Kiehtan, but they hold it a great charge and dutie, that one age teach another; and to him they make feasts, and cry and sing for plentie and victorie, or any thing is good. They have another Power they call Hobamock, which wee conceive the Devill, and upon him they call to cure their wounds and diseases: when they are curable he perswades them he sent them, because they have displeased him; but if they be mortall, then he saith, Kiehtan sent them, which makes them never call on him in their sicknesse. They say this Hobamock appeares to them somtimes like a Man, a Deere, or an Eagle, but most commonly like a Snake; not to all, but only to their Powahs to cure diseases, and Undeses, which is one of the chiefe next the King, and so bold in the warres, that they thinke no weapon can kill them: and those are such as conjure in Virginia, and cause the people to doe what they list.

Their Government.

For their Government: every Sachem is not a King, but their great Sachems have divers Sachems under their protection, paying them tribute, and dare make no warres without his knowledge; but every Sachem taketh care for the Widowes, Orphans, the aged and maimed, nor will they take any to first wife, but them in birth equall to themselves, although they have many inferior Wives and Concubins that attend on the principall; from whom he never parteth, but any of the rest when they list, they inherit by succession, and every one knowes their owne bounds. To his men, hee giveth them land, also bounded, and what Deere they kill in that circuit, he hath the fore-part; but if in the water, onely the skin: But they account none a man, till hee hath done some notable exploit: the men are most imploied in hunting, the women in slavery; the younger obey the elders: their names are variable; they have harlots and honest women: the harlots never marrie, or else are widowes. They use divorcement, and the King commonly punisheth all offenders himselfe: when a maid is maried, she cutteth her haire, and keepes her head covered till it be growne againe. Their arts, games, musicke, attire, burials, and such like, differ very little from the Virginians, onely for their Chronicles they make holes in the ground, as the others set up great stones. Out of the Relations of Master Edward Winslow.

An answer to Objections.

Now I know the common question is, For all those miseries, where is the wealth they have got, or the Gold or Silver Mines? To such greedy unworthy minds I say once againe: The Sea is better then the richest Mine knowne, and of all the fishing ships that went well provided, there is no complaint of losse nor misery, but rather an admiration of wealth, profit, and health. As for the land were it never so good, in two yeeres so few of such small experience living without supplies so well, and in health, it was an extraordinary blessing from God. But

that with such small meanes they should subsist, and doe so much, to any understanding judgement is a wonder. Notwithstanding, the vaine expectation of present gaine in some, ambition in others, that to be great would have all else slaves, and the carelesnesse in providing supplies, hath caused those defailements in all those Plantations, and
[VI. 241.] how ever some bad conditions will extoll the actions of any Nation but their owne: yet if we may give credit to the Spaniards, Portugals, and French writings, they indured as many miseries, and yet not in twenty yeeres effected so much, nay scarce in fortie.

The ordinary voyage to goe to Virginia or New-England.

Thus you may see plainly the yeerely successe from New England by Virginia, which hath beene so costly to this Kingdome, and so deare to me, which either to see perish, or but bleed; Pardon me though it passionate me beyond the bounds of modesty, to have beene sufficiently able to fore-see their miseries, and had neither power nor meanes to prevent it. By that acquaintance I have with them, I call them my children, for they have beene my Wife, my Hawks, Hounds, my Cards, my Dice, and in totall, my best content, as indifferent to my heart, as my left hand to my right. And notwithstanding, all those miracles of disasters have crossed both them and me, yet were there not an Englishman remaining, as God be thanked notwithstanding the massacre there are some thousands; I would yet begin againe with as small meanes as I did at first, not that I have any secret encouragement (I protest) more then lamentable experience; for all their discoveries I have yet heard of, are but Pigs of my owne Sow, nor more strange to me, then to heare one tell me hee hath gone from Billingsgate and discovered Gravesend, Tilbury, Quinborow, Lee, and Margit, which to those did never heare of them, though they dwell in England, might bee made some rare secrets and great Countries unknowne, except some few Relations of Master Dirmer. In England, some are held great travellers that have seene Venice, and Rome, Madrill, Toledo, Sivill, Algere, Prague, or Ragonsa, Constantinople, or Jerusalem, and the

Piramides of Egypt; that thinke it nothing to goe to Summer Iles, or Virginia, which is as far as any of them; and I hope in time will prove a more profitable and a more laudable journey: as for the danger, you see our Ladies and Gentlewomen account it nothing now to goe thither; and therefore I hope all good men will better apprehend it, and not suffer them to languish in despaire, whom God so wonderfully and oft hath preserved.

What here I have writ by Relation, if it be not right I humbly intreat your pardons, but I have not spared any diligence to learne the truth of them that have beene actors, or sharers in those voyages; In some particulars they might deceive mee, but in the substance they could not: for few could tell me any thing, except where they fished. But seeing all those have lived there, doe confirme more then I have writ, I doubt not but all those testimonies with these new begun examples of Plantation, will move both Citie and Country, freely to adventure with me more then promises.

The objections against me.

But because some Fortune-tellers say, I am unfortunate; had they spent their time as I have done, they would rather beleeve in God then their calculations, and peradventure have given as bad an account of their actions, and therefore I intreat leave to answer those objecters, that thinke it strange, if this be true, I have made no more use of it, rest so long without imploiment, nor have no more reward nor preferment: To which I say;

My answer.

I thinke it more strange they should tax me, before they have tried as much as I have, both by land and sea, as well in Asia and Affrica, as Europe and America, where my Commanders were actors or spectators, they alwaies so freely rewarded me, I never needed bee importunate, or could I ever learne to beg: What there I got, I have spent; yet in Virginia I staied, till I left five hundred behinde me better provided then ever I was, from which blessed Virgin (ere I returned) sprung the fortunate habitation of Summer Iles.

This Virgins Sister, now called New England, at my

humble sute, by our most gracious Prince Charles, hath beene neere as chargeable to me and my friends: for all which, although I never got shilling but it cost mee a pound, yet I would thinke my selfe happy could I see their prosperities.

Considerations. But if it yet trouble a multitude to proceed upon these certainties, what thinke you I undertooke when nothing [VI. 242.] was knowne but that there was a vast land? I never had power and meanes to doe any thing, though more hath beene spent in formall delaies then would have done the businesse, but in such a penurious and miserable manner, as if I had gone a begging to build an Universitie: where had men beene as forward to adventure their purses, and performe the conditions they promised mee, as to crop the fruits of my labours, thousands ere this had beene bettered by these designes. Thus betwixt the spur of desire and the bridle of reason, I am neere ridden to death in a ring of despaire; the reines are in your hands, therefore I intreat you ease me, and those that thinke I am either idle or unfortunate, may see the cause and know: unlesse I did see better dealing, I have had warning enough not to be so forward againe at every motion upon their promises, unlesse I intended nothing but to carie newes; for now they dare adventure a ship, that when I went first would not adventure a groat, so they may be at home againe by Michaelmas, which makes me remember and say with Master Hackluit; Oh incredulitie the wit of fooles, that slovingly doe spit at all things faire, a sluggards Cradle, a Cowards Castle, how easie it is to be an Infidell. But to the matter: By this all men may perceive, the ordinary performance of this voyage in five or six moneths, the plentie of fish is most certainly approved; and it is certaine, from Cannada and New England, within these six yeeres hath come neere twenty thousand Bever skinnes: Now had each of these ships transported but some small quantitie of the most increasing Beasts, Fowles, Fruits, Plants, and Seeds, as I projected; by this time their increase might have beene

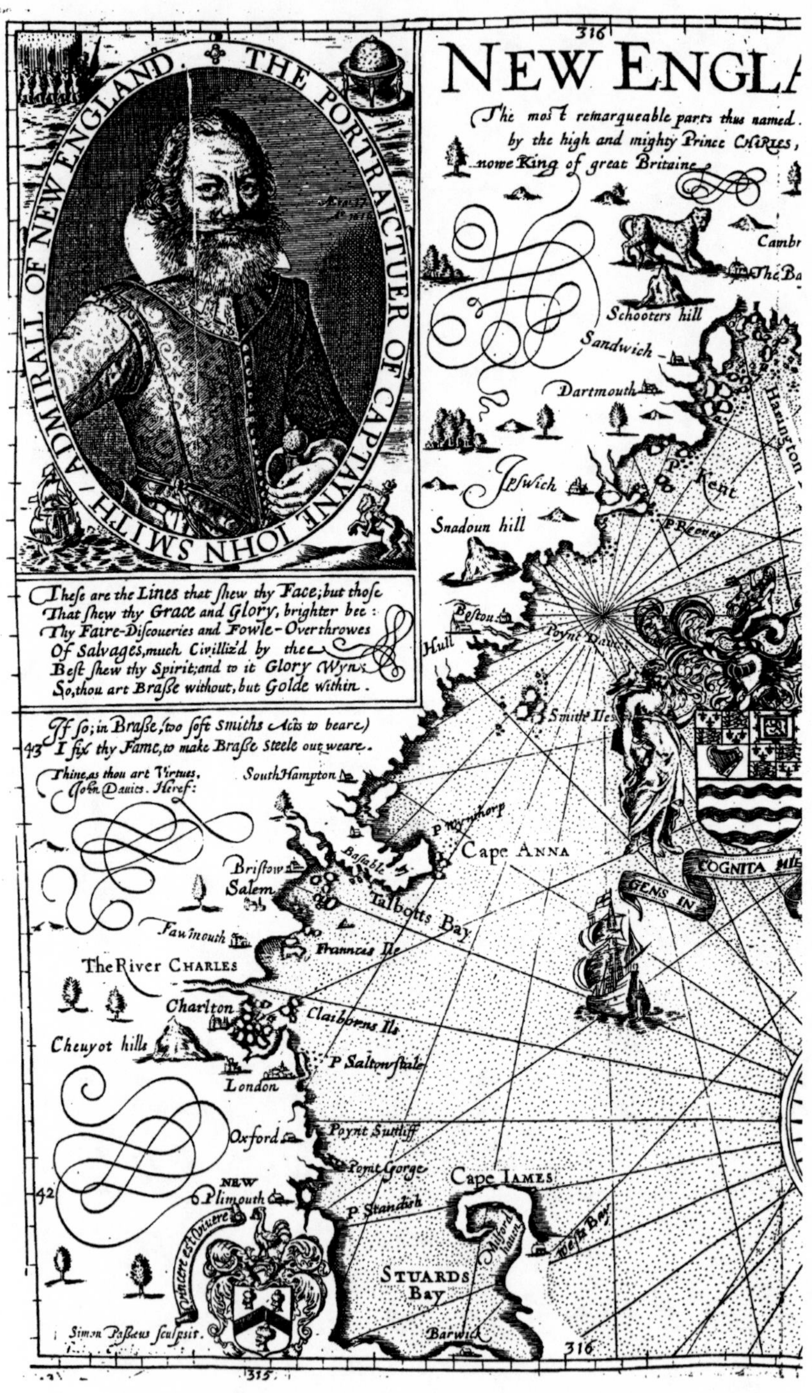
316
NEW ENGLA
The most remarqueable parts thus named by the high and mighty Prince CHARLES, nowe King of great Britaine
THE PORTRAICTUER OF CAPTAYNE IOHN SMITH ADMIRALL OF NEW ENGLAND
These are the Lines that shew thy Face; but those
That shew thy Grace and Glory, brighter bee:
Thy Faire-Discoueries and Fowle-Overthrowes
Of Salvages, much Civilliz'd by thee
Best shew thy Spirit; and to it Glory Wyn;
So, thou art Brasse without, but Golde within.
If so; in Brasse, (too soft Smiths Acts to beare)
I fix thy Fame, to make Brasse Steele out weare.
Thine, as thou art Virtues,
John Dauies. Heref:
Schooters hill
Sandwich
Dartmouth
Ipswich
Kent
Snadoun hill
Hull
Smiths Iles
SouthHampton
Cape Anna
Bristow
Salem
Talbotts Bay
Fawmouth
Frannces Ile
The River CHARLES
Charlton
Claibborns Ils
Cheuyot hills
P Saltonstale
London
Oxford
Poynt Suttliff
Poynt Gorge
NEW Plimouth
P Standish
Cape IAMES
STUARDS Bay
Barwick
Simon Passeus sculpsit.
316
315
43
42

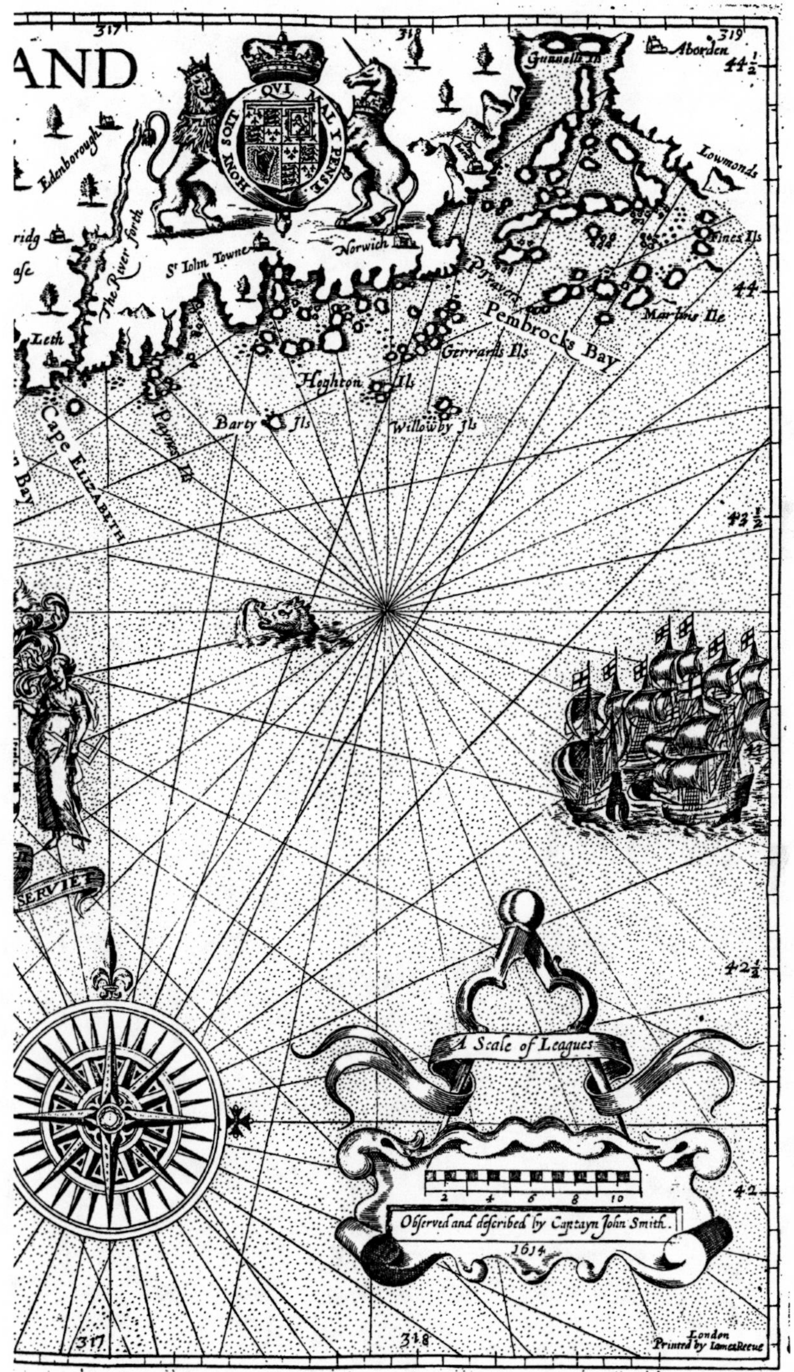

AND
Edenborough
The River forth
St Iohn Towne
Norwich
Leth
Cape Elizabeth
Pembrocks Bay
Gerrards Ils
Hoghton Ils
Barty Ils
Willowby Ils
Aborden
Lowmonds
Fines Ils
Marlins Ile
Gunnells Ils
HONY SOIT QVI MAL Y PENSE
A Scale of Leagues
2 4 6 8 10
Observed and described by Captayn John Smith.
1614
London
Printed by Iames Reeue

sufficient for more then one thousand men: But the desire of present gaine (in many) is so violent, and the endevours of many undertakers so negligent, every one so regarding their private gaine, that it is hard to effect any publike good, and impossible to bring them into a body, rule, or order, unlesse both honesty, as well as authoritie and money, assist experience. But your home-bred ingrossing Projecters will at last finde, there is a great difference betwixt saying and doing, or those that thinks their directions can be as soone and easily performed, as they can conceit them; or that their conceits are the fittest things to bee put in practise, or their countenances maintaine Plantations. But to conclude, the fishing will goe forward whether you plant it or no; whereby a Colony may be then transported with no great charge, that in short time might provide such fraughts, to buy on us there dwelling, as I would hope no ship should goe or come emptie from New England.

The charge. The charge of this is onely Salt, Nets, Hookes, Lines, Knives, Irish-rugges, course cloth, Beads, Glasse, and such trash, onely for fishing and trade with the Salvages, besides our owne necessarie provisions, whose endevours would quickly defray all this charge, and the Salvages did intreat me to inhabit where I would. Now all those ships till these last two yeeres, have beene fishing within a square of two or three leagues, and scarce any one yet will goe any further in the Port they fish in, where questionlesse five hundred may have their fraught as well as elsewhere, and be in the market ere others can have the fish in their ships, because New Englands fishing begins in February, in Newfoundland not till the midst of May; the progression hereof tends much to the advancement of Virginia and Summer Iles, whose empty ships may take in their fraughts there, and would be also in time of need a good friend to the Inhabitants of Newfoundland.

The order of the westerne men. The returnes made by the Westerne men, are commonly divided in three parts; one for the owner of the ship; another for the Master and his Company; the third for the victualers, which course being still permitted, will be no hinderance to the Plantation as yet goe there never so many, but a meanes of transporting that yeerely for little or nothing, which otherwise wil cost many hundreds of pounds. If a ship can gaine twenty, thirty, fifty in the hundred; nay three hundred for one hundred in seven or ten moneths, as you see they have done, spending twice so much time in comming and going as in staying there: were I there planted, seeing the variety of the fishings serve the most part of the yeere, and with a little labour we might make all the Salt we need use, as is formerly said, and can conceive no reason to distrust of good successe by Gods assistance; besides for the building of ships, no place hath more convenient Harbours, ebbe, nor floud, nor better timber; and no Commoditie in Europe doth more decay then wood.

The gaines.

[VI. 243.]

Master Dee his opinion for the building of ships.

The effects of shipping.

MAster Dee recordeth in his Brittish Monarchy, that King Edgar had a Navy of foure thousand saile, with which he yeerely made his progresse about this famous Monarchy of Great Britaine, largely declaring the benefit thereof; whereupon hee projected to our most memorable Queene Elizabeth, the erecting of a Fleet of sixty Saile, he called a little Navy Royall: imitating that admired Pericles Prince of Athens, that could never secure that tormented estate, untill he was Lord and Captaine of the Sea. At this none need wonder, for who knowes not her Royall Majestie during her life, by the incredible adventures of her Royall Navy, and valiant Souldiers and Sea-men, notwithstanding all treacheries at home, the protecting and defending France and Holland, and reconquering Ireland; yet all the world by Sea and Land both feared or loved, and admired good Queene Elizabeth. Both to maintaine and increase that incomparable honour (God be thanked) to her incomparable Successor, our most Royall Lord and Soveraigne King James, this great

Philosopher hath left this to his Majestie and his Kingdomes consideration: that if the tenths of the earth be proper to God, it is also due by Sea. The Kings high waies are common to passe, but not to dig for Mines or any thing: So Englands Coasts are free to passe, but not to fish, but by his Majesties Prerogative.

The Popes order for the East and West Indies.

His Majesty of Spaine permits none to passe the Popes order, for the East and West Indies but by his permission, or at their perils; if all that world be so justly theirs, it is no injustice for England to make as much use of her owne shores as strangers doe, that pay to their owne Lords the tenth, and not to the owner of those liberties any thing to speake of, whose subjects may neither take nor sell any in their Teritories: which small tribute would maintaine this little Navy Royall, and not cost his Majesty a peny, and yet maintaine peace with all Forrainers, and allow them more courtesie then any Nation in the world affords to England. It were a shame to alleage, that Holland is more worthy to enjoy our fishing as Lords thereof, because they have more skill to handle it then we, as they can our wooll and undressed Cloth, notwithstanding all their warres and troublesome disorders.

How to get money to build this little Navy.

To get money to build this Navy, he saith, who would not spare the one hundreth penny of his rents, and the five hundreth penny of his goods; each servant that taketh forty shillings wages, foure pence; and every forrainer of seven yeeres of age foure pence, for seven yeeres; not any of these but they will spend three times so much in pride, wantonnesse, or some superfluitie: And doe any men love the securitie of their estates, that of themselves would not bee humble suters to his Majesty to doe this of free will as a voluntary benevolence, or but the one halfe of this (or some such other course as I have propounded to divers of the Companies) free from any constraint, tax, lottery, or imposition; so it may be as honestly and truly imploied, as it is projected, the poorest Mechanicke in this Kingdome would gaine by it. Then you might build ships of any proportion and numbers you please, five times cheaper then you can doe here, and have good merchandize for their fraught in this unknowne Land, to the advancement of Gods glory, his Church and Gospel, and the strengthning and releefe of a great part of Christendome without hurt to any, to the terror of Pirats, the amazement of enemies, the assistance of friends, the securing Merchants, and so much increase of Navigation, to make Englands trade and shipping as much as any Nations in the world, besides a hundred other benefits, to the generall good of all true subjects, & would cause thousands yet unborne to blesse the time, and all them that first put it in practise.

[VI. 244.] *Contention for New-Englands goods, not her good.*

Now lest it should be obscured as it hath beene to privat ends, or so weakely undertaken by our overweening incredulity, that strangers may possesse it whilest we contend for New-Englands goods, but not Englands good; I have presented it as I have said, to the Prince and Nobility, the Gentry and Commonalty, hoping at last it will move the whole land to know it and consider of it; since I can finde them wood and halfe victuall, with the foresaid advantages: were this Country planted, with what facility they may build and maintaine this little Navy Royall, both with honour, profit and content, and inhabit as good a Country as any in the world within that paralell, which with my life and what I have, I will endevour to effect, if God please and you permit. But no man will goe from hence to have lesse freedome there then here, nor adventure all they have to prepare the way for them will scarce thanke them for it; and it is too well knowne there have beene so many undertakers of Patents, and such sharing of them, as hath bred no lesse discouragement then wonder, to heare such great promises and so little performance; in the Interim, you see the French and Dutch already frequent it, and God forbid they in Virginia, or any of his Majesties subjects, should not have as free liberty as they. To conclude, were it not for Master Cherley and a few private adventurers with them, what have we there for all these inducements? As for them whom pride or covetousnesse lulleth asleepe in a Cradle of slothfull carelesnesse, would they but consider how all the great Monarchies of the earth have beene brought to confusion, or but remember the late lamentable experiences of Constantinople, and how many Cities, Townes and Provinces, in the faire rich Kingdoms of Hungaria, Transilvania, Wallachia & Moldavia, and how many thousands of Princes, Earles, Barons, Knights, Merchants, and others, have in one day lost goods, lives and honours, or sold for slaves like beasts in a market place, their wives, children and servants slaine, or wandring they knew not whither, dying or living in all extremities of extreme miseries and calamities, surely they would not onely doe this, but give all they have to enjoy peace and liberty at home, or but adventure their persons abroad; to prevent the conclusions of a conquering Foe, who commonly assaulteth and best prevaileth where he findeth wealth and plenty, most armed with ignorance and security.

The necessity of martiall power.

Though the true condition of warre is onely to suppresse the proud and defend the innocent, as did that most generous Prince Sigismundus, Prince of those Countries, against them whom under the colour of justice and piety, to maintaine their superfluity of ambitious pride, thought all the world too little to maintaine their vice, and undoe them, or keepe them from ability to doe any thing, that would not admire and adore their honours, fortunes, covetousnesse, falshood, bribery, cruelty, extortion, and ingratitude, which is worse then cowardize or ignorance, and all manner of vildnesse, cleane contrary to all honour, vertue, and noblenesse. John Smith writ this with his owne hand.

Here follow certaine notes and observations of Captaine Charles Whitbourne concerning New-found land, which although every master trained up in fishing, can make their proportions of necessaries according to their custome, yet it is not much amisse here to insert them, that every one which desires the good of those actions know them also. Besides in his Booke intituled, A discovery of New-found land, and the commodities thereof, you shall finde many excellent good advertisements for a Plantation; and how that most yeeres this Coast hath beene frequented with 250. saile of his Majesties subjects, which supposing but 60. tunnes a peece, one with another, they amount to 15000. tunnes, and allowing 25. men and boies to every Barke, they will make 5000. persons, whose labours returne yeerely to about 135000. pound sterling, besides the great numbers of Brewers, Bakers, Coupers, Ship-Carpenters, Net-makers, Rope-makers, Hooke-makers, and the most of all other mecanicall trades in England.

[VI. 245.] The charge of setting forth a ship of 100. tuns with 40. persons, both to make a fishing voyage, and increase the Plantation.

	£.	s.	d.
INprimis, 10000. weight of Bisket at 15.s. a 100. weight.	82.	10.	
26 Tun of Beere and Sider at 53.s. 4.d. a Tun.	69.	7.	
2 Hogsheads of English Beefe.	10.		
2 Hogsheads of Irish Beefe.	5.		
10 Fat Hogs salted with Salt and Caske.	10.	10.	
30 Bushels of Pease.	6.		
2 Ferkins of Butter.	3.		
200 Waight of Cheese.	2.	10.	
1 Bushell of Mustard-seed.		6.	
1 Hogshead of Vinegar.	1.	5.	
Wood to dresse meat withall.	1.		
1 Great Copper Kettle.	2.		
2 Small Kettles.	2.		
2 Frying-pans.		3.	4.
Platters, Ladles and Cans.	1.		
a paire of Bellowes for the Cooke.		2.	6.
Taps, Boriers and Funnels.		2.	

	£.	s.	d.
Locks for the Bread roomes.		2.	6.
100 weight of Candles.	2.	10.	
130 quarters of Salt at 2.s. the Bushell.	10.	4.	
Mats & dinnage to lie under it.	2.	10.	
Salt Shovels.		10.	
Particulars for the 40. persons to keepe 8. fishing boats at Sea, with 3. men in every boat, imploies 24. and 500. foot of Elme boords of an inch thicke, 8.s. each one.	2.		
2000 Nailes for the 8. Boats, at 13.s. 4.d. a 1000.	1.	6.	8.
4000 Nailes at 6.s. 8.d. 1000.	1.	6.	8.
2000 Nailes at 5.d. 100.		8.	
500 weight of pitch at 8.s. 100.	2.		
2000 of good orlop nailes.	2.	5.	
More for other small necessaries.	3.		
A barrell of Tar.		10.	
200 weight of black Ocome.	1.		
Thrums for pitch Maps.		1.	6.
Bolls, Buckets and Pumps.	1.		
2 brazen Crocks.	2.		
Canvas to make Boat sailes & small ropes, at 25.s. for each saile.	12.	10.	
10 rode Ropes which containe 600. weight at 30.s. the 100.	10.		
12 dozen of fishing lines.	6.		
24 dozen of fishing hookes.	2.		
for Squid line.		3.	
For Pots and liver maunds.		18.	
Iron works for the boats ruthers.	2.		
10 Kipnet Irons.		10.	
Twine to make kipnets and gagging hooks.		6.	
10 good Nets at 26.s. a net.	13.		
2 Saynes, a great and a lesse.	12.		
200 weight of Sow-lead.	1.		

	£.	s.	d.
2 couple of ropes for the Saynes.	1.		
Dry-fats to keepe them in.		6.	
Twine for store.		5.	
Flaskets and bread Baskets.		15.	
For haire cloth.	10.		
3. Tuns of Vinegar caske for water.	1.	6.	8.
1 douzen of Deale Bourds.		10.	
2 Barrels of Oatmeale.	1.	6.	
100 weight of Spikes.	2.	5.	
2 good Axes, 4. hand Hatchets, 4. Drawers, 2. drawing Irons.		16.	
3 yards of wollen cloth for cuffs.		10.	
8 yards of good Canvasse.		10.	
A Grind-stone or two.		6.	
2000 of poore John to spend in going.	6.	10.	
1 Hogshead of Aquavitæ.	4.		
4 arme Sawes, 4. Handsawes, 4. thwart Sawes, 3. Augers, 2. Crowes of Iron, 3. Sledges, 4. shod Shovels, 2. Picaxes, 4. Matocks, and 4. Hammers.	5.		
The totall summe is	420.	11.	0.

All these provisions the Master or Purser is to be accountable what is spent and what is left, with those which shall continue there to plant, and of the 40. thus provided for the voyage, ten may well be spared to leave behind them, with 500. weight of Bisket, 5. hogsheads of Sider or beere, halfe a hogshead of Beefe, 4. sides of dry Bakon, 4. bushell of Pease, halfe a ferkin of Butter, halfe 100. weight of Cheese, a pecke of Mustard-seed, a barrell of Vinegar, 12. pound of Candles, 2. pecks of Oatmeale, halfe a hogshead of Aquavitæ, 2. copper Kettles, 1. brasse Crock, 1. Frying-pan, a Grindstone, and all the Hatchets, Woodhooks, Sawes, Augers, &c. and all other iron tooles, with the 8. Boats and their
[VI. 246.] implements, and spare salt, and what else they use not

in a readinesse from yeere to yeere, and in the meane time served them to helpe to build their houses, cleanse land, and further their fishing whilst the ships are wanting.

By his estimation and calculation these 8. Boats with 22. men in a Summer doe usually kill 25000. fish for every Boat, which may amount to 200000. allowing 120. fishes to the 100. sometimes they have taken above 35000. for a Boat, so that they load not onely their owne ship, but provide great quantities for sacks, or other spare ships which come thither onely to buy the overplus: if such ships come not, they give over taking any more, when sometimes there hath beene great abundance, because there is no fit houses to lay them in till another yeere, now most of those sacks goeth empty thither, which might as well transport mens provision and cattle at an easie rate as nothing, either to New-England or New-found land, but either to transport them for nothing or pay any great matter for their liberty to fish, will hardly effect so much as freedome as yet; nor can this be put in practice as before I said, till there be a power there well planted and setled to entertaine and defend them, assist and releeve them as occasion shall require, otherwaies those small divisions will effect little, but such miserable conclusions as both the French and we too long have tried to our costs. Now commonly 200000. fish will load a ship of 100. tunnes in New-found land, but halfe so many will neere doe it in New-England, which carried to Toloune or Merselus, where the custome is small, and the Kintall lesse then 90. English pounds weight, and the prise when least, 12. shillings the Kintall, which at that rate amounts to 1320. l. starling; and the ship may either there be discharged or imployed as hath beene said to refraught for England, so that the next yeere she may be ready to goe her fishing voyage againe, at a farre cheaper rate then before.

To this adde but 12. tuns of traine oile, which delivered in New-found land, is 10. l. the tun, makes 120. l. then it is hard if there be not 10000. of Cor-fish, which also sold there at 5. l. the 1000. makes 50. l. which brought to England, in somes places yeelds neere halfe so much more; but if at Merselus it be sold for 16. s. the Kentall, as commonly it is, and much dearer, it amounts to 1760. l. and if the Boats follow the fishing till the 15. of October, they may take 80000. more, which with their traine in New-found land at 4. l. the 1000. will amount to 320. l. which added to 1320. l. with 120. l. for Oile, and 10000. of Cor-fish 50. l. and the overplus at Merselus, which will be 440. l. make the totall 2250. l. which divided in three parts according to their custome, the Victualer hath for the former particulars, amounting to 420. l. 751. l. so all the charge defraied, hee gaines 331. l. 11. s. then for the fraught of the ship there is 751. l. and so much for the Master and his company, which comparing with the voiages hath beene made to New-England, you may easily finde which is the better though both bee good. But now experience hath taught them at New-Plimoth, that in Aprill there is a fish much like a Herring that comes up into the small Brookes to spawne, and where the water is not knee deepe, they will presse up through your hands, yea though you beat at them with Cudgels, and in such abundance as is incredible, which they take with that facility they manure their land with them when they have occasion; after those the Cod also presseth in such plenty, even into the very Harbours, they have caught some in their armes, and hooke them so fast, three men oft loadeth a Boat of two tuns in two houres, where before they used most to fish in deepe water.

The facility of the fishing lately observed.

[VI. 247.]

The present estate of New-Plimoth.

The present estate of the plantation at New-Plimoth. 1624.

AT New-Plimoth there is about 180 persons, some cattell and goats, but many swine and poultry, 32 dwelling houses, whereof 7 were burnt the last winter, and the value of five hundred pounds in other goods; the Towne is impailed about halfe a mile compasse. In the towne upon a high Mount they have a Fort well built with wood, lome, and stone, where is planted their Ordnance: Also a faire Watch-tower, partly framed for the Sentinell, the place it seemes is healthfull, for in these last three yeeres, notwithstanding their great want of most necessaries, there hath not one died of the first planters, they have made a saltworke, and with that salt preserve the fish they take, and this yeare hath fraughted a ship of 180. tunnes. The Governour is one Mr. William Bradford, their Captaine Miles Standish, a bred Souldier in Holland; the chiefe men for their assistance is Master Isaak Alderton, and divers others as occasion serveth; their Preachers are Master William Bruster and Master John Layford.

Their order of government.

The most of them live together as one family or houshold, yet every man followeth his trade and profession both by sea and land, and all for a generall stocke, out of which they have all their maintenance, untill there be a divident betwixt the Planters and the Adventurers. Those Planters are not servants to the Adventurers here, but have onely councells of directions from them, but no injunctions or command, and all the masters of families are partners in land or whatsoever, setting their labours against the stocke, till certaine yeeres be expired for the division: they have young men and boies for their Apprentises and servants, and some of them speciall families, as Ship-carpenters, Salt-makers, Fish-masters, yet as servants upon great wages. The Adventurers which raised the stocke to begin and supply this Plantation were about 70. some Gentlemen, some Merchants, some handy-crafts men, some adventuring great summes, some small, as their estates and affection served. The generall stocke already imploied is about 7000. l. by reason of which charge and many crosses, many of them would adventure no more, but others that knowes so great a designe cannot bee effected without both charge, losse and crosses, are resolved to goe forward with it to their powers; which deserve no small commendations and encouragement. These dwell most about London, they are not a corporation, but knit together by a voluntary combination in a society without constraint or penalty, aiming to doe good & to plant Religion; they have a President & Treasurer, every yeere newly chosen by the most voices, who ordereth the affaires of their Courts and meetings, and with the assent of the most of them, undertaketh all ordinary businesses, but in more weighty affaires, the assent of the whole Company is required. There hath beene a fishing this yeere upon the Coast about 50. English ships: and by Cape Anne, there is a Plantation a beginning by the Dorchester men, which they hold of those of New-Plimoth, who also by them have set up a fishing worke; some talke there is some other pretended Plantations, all whose good proceedings the eternal God protect and preserve. And these have beene the true proceedings and accidents in those Plantations.

Now to make a particular relation of all the acts and orders in the Courts belonging unto them, of the anihilating old Patents and procuring new; with the charge, paines and arguments, the reasons of such changes, all the treaties, consultations, orations, and dissentions about the sharing and dividing those large territories, confirming of Counsailers, electing all sorts of Officers, directions, Letters of advice, and their answers, disputations about the Magazines and Impositions, suters for Patents, positions for Freedomes, and confirmations with complaints of injuries here, and also the mutinies, examinations, arraignements, executions, and the cause of the so oft revolt of the Salvages at large, as many
[VI. 248.] would have had, and it may be some doe expect it would make more quarrels then any of them would willingly answer, & such a volume as would tire any wise man but to read the contents; for my owne part I rather feare the unpartiall Reader wil thinke this rather more tedious then necessary: but he that would be a practitioner in those affaires, I hope will allow them not only needfull but expedient: but how ever, if you please to beare with

those errors I have committed, if God please I live, my care and paines shall endevour to be thankfull: if I die, accept my good will: If any desire to be further satisfied, what defect is found in this, they shall finde supplied in me, that thus freely have throwne my selfe with my mite into the Treasury of my Countries good, not doubting but God will stirre up some noble spirits to consider and examine if worthy Columbus could give the Spaniards any such certainties for his designe, when Queene Isabel of Spaine set him forth with 15. saile, and though I promise no Mines of gold, yet the warlike Hollanders let us imitate but not hate, whose wealth and strength are good testimonies of their treasury gotten by fishing; and New-England hath yeelded already by generall computation one hundred thousand pounds at the least. Therefore honourable and worthy Country men, let not the meannesse of the word fish distaste you, for it will afford as good gold as the Mines of Guiana or Potassie, with lesse hazard and charge, and more certainty and facility. J. S.

FINIS.

[The True

The True Travels, Adventures, and Observations of Captaine John Smith

THE TRUE TRAVELS, ADVENTURES, AND OBSERVATIONS OF

CAPTAINE JOHN SMITH,

In Europe, Asia, Affrica, and America, from Anno Domini 1593 to 1629.

LONDON,
Printed by J. H. for Thomas Slater, and are to bee sold at the Blew Bible in Greene Arbour.
1630.

To the Right Honourable WILLIAM, Earle of Pembroke, Lord Steward of his Majesties most Honourable Houshold. ROBERT, Earle of Lindsey, Great Chamberlaine of England. HENRIE, Lord Hunsdon, Vicount Rochford, Earle of Dover. And all your Honourable Friends and Well-willers.

My Lords:

SIr Robert Cotton, that most learned Treasurer of Antiquitie, having by perusall of my Generall Historie, and others, found that I had likewise undergone divers other as hard hazards in the other parts of the world, requested me to fix the whole course of my passages in a booke by it selfe: whose noble desire I could not but in part satisfie; the rather, because they have acted my fatall Tragedies upon the Stage, and racked my Relations at their pleasure. To prevent therefore all future misprisions, I have compiled this true discourse. Envie hath taxed me to have writ too much, and done too little: but that such should know, how little I esteeme them, I have writ this; more for the satisfaction of my friends, and all generous and well disposed Readers. To speake only of my selfe were intolerable ingratitude; because, having had so many co-partners with me; I cannot make a Monument for my selfe, and leave them unburied in the fields, whose lives begot me the title of a Souldier; for as they were companions with me in my dangers, so shall they be partakers with me in this Tombe.

For my Sea Grammar (caused to bee printed by my worthy friend, Sir Samuel Saltonstall) hath found such good entertainment abroad, that I have beene importuned by many noble persons, to let this also passe the Presse. Many of the most eminent Warriers, and others, what their swords did, their penns writ. Though I bee never so much their inferiour, yet I hold it no great errour, to follow good examples; nor repine at them, will doe the like.

And now my most Honourable good Lords, I know not to whom I may better present it, than to your Lordships, whose friendships, as I conceive, are as much to each others, as my duty is to you all; and because you are acquainted both with my endevours, and writings, I doubt not, but your honours will as well accept of this, as of the rest, and Patronize it under the shadow of your most noble vertues, which I am ever bound in all duty to reverence, and under which I hope to have shelter, against all stormes that dare threaten.

Your Honours to be commanded,

John Smith.

The Contents of the severall Chapters

THE CONTENTS

THE CONTENTS

THE CONTENTS

PANEGYRICK VERSES

To my worthy friend, Captaine John Smith.

TWo greatest Shires of England did thee beare,
Renowned Yorkshire, Gaunt-stild Lancashire;
But what's all this? even Earth, Sea, Heaven above,
Tragabigzanda, Callamata's love,
Deare Pocahontas, Madam Shanoi's too,
Who did what love with modesty could doe:
Record thy worth, thy birth, which as I live,
Even in thy reading such choice solace give,
As I could wish (such wishes would doe well)
Many such Smiths in this our Israel.

R. BRATHWAIT.

To my noble brother and friend, Captaine John Smith.

THou hast a course so full of honour runne,
Envy may snarle, as dogges against the Sunne
May barke, not bite: for what deservedly
With thy lifes danger, valour, pollicy,
Quaint warlike stratagems, abillity
And judgement, thou hast got, fame sets so high
Detraction cannot reach: thy worth shall stand
A patterne to succeeding ages, and
Cloth'd in thy owne lines, ever shall adde grace,
Unto thy native Country and thy race;
And when dissolv'd, laid in thy mothers wombe,
These, Cæsar-like, Smiths Epitaph and tombe.

ANTHONY FEREBY.

To his valiant and deserving friend, Captaine John Smith.

MOngst Frenchmen, Spanyards, Hungars, Tartars, Turks,
And wilde Virginians too, this tells thy works:
Now some will aske, what benefit? what gaine?
Is added to thy store for all this paine?
Th' art then content to say, content is all,
Th' ast got content for perils, paine and thrall;
Tis lost to looke for more: for few men now
Regard Wit, Learning, Valour; but allow
The quintessence of praise to him that can
Number his owne got gold, and riches, than
Th' art Valiant, Learned, Wise; Pauls counsell will,
Admire thy merits, magnifie thy skill.
The last of thine to which I set my hand
Was a Sea Grammar; this by Sea and Land,
Serves us for imitation: I know none,
That like thy selfe hast come, and runne, and gone,
To such praise-worthy actions: bee't approv'd,
Th' ast well deserv'd of best men to be lov'd:
If France, or Spaine, or any forren soile
Could claime thee theirs, for these thy paines and toile,
Th' adst got reward and honour: now adayes,
What our owne natives doe, we seldom praise.

Good men will yeeld thee praise; then sleight the rest;
Tis best praise-worthy to have pleas'd the best.

Tuissimus Ed. Jorden.

To my worthy friend, Captaine John Smith.

DEare noble Captaine, who by Sea and Land,
To act the earnest of thy name hast hand
And heart; who canst with skill designe the Fort,
The Leaguer, Harbour, City, Shore, and Port:

Whose sword and pen in bold, ruffe, Martiall wise,
Put forth to try and beare away the prize,
From Cæsar and Blaize Monluc: Can it be,
That Men alone in Gonnels fortune see
Thy worth advanc'd? no wonder since our age,
Is now at large a Bedlem or a Stage.

RICH. JAMES.

To his worthy friend, Captaine John Smith.

THou that hast had a spirit to flie like thunder,
  Without thy Countries charge through those strange dangers,
Doth make my muse amaz'd, and more to wonder
  That thy deserts should shared be by strangers,
And thou neglected; (ah miracle!) most lamented,
  At thy great patience thus to rest contented.
For none can truly say thou didst deceive,
  Thy Souldiers, Sailers, Merchants, nor thy friends,
But all from thee a true account receive,
  Yet nought to thee all these thy vertues brings;
Is none so noble to advance thy merit,
  If any be, let him thy praise inherit.

MA. HAWKINS.

To my worthy friend, Captaine John Smith.

TO combate with three Turks in single du'le,
  Before two Armies, who the like hath done?
Slaine thy great Jailor; found a common weale
  In faire America where thou hast wonne
No lesse renowne amongst their Savage Kings,
  Than Turkish warres, that thus thy honour sings.

Could not those tyrants daunt thy matchlesse spirit,
  Nor all the cruelty of envies spight:

Will not thy Country yet reward thy merit,
  Nor in thy acts and writings take delight?
Which here in so few sheets doth more expresse
  Than volumes great, this is thy happinesse.

RICHARD MEADE.

To my well deserving friend, Captaine John Smith.

THou hast no need to covet new applause,
  Nor doe I thinke vaine-glory moves thee to it;
But since it is thy will (though without cause)
  To move a needlesse thing, yet will I doe it:
Doe it in briefe I will, or else I doe the wrong,
  And say, rend o're Captaine Smiths former song;
His first then will invite thee to his latter:
  Reader 'tis true; I am not brib'd to flatter.

EDW. INGHAM.

To his approved friend, the Authour; Captaine John Smith.

THe old Greeke Beard,* counts him the onely man,
  Who knowes strange Countries, like his Ithacan,
  And wise, as valiant, by his observation,
  Can tell the severall customes of each Nation:
All these are met in thee, who will not then
Repute thee in the ranke of worthiest men?

  To th'Westerne world to former times unknowne,
  Thy active spirit hath thy valour showne:
  The Turks and Tartars both can testifie,
  Thee t'have deserv'd a Captaines dignity;
But verse thou need'st not to expresse thy worth,
Thy acts, this booke doe plainly set it forth.

M. CARTNER.

*i.e. Bard.

To the Valourous and truly-vertuous souldier, Captaine John Smith.

NO* Faith in Campe? tis false: see pious Smith
Hath brought stragling Astræa backe, and with
An all outdaring spirit made Valour stand
Upheld by Vertue in bold Mars his land:
If Valourous, be praise; how great's his Name?
Whose Valour joynd with Vertue laud's his Fame.
T'was Homers boast of wise Laertes sonne,
†Well-read in men and Cities: than thou none
(Great Smith) of these can more true tales rehearse;
What want thy praises then, but Homers verse?

**Nulla fides pietasque viris, qui castra sequuntur.*

†πολλῶν δ' ἀνθρώπων ἴδεν ἄστεα καὶ νόον ἔγνω *Hom. Odyss. a.*

In Smithum Distichon.

Quisque suæ sortis* Faber: an Faber exstitit unquam
Te (Smithe) fortunæ verior usque suæ?

J. C.
C. P.

To his noble friend, Captaine John Smith.

TO see bright honour sparkled all in gore,
Would steele a spirit that ne're fought before:
And that's the height of Fame, when our best bloud,
Is nobly spilt in actions great and good:
So thou hast taught the world to purchase Fame,
Rearing thy story on a glorious frame,
And such foundation doth thy merits make it,
As all detractions rage shall never shake it;
Thy actions crowne themselves, and thy owne pen,
Gives them the best and truest Epiphonem.

Brian O Rourke.

To his truly deserving friend, Captaine John Smith.

CAn one please all? there's none from Censure free,
To looke for'it then it were absurd in thee;
It's easie worke to censure sweetest Layes,
Where Ignorance is Judge thou'd have no praise:
Wisdome I know will mildly judge of all,
Envious hearts, tongues, pennes, are dippt in Gall.
Proud malignant times will you now bring forth
Monsters at least to snarle at others worth;
O doe not so, but wisely looke on him
That wrought such Honours for his Countries King:
Of Turks and Tartars thou hast wonne the field,
The great Bashaw his courage thou hast quel'd;
In the Hungarian warre thou'st shewd thy Arts,
Prov'd thy Selfe a Souldier true in all parts:
Thy Armes are deckt with that thy Sword hath wonne,
Which mallice can't out-weare till day be done:
For three proud Turks in single fight thou'st slue,
Their Heads adorne thy Armes, for witnesse true;
Let Mars and Neptune both with Pregnant wit,
Extoll thy due deserts, Ile pray for it.

SALO. TANNER.

The True Travels, [P. 1]

Adventures, and Observations of Captaine John Smith, in Europe, Asia, Africke, and America: beginning about the yeere 1593. and continued to this present 1629.

Chap. I.

His birth; Apprentiship; Going into France; His beginning with ten shillings and three pence; His Service in Netherlands; His bad passage into Scotland; His returne to Willoughby; And how he lived in the Woods.

HE was borne in Willoughby in Lincolneshire, and a Scholler in the two Freeschooles of Alford and Louth. His father anciently descended from the ancient Smiths of Crudley in Lancashire; his mother from the Rickands at great Heck in York-shire. His parents dying when he was about thirteene yeeres of age, left him a competent meanes, which hee not being capable to manage, little regarded; his minde being even then set upon brave adventures, sould his Satchell, bookes, and all he had, intending secretly to get to Sea, but that his fathers death [P. 2] stayed him. But now the Guardians of his estate more regarding it than him, he had libertie enough, though no meanes, to get beyond the Sea. About the age of fifteene yeeres hee was bound an Apprentice to Master Thomas Sendall of Linne, the greatest Merchant of all those parts; but because hee would not presently send him to Sea, he never saw his master in eight yeeres after. At last, he found meanes to attend Master Perigrine Barty into France, second sonne to the Right Honourable Perigrine, that generous Lord Willoughby and famous Souldier; where comming to his brother Robert, then at Orleans, now Earle of Linsey, and Lord great Chamberlaine of England; being then but little youths under Tutorage: his service being needlesse, within a moneth or six weeks they sent him backe againe to his friends. Who when he came from London, they liberally gave him (but out of his owne estate) ten shillings to be rid of him; such oft is the share of fatherlesse children: but those two Honourable Brethren gave him sufficient to returne for England. But it was the least thought of his determination, for now being freely at libertie in Paris, growing acquainted with one Master David Hume, who making some use of his purse, gave him Letters to his friends in Scotland to preferre him to King James. Arriving at Roane, he better bethinkes himselfe, seeing his money neere spent, downe the River he went to Haver de grace, where he first began to learne the life of a souldier. Peace being concluded in France, he went with Captaine Joseph Duxbury into the Low-countries, under whose Colours having served three or foure yeeres, he tooke his journey for Scotland, to deliver his Letters. At Ancusan he imbarked himselfe for Lethe, but as much danger as shipwracke and sicknesse could endure, hee had at the holy Ile in Northumberland neere Barwicke: (being recovered) into Scotland he went to deliver his Letters. After much kinde usage amongst those honest Scots at Ripweth and Broxmoth, but neither money nor meanes to make him a Courtier; he returned to Willoughby in

THE TRUE TRAVELS, ADVENTVRES, AND OBSERVATIONS OF Captaine IOHN SMITH,

In *Europe*, *Asia*, *Affrica*, and *America*, from *Anno Domini* 1593. to 1629.

His Accidents and Sea-fights in the Straights; his Service and Stratagems of warre in *Hungaria*, *Transilvania*, *Wallachia*, and *Moldavia*, against the *Turks*, and *Tartars*; his three single combats betwixt the *Christian* Armie and the *Turkes*.

After how he was taken prisoner by the *Turks*, sold for a Slave, sent into *Tartaria*; his description of the *Tartars*, their strange manners and customes of Religions, Diets, Buildings, Warres, Feasts, Ceremonies, and Living; how hee slew the Bashaw of *Nalbrits* in *Cambia*, and escaped from the *Turkes* and *Tartars*.

Together with a continuation of his generall History of *Virginia*, *Summer-Iles*, *New England*, and their proceedings, since 1624. to this present 1629; as also of the new Plantations of the great River of the *Amazons*, the Iles of S^t. *Christopher*, *Mevis*, and *Barbados* in the *West Indies*.

All written by actuall Authours, whose names you shall finde along the History.

LONDON,

Printed by *J. H.* for *Thomas Slater*, and are to bee sold at the Blew Bible in *Greene Arbour*. 1630.

Lincolne-shire; where within a short time being glutted with too much company, wherein he took small delight, he retired himselfe into a little wooddie pasture, a good way from any towne, invironed with many hundred Acres of other woods: Here by a faire brook he built a Pavillion of boughes, where only in his cloaths he lay. His studie was Machiavills Art of warre, and Marcus Aurelius; his exercise a good horse, with his lance and Ring; his food was thought to be more of venison than any thing else; what he wanted, his man brought him. The countrey wondering at such an Hermite; His friends perswaded one Seignior Theadora Polaloga, Rider to Henry Earle of Lincolne, an excellent Horse-man, and a noble Italian Gentleman, to insinuate into his wooddish acquaintances, whose Languages and good discourse, and exercise of riding, drew him to stay with him at Tattersall. Long these pleasures could not content him, but hee returned againe to the Low-Countreyes.

Chapter II.

[P. 3]

The notable villany of foure French Gallants, and his revenge; Smith throwne over-board; Captaine La Roche of Saint Malo releeves him.

Hus when France and Netherlands had taught him to ride a Horse and use his Armes, with such rudiments of warre as his tender yeeres in those martiall Schooles could attaine unto; he was desirous to see more of the world, and trie his fortune against the Turkes: both lamenting and repenting to have seene so many Christians slaughter one another. Opportunitie casting him into the company of foure French Gallants well attended, faining to him the one to be a great Lord, the rest his Gentlemen, and that they were all devoted that way; over-perswaded him to goe with them into France, to

A notable villany of foure French Gallants.

the Dutchesse of Mercury, from whom they should not only have meanes, but also Letters of favour to her noble Duke, then Generall for the Emperour Rodolphus in Hungary: which he did, with such ill weather as winter affordeth, in the darke night, they arrived in the broad shallow In-let of Saint Valleries sur Some in Picardie; his French Lord knowing he had good apparell, and better furnished with money than themselves, so plotted with the Master of the ship to set his and their owne truncks a shore, leaving Smith aboard till the boat could returne, which was the next day after towards evening: the reason hee alleaged was the sea went so high hee could come no sooner, and that his Lord was gone to Amiens where they would stay his comming; which treacherous villany, when divers other souldiers and passengers understood, they had like to have slaine the Master, and had they knowne how, would have runne away with the ship.

A Carralue is in value a penny.

Comming on shore hee had but one Carralue, was forced to sell his cloake to pay for his passage. One of the souldiers, called Curzianvere, compassionating his injury, assured him this great Lord Depreau was only the sonne of a Lawyer of Mortaigne in base Britany; and his Attendants Cursell, La Nelie, and Monferrat, three young citizens, as arrant cheats as himselfe; but if he would accompany him, he would bring him to their friends; but in the interim supplied his wants: thus travelling by Deepe, Codebeck, Humphla, Pountdemer in Normandie, they came to Cane in base Normandie; where both this noble Curzianvere, and the great Prior of the great Abbey of S. Steven (where is the ruinous Tombe of William the Conquerour,) and many other of his friends kindly welcomed him, and brought him to Mortaigne; where hee found Depreau and the rest, but to small purpose; for Master Curzianvere was a banished man, and durst not be seene, but to his friends: yet the bruit of their cosenage occasioned the Lady Collumber, the Baron Larshan, the Lord Shasghe, and divers other honourable persons, to supply his wants, and with them to recreate himselfe so long as hee would: but such pleasant pleasures suited little with his poore estate, and his restlesse spirit, that could never finde content, to receive such noble favours, as he could neither deserve nor requite: but wandring [P. 4] from Port to Port to finde some man of war, spent that he had; and in a Forest, neere dead with griefe and cold, a rich Farmer found him by a faire Fountaine under a tree. This kinde Pesant releeved him againe to his content, to follow his intent. Not long after, as he passed thorow a great grove of trees, betweene Pounterson and Dina in Britaine, it was his chance to meet Cursell, more miserable than himselfe. His piercing injuries had so small patience, as without any word they both drew, and in a short time Cursell fell to the ground, where from an old ruinated Tower the inhabitants seeing them, were satisfied, when they heard Cursell confesse what had formerly passed; and that how in the dividing that they had stolne from him, they fell by the ears amongst themselves, that were actors in it: but for his part, he excused himselfe to be innocent as well of the one, as of the other. In regard of his hurt, Smith was glad to be so rid of him, directing his course to an honourable Lord, the Earle of Ployer; who during the warre in France, with his two brethren, Viscount Poomory, and Baron d'Mercy, who had beene brought up in England; by him he was better refurnished than ever. When they had shewed him Saint Malo Mount, Saint Michael, Lambal, Simbreack, Lanion, and their owne faire Castle of Tuncadeck, Gingan, and divers other places in Britanny (and their Brittish Cornwaile), taking his leave, he tooke his way to Raynes, the Britaines chiefe Citie, and so to Nantes, Poyters, Rochell, and Burdeaux. The rumour of the strength of Bayon in Biskay, caused him to see it; and from thence tooke his way from Leskar in Biearne, and Paw in the kingdom of Navar to Tolouza in Gascoigne, Bezers and Carcassone, Narbone, Montpellier, Nimes in Languedock, and thorow the Country of Avignion, by

Here he incountred one of the theeves.

The noblenesse of the Earle of Ployer.

Arles to Marcellos in Province, there imbarking himselfe for Italy, the ship was enforced to Tolonne, and putting againe to sea, ill weather so grew upon them, they anchored close aboard the shore, under the little Isle of S. Mary, against Neice in Savoy. Here the inhumane Provincialls, with a rabble of Pilgrimes of divers Nations going to Rome, hourely cursing him, not only for a Hugonoit, but his Nation they swore were all Pyrats, and so vildly railed on his dread Soveraigne Queene Elizabeth, and that they never should have faire weather so long as hee was aboard them; their disputations grew to that passion, that they threw him over-board: yet God brought him to that little Isle, where was no inhabitants, but a few kine and goats. The next morning, he espied two ships more riding by them, put in by the storme, that fetched him aboard, well refreshed him, and so kindly used him, that he was well contented to trie the rest of his fortune with them. After he had related unto them his former discourse, what for pitie, and the love of the Honourable Earle of Ployer, this noble Britaine his neighbour, Captaine la Roche of Saint Malo, regarded and entertained him for his well respected friend. With the next faire wind they sailed along by the Coast of Corsica and Sardinia, and crossing the gulfe of Tunis, passed by Cape Bona to the Isle of Lampadosa, leaving the coast of Barbary till they came at Cape Rosata, and so along the African shore, for Alexandria in Ægypt. There delivering their fraught, they went to Scandaroone; rather to view what ships was in the Roade, than any thing else:
[P. 5] keeping their course by Cypres and the coast of Asia, sayling by Rhodes, the Archipellagans, Candia, and the coast of Gretia, and the Isle of Zaffalonia. They lay to and againe a few days betwixt the Isle of Corfue and the Cape of Otranto in the Kingdome of Naples, in the Entrance of the Adriatike sea.

An inhumane act of the Provincialls in casting him overboard.

Captaine La Roche releeves him.

Chapter III.

A desperate Sea-fight in the Straights; His passage to Rome, Naples, and the view of Italy.

Etwixt the two Capes they meet with an Argosie of Venice, it seemed the Captaine desired to speake with them, whose untoward answer was such, as slew them a man; whereupon the Britaine presently gave them the broad-side, then his Sterne, and his other broad-side also, and continued the chase, with his chase peeces, till he gave them so many broad-sides one after another, that the Argosies sayles and tackling was so torne, she stood to her defence, and made shot for shot; twice in one houre and a halfe the Britaine boarded her, yet they cleared themselves: but clapping her aboard againe, the Argosie fired him, which, with much danger to them both, was presently quenched. This rather augmented the Britaines rage, than abated his courage: for having reaccommodated himselfe againe, shot her so oft betweene wind and water, shee was readie to sinke; then they yeelded; the Britaine lost fifteene men, she twentie, besides divers were hurt, the rest went to worke on all hands; some to stop the leakes, others to guard the prisoners that were chained, the rest to rifle her. The Silkes, Velvets, Cloth of gold and Tissue, Pyasters Chicqueenes and Sultanies, which is gold and silver, they unloaded in foure and twentie houres, was wonderfull: whereof having sufficient, and tired with toile, they cast her off with her company, with as much good merchandize as would have fraughted such another Britaine, that was but two hundred Tunnes, she foure or five hundred.

A desperate sea-fight.

To repaire his defects, hee stood for the coast of Calabria, but hearing there was six or seven Galleyes at Mesina, hee departed thence for Malta, but the wind comming faire, he kept his course along the coast of the

Kingdome of Sicilia by Sardinia and Corsica, till he came to the Road of Antibo in Peamon, where he set Smith on shore with five hundred chicqueenes, and a little box God sent him worth neere as much more.

Here he left this noble Britaine, and embarked himselfe for Lygorne, being glad to have such opportunitie and meanes to better his experience by the view of Italy; and having passed Tuskany, and the Countrey of Sieana, where hee found his deare friends, the two Honourable Brethren, the Lord Willoughby and his Brother cruelly wounded, in a desperate fray, yet to their exceeding great honour. Then to Viterbo and many other Cities, he came to Rome: where it was his chance to see Pope Clement the eight, with many Cardinalls, creepe up the holy Stayres, which they say are those our Saviour Christ went up to Pontius Pilate, where bloud falling from his head, being pricked with his crowne of thornes, the drops are marked with nailes of steele, upon them none dare goe but in that manner, saying so many Ave-Maries and Paternosters, as is their devotion, and to kisse the nailes of steele. But on each side is a paire of such like staires, up which you may goe, stand, or kneele, but divided from the holy Staires by two walls: right against them is a Chappell, where hangs a great silver Lampe, which burneth continually, yet they say the oyle neither increaseth nor diminisheth. A little distant is the ancient Church of Saint John de Laterane, where he saw him say Masse, which commonly he doth upon some Friday once a moneth. Having saluted Father Parsons, that famous English Jesuite, and satisfied himselfe with the rarities of Rome, he went downe the River of Tiber to Civita Vechia, where he embarked himselfe to satisfie his eye with the faire Citie of Naples, and her Kingdomes nobilitie; returning by Capua, Rome and Seana, he passed by that admired Citie of Florence, the Cities and Countries of Bolonia, Ferrara, Mantua, Padua, and Venice, whose Gulfe he passed from Malamoco and the Adriatike Sea for Ragouza, spending some time to see that barren broken

The Popes holy Staires brought from Jerusalem, whereon (they say) Christ went up to Pontius Pilate. [P. 6]

coast of Albania and Dalmatia, to Capo de Istria, travelling the maine of poore Slavonia by Lubbiano, till he came to Grates in Steria, the Seat of Ferdinando Archduke of Austria, now Emperour of Almania: where he met an English man, and an Irish Jesuite, who acquainted him with many brave Gentlemen of good qualitie, especially with the Lord Ebersbaught, with whom trying such conclusions, as he projected to undertake, preferred him to Baron Kisell, Generall of the Artillery, and he to a worthy Collonell, the Earle of Meldritch, with whom going to Vienne in Austria, under whose Regiment, in what service, and how he spent his time, this ensuing Discourse will declare.

Chapter IV.

The Siege of Olumpagh: An excellent Stratagem by Smith; Another not much worse.

The siege of Olumpagh.

AFter the losse of Caniza, the Turkes with twentie thousand besieged the strong Towne of Olumpagh so straightly, as they were cut off from all intelligence and hope of succour; till John Smith, this English Gentleman, acquainted Baron Kisell, Generall of the Archdukes Artillery, he had taught the Governour, his worthy friend, such a Rule, that he would undertake to make him know any thing he intended, and have his answer, would they bring him but to some place where he might make the flame of a Torch seene to the Towne; Kisell inflamed with this strange invention; Smith made it so plaine, that forthwith hee gave him guides, who in the darke night brought him to a mountaine, where he shewed three Torches equidistant from other, which plainly appearing to the Towne, the Governour presently apprehended, and answered againe with three other fires in like manner; each knowing the others being and intent; Smith, though distant seven miles, signified to him these words: On

[P. 7] Thursday at night I will charge on the East, at the Alarum, salley you; Ebersbaught answered he would, and thus it was done: First he writ his message as briefe, you see, as could be, then divided the Alphabet in two parts thus;

A. b. c. d. e. f. g. h. i. k. l.
1. 1. 1. 1. 1. 1. 1. 1. 1. 1. 1.
m. n. o. p. q. r. s. t. v. w. x.
2. 2. 2. 2. 2. 2. 2. 2. 2. 2. 2.
y. z.
2. 2.

An excellent Stratagem.

The first part from A. to L. is signified by shewing and hiding one linke, so oft as there is letters from A. to that letter you meane; the other part from M. to Z. is mentioned by two lights in like manner. The end of a word is signified by shewing of three lights, ever staying your light at that letter you meane, till the other may write it in a paper, and answer by his signall, which is one light, it is done, beginning to count the letters by the lights, every time from A. to M. by this meanes also the other returned his answer, whereby each did understand other. The Guides all this time having well viewed the Campe, returned to Kisell, who, doubting of his power being but ten thousand, was animated by the Guides, how the Turkes were so divided by the River in two parts, they could not easily second each other. To which Smith added this conclusion; that two or three thousand pieces of match fastened to divers small lines of an hundred fathome in length being armed with powder, might all be fired and stretched at an instant before the Alarum, upon the Plaine of Hysnaburg, supported by two staves, at each lines end, in that manner would seeme like so many Musketteers; which was put in practice: and being discovered by the Turkes, they prepared to encounter these false fires, thinking there had beene some great Armie: whilest Kisell with his ten thousand being entred the Turks quarter, who ranne up and downe as men amazed. It was not long ere Ebersbaught was pell-mell with them

Another Stratagem.

in their Trenches; in which distracted confusion, a third part of the Turkes, that besieged that side towards Knousbruck, were slaine; many of the rest drowned, but all fled. The other part of the Armie was so busied to resist the false fires, that Kisell before the morning put two thousand good souldiers in the Towne, and with small losse was retired; the Garrison was well releeved with that they found in the Turkes quarter, which caused the Turkes to raise their siege and returne to Caniza: and Kisell with much honour was received at Kerment, and occasioned the Author a good reward and preferment, to be Captaine of two hundred and fiftie Horse-men, under the Conduct of Colonell Voldo, Earle of Meldritch.

Chapter V.

[P. 8]

The siege of Stowlle-wesenburg; The effects of Smiths Fireworkes: A worthy exploit of Earle Rosworme; Earle Meldritch takes the Bashaw prisoner.

A Generall rumour of a generall peace, now spred it selfe over all the face of those tormented Countries: but the Turke intended no such matter, but levied souldiers from all parts he could. The Emperour also, by the assistance of the Christian Princes, provided three Armies, the one led by the Arch-duke Mathias, the Emperours brother, and his Lieutenant Duke Mercury to defend Low Hungary, the second, by Ferdinando the Arch-duke of Steria, and the Duke of Mantua his Lieutenant to regaine Caniza; the third by Gonzago, Governour of High Hungary, to joyne with Georgia Busca, to make an absolute conquest of Transilvania.

The siege of Alba Regalis.

Duke Mercury with an Armie of thirtie thousand, whereof neere ten thousand were French, besieged Stowlle-wesenburg, otherwise called Alba Regalis, a place so strong by Art and Nature, that it was thought impregnable.

At his first comming, the Turkes sallied upon the Germane quarter, slew neere five hundred, and returned before they were thought on. The next night, in like manner they did neere as much to the Bemers, and Hungarians; of which fortune still presuming, thinking to have found the French quarter as carelesse, eight or nine hundred of them were cut in pieces and taken prisoners. In this encounter Mousier Grandvile, a brave French Colonell, received seven or eight cruell wounds, yet followed the enemie to the Ports; he came off alive, but within three or foure dayes died.

Earle Meldritch, by the information of three or foure Christians (escaped out of the Towne), upon every Alarum, where there was greatest assemblies and throng of people, caused Captaine Smith to put in practice his fiery Dragons, hee had demonstrated unto him, and the Earle Von Sulch at Comora, which hee thus performed: Having prepared fortie or fiftie round-bellied earthen pots, and filled them with hand Gunpowder, then covered them with Pitch, mingled with Brimstone and Turpentine; and quartering as many Musket-bullets, that hung together but only at the Center of the division, stucke them round in the mixture about the pots, and covered them againe with the same mixture, over that a strong Searcloth, then over all a good thicknesse of Towze-match well tempered with oyle of Lin-seed, Campheer, and powder of Brimstone, these he fitly placed in Slings, graduated so neere as they could to the places of these Assemblies. At midnight upon the Alarum, it was a fearfull sight to see the short flaming course of their flight in the aire: but presently after their fall, the lamentable noise of the miserable slaughtered Turkes was most wonderfull to heare: Besides, they had fired that Suburbe at the Port of Buda, in two or three places, which so troubled the Turkes to quench, that had there beene any meanes to have assaulted them, they could hardly have resisted the fire, and their enemies. The Earle Rosworme, contrary to the opinion of all men, would needs undertake to finde

The effect of good fire-works.

[P. 9]

A worthy exploit of Earle Rosworme.

meanes to surprize the Segeth and Suburbe of the Citie, strongly defended by a muddie Lake, which was thought unpassable.

The Duke having planted his Ordnance, battered the other side, whilest Rosworme, in the darke night, with every man a bundle of sedge and bavins still throwne before them, so laded up the Lake, as they surprized that unregarded Suburbe before they were discovered: upon which unexpected Alarum, the Turkes fled into the Citie; and the other Suburbe not knowing the matter, got into the Citie also, leaving their Suburbe for the Duke, who with no great resistance, tooke it, with many peeces of Ordnance; the Citie, being of no such strength as the Suburbs, with their owne Ordnance was so battered, that it was taken perforce, with such a mercilesse execution, as was most pitifull to behold. The Bashaw notwithstanding drew together a partie of five hundred before his owne Pallace, where he intended to die; but seeing most of his men slaine before him, by the valiant Captaine Earl Meldritch, who tooke him prisoner with his owne hands; and with the hazard of himselfe saved him from the fury of other troopes, that did pull downe his Pallace, and would have rent him in peeces, had he not beene thus preserved. The Duke thought his victory much honoured with such a Prisoner; tooke order hee should bee used like a Prince, and with all expedition gave charge presently to repaire the breaches, and the ruines of this famous Citie, that had beene in the possession of the Turkes neere threescore yeares.

Earle Meldritch takes the Bashaw prisoner.

[Chapter VI.

Chapter VI.

A brave encounter of the Turkes Armie with the Christians; Duke Mercury overthroweth Assan Bashaw; Hee divides the Christian Armie; His noblenesse and death.

Ahomet, the great Turke, during the siege, had raised an Armie of sixtie thousand men to have releeved it; but hearing it was lost, he sent Assan Bashaw Generall of his Armie, the Bashaw of Buda, Bashaw Amaroz, to see if it were possible to regaine it; The Duke understanding there could be no great experience in such a new levied Armie as Assan had; having put a strong Garrison into it: and with the brave Colonell Rosworme, Culnits, Meldritch, the Rhine-Grave, Vahan and many others; with twenty thousand good souldiers, set forward to meet the Turke in the Plaines of Girke. Those two Armies encountred as they marched, where began a hot and bloudy Skirmish betwixt them, Regiment against Regiment, as they came in order, till the night parted them: Here Earle Meldritch was so invironed amongst those halfe circuler Regiments of Turkes, they supposed him their Prisoner, and his Regiment lost; but his two most couragious friends, Vahan and Culnits, made such a passage amongst them, that it was a terror to see how horse and man lay sprawling and tumbling, some one way, some another on the ground. The Earle there at that time made his valour shine more bright than his armour, which seemed then painted with Turkish bloud, he slew the brave Zanzack Bugola, and made his passage to his friends, but neere halfe his Regiment was slaine.

A brave encounter of the Turkes Armie with the Christians.

[P. 10]

Captain Smith had his horse slaine under him, and himselfe sore wounded; but he was not long unmounted, for there was choice enough of horses that wanted masters. The Turke thinking the victory sure against the Duke, whose Armie, by the Siege, and the Garrison, he had left behind him, was much weakened, would not be content with one, but he would have all; and lest the Duke should returne to Alba Regalis, he sent that night twenty thousand to besiege the Citie, assuring them he would keepe the Duke or any other from releeving them. Two or three dayes they lay each by other, entrenching themselves; the Turkes daring the Duke daily to a sett battell, who at length drew out his Army, led by the Rhine-Grave, Culnits and Meldritch, who upon their first encounter, charged with that resolute and valiant courage, as disordered not only the formost squadrons of the Turkes, but enforced all the whole Armie to retire to the Campe, with the losse of five or six thousand, with the Bashaw of Buda, and foure or five Zanzacks, with divers other great Commanders, two hundred Prisoners, and nine peeces of Ordnance. At that instant appeared, as it were, another Armie comming out of a valley over a plaine hill, that caused the Duke at that time to be contented, and to retire to his Trenches; which gave time to Assan to reorder his disordered squadrons.

Duke Mercury overthroweth Assan Bassa.

Here they lay nine or ten dayes, and more supplies repaired to them, expecting to try the event in a sett battell; but the souldiers on both parties, by reason of their great wants and approach of winter, grew so discontented, that they were ready of themselves to breake up the Leager: the Bashaw retiring himselfe to Buda, had some of the Reare Troopes cut off. Amaroz Bashaw hearing of this, found such bad welcome at Alba Regalis, and the Towne so strongly repaired, with so brave a Garrison, raised his siege and retired to Zigetum. The Duke understanding that the Arch-duke Ferdinando had so resolutely besieged Caniza, as what by the losse of Alba Regalis, and the Turks retreat to Buda, being void of hope of any reliefe, doubted not but it would become againe the Christians. To the furtherance whereof, the Duke divided his Armie into three parts. The Earle of Rosworme went with seven thousand to Caniza; the

Duke Mercury divideth his Armie.

Earle of Meldritch with six thousand he sent to assist Georgio Busca against the Transilvanians, the rest went with himselfe to the Garrisons of Strigonium and Komara; having thus worthily behaved himselfe, he arrived at Vienne, where the Arch-dukes and the Nobilitie with as much honour received him, as if he had conquered all Hungaria; his very Picture they esteemed would make them fortunate, which thousands kept as curiously as a precious relique. To requite this honour, preparing himselfe to returne into France, to raise new Forces against the next yeare, with the two Arch-dukes Mathias and Maximilian and divers others of the Nobilitie, was with
[P. 11] great magnificence conducted to Nurenburg, there by them royally feasted, (how it chanced is not knowne;) but the next morning he was found dead, and his brother in law died two dayes after; whose hearts, after this great triumph, with much sorrow were carried into France.

Duke Mercury and his brother in law die suddenly.

Chapter VII.

The unhappie Siege of Caniza; Earle Meldritch serveth Prince Sigismundus; Prince Moyses besiegeth Regall; Smiths three single combats; His Patent from Sigismundus, and reward.

The unhappie siege of Caniza.

THe worthy Lord Rosworme had not a worse journey to the miserable Seige of Caniza, (where by the extremitie of an extraordinary continuing tempest of haile, wind, frost and snow, in so much that the Christians were forced to leave their Tents and Artillery, and what they had; it being so cold that three or foure hundred of them were frozen to death in a night, and two or three thousand lost in that miserable flight in the snowie tempest, though they did know no enemie at all to follow them:) than the noble Earle of Meldritch had to Transilvania: where hearing of the death of Michael and the brave Duke Mercury, and knowing the policie of Busca, and the Prince his Roialtie, being now beyond all beleefe of men, in possession of the best part of Transilvania; perswaded his troopes, in so honest a cause, to assist the Prince against the Turke, rather than Busca against the Prince.

Earle Meldritch serveth Prince Sigismundus.

The souldiers being worne out with those hard payes and travells, upon hope to have free libertie to make bootie upon what they could get possession of from the Turkes, was easily perswaded to follow him whithersoever. Now this noble Earle was a Transilvanian borne, and his fathers Countrey yet inhabited by the Turkes; for Transilvania was yet in three divisions, though the Prince had the hearts both of Country and people; yet the Frontiers had a Garrison amongst the unpassable mountaines, some for the Emperour, some for the Prince, and some for the Turke: to regaine which small estate, hee desired leave of the Prince to trie his fortunes, and to make use of that experience, the time of twentie yeares had taught him in the Emperours service, promising to spend the rest of his dayes for his countries defence in his Excellencies service. The Prince glad of so brave a Commander, and so many expert and ancient souldiers, made him Campe-master of his Armie, gave him all necessary releefe for his troopes and what freedome they desired to plunder the Turkes.

Earle Meldritch maketh incursions to discover Regall.

The Earle having made many incursions into the Land of Zarkam among those rockie mountains, where were some Turks, some Tartars, but most Bandittoes, Rennegadoes, and such like, which sometimes hee forced into the Plaines of Regall, where is a Citie not only of men and fortifications, strong of it selfe, but so environed with mountaines, that made the passages so difficult, that in all these warres no attempt had beene made upon it to any purpose: Having satisfied himselfe with the Situation, [P. 12] and the most convenient passages to bring his Armie unto it: The earth no sooner put on her greene habit, than the Earle overspread her with his armed troopes. To possesse himselfe first of the most convenient passage, which was a narrow valley betwixt two high mountaines;

he sent Colonell Veltus with his Regiment, dispersed in companies to lye in Ambuscado, as he had directed them, and in the morning to drive all the cattell they could finde before a Fort in that passage, whom he supposed would sally, seeing but some small partie, to recover their prey: which tooke such good successe, that the Garrison was cut off by the Ambuscado, and Veltus seized on the Skonces, which was abandoned. Meldritch glad of so fortunate a beginning, it was six dayes ere he could with six thousand Pioners make a passage for his Ordnance: The Turkes having such warning, strengthned the Towne so with men and provision, that they made a scorne of so small a number as Meldritch brought with him before the Citie, which was but eight thousand. Before they had pitched their Tents, the Turkes sallied in such abundance, as for an houre they had rather a bloudy battell than a skirmish, but with the losse of neere fifteene hundred on both sides. The Turkes were chased till the Cities Ordnance caused the Earle to retire. The next day Zachel Moyses, Generall of the Armie, pitched also his tents with nine thousand foot and horse, and six and twenty peeces of Ordnance; but in regard of the situation of this strong Fortresse, they did neither feare them nor hurt them, being upon the point of a faire promontory, environed on the one side within halfe a mile with an un-usefull mountaine, and on the other side with a faire Plaine, where the Christians encamped, but so commanded by their Ordnance, they spent neere a month in entrenching themselves, and raising their mounts to plant their batteries; which slow proceedings the Turkes oft derided, that the Ordnance were at pawne, and how they grew fat for want of exercise, and fearing lest they should depart ere they could assault their Citie, sent this Challenge to any Captaine in the Armie. That to delight the Ladies, who did long to see some court-like pastime, the Lord Turbashaw did defie any Captaine, that had the command of a Company, who durst combate with him for his head: The matter being discussed, it was accepted, but so many

Moyses besiegeth Regall.

Cecill ſcul

questions grew for the undertaking, it was decided by lots, which fell upon Captaine Smith, before spoken of.

Three single Combates.

Truce being made for that time, the Rampiers all beset with faire Dames, and men in Armes, the Christians in Battalio; Turbashaw with a noise of Howboyes entred the fields well mounted and armed; on his shoulders were fixed a paire of great wings, compacted of Eagles feathers within a ridge of silver, richly garnished with gold and precious stones, a Janizary before him, bearing his Lance, on each side another leading his horse; where long hee stayed not, ere Smith with a noise of Trumpets, only a Page bearing his Lance, passing by him with a courteous salute, tooke his ground with such good successe, that at the sound of the charge, he passed the Turke throw the sight of his Beaver, face, head, and all, that he fell dead to the ground, where alighting and unbracing his Helmet, [P. 13] cut off his head, and the Turkes tooke his body; and so returned without any hurt at all. The head hee presented to the Lord Moses, the Generall, who kindly accepted it; and with joy to the whole armie he was generally welcomed.

The death of this Captaine so swelled in the heart of one Grualgo, his vowed friend, as, rather inraged with madnesse than choller, he directed a particular challenge to the Conquerour, to regaine his friends head, or lose his owne, with his horse and Armour for advantage, which according to his desire, was the next day undertaken: as before, upon the sound of the Trumpets, their Lances flew in peeces upon a cleare passage; but the Turke was neere unhorsed. Their Pistolls was the next, which marked Smith upon the placard; but the next shot the Turke was so wounded in the left arme, that being not able to rule his horse, and defend himselfe, he was throwne to the ground; and so bruised with the fall, that he lost his head, as his friend before him; with his horse and Armour; but his body and his rich apparell was sent backe to the Towne.

Every day the Turkes made some sallies, but few

skirmishes would they endure to any purpose. Our workes and approaches being not yet advanced to that height and effect which was of necessitie to be performed; to delude time, Smith, with so many incontradictible perswading reasons, obtained leave that the Ladies might know he was not so much enamoured of their servants heads, but if any Turke of their ranke would come to the place of combate to redeeme them, should have his also upon the like conditions, if he could winne it.

The challenge presently was accepted by Bonny Mulgro.

The next day both the Champions entring the field as before, each discharging their Pistoll having no Lances, but such martiall weapons as the defendant appointed, no hurt was done; their Battle-axes was the next, whose piercing bils made sometime the one, sometime the other to have scarce sense to keepe their saddles, specially the Christian received such a blow that he lost his Battle-axe, and failed not much to have fallen after it, whereat the supposing conquering Turk, had a great shout from the Rampiers. The Turk prosecuted his advantage to the uttermost of his power; yet the other, what by the readinesse of his horse, and his judgement and dexterity in such a businesse, beyond all mens expectation, by Gods assistance, not onely avoided the Turkes violence, but having drawne his Faulchion, pierced the Turke so under the Culets thorow backe and body, that although he alighted from his horse, he stood not long ere hee lost his head, as the rest had done.

Chapter VIII. [P. 14]

Georgio Busca an Albane his ingratitude to Prince Sigismundus; Prince Moyses, his Lieutenant, is overthrowne by Busca, Generall for the Emperour Rodolphus; Sigismundus yeeldeth his Countrey to Rodolphus; Busca assisteth Prince Rodoll in Wallachia.

His good successe gave such great encouragement to the whole Armie, that with a guard of six thousand, three spare horses, before each a Turkes head upon a Lance, he was conducted to the Generalls Pavillion with his Presents. Moyses received both him and them with as much respect as the occasion deserved, embracing him in his armes, gave him a faire Horse richly furnished, a Semitere and belt worth three hundred ducats; and Meldritch made him Sergeant major of his Regiment. But now to the siege, having mounted six and twenty peeces of Ordnance fifty or sixty foot above the Plaine, made them so plainly tell his meaning, that within fifteene dayes two breaches were made, which the Turkes as valiantly defended as men could; that day was made a darksome night, but by the light that proceeded from the murdering Muskets, and peacemaking Canon, whilest their slothfull Governour lay in a Castle on the top of a high mountaine, and like a valiant Prince asketh what's the matter, when horrour and death stood amazed each at other, to see who should prevaile to make him victorious: Moyses commanding a generall assault upon the sloping front of the high Promontory, where the Barons of Budendorfe and Oberwin lost neere halfe their Regiments, by logs, bags of powder, and such like, tumbling downe the hill, they were to mount ere they could come to the breach; notwithstanding with an

Regall assaulted and taken.

incredible courage they advanced to the push of the Pike with the defendants, that with the like courage repulsed, till the Earle Meldritch, Becklefield and Zarvana, with their fresh Regiments seconded them with that fury, that the Turks retired and fled into the Castle, from whence by a flag of truce they desired composition. The Earle remembring his fathers death, battered it with all the Ordnance in the Towne, and the next day tooke it; all he found could beare Armes he put to the sword, and set their heads upon stakes round about the walles, in the same manner they had used the Christians, when they tooke it. Moyses having repaired the Rampiers, and throwne downe the worke in his Campe, he put in it a strong Garrison, though the pillage he had gotten in the Towne was much, having beene for a long time an impregnable den of theeves; yet the losse of the Armie so intermingled the sowre with the sweet, as forced Moyses to seek a further revenge, that he sacked Veratio, Solmos, and Kupronka, and with two thousand prisoners, most women and children, came to Esenberg, not farre from the Princes Palace, where he there Encamped.

Sigismundus comming to view his Armie, was presented [P. 15] with the Prisoners, and six and thirtie Ensignes; where celebrating thankes to Almightie God in triumph of those victories, hee was made acquainted with the service Smith had done at Olumpagh, Stowle-Wesenburg and Regall, for which with great honour hee gave him three Turkes heads in a Shield for his Armes, by Patent, under his hand and Seale, with an Oath ever to weare them in his Colours, his Picture in Gould, and three hundred Ducats, yearely for a Pension.

The Patent. Sigismundus Bathori, Dei gratia Dux Transilvaniæ, Wallachiæ, et Vandalorum; Comes Anchard, Salford, Growenda; Cunctis his literis significamus qui eas lecturi aut audituri sunt, concessam licentiam aut facultatem Johanni Smith, natione Anglo Generoso, 250. militum Capitaneo sub Illustrissimi et Gravissimi Henrici Volda,

Comitis de Meldri, Salmariæ, et Peldoiæ primario, et 1000 equitibus et 1500. peditibus bello Ungarico conductione in Provincias suprascriptas sub Authoritate nostra: cui servituti omni laude, perpetuaque memoria dignum præbuit sese erga nos, ut virum strenuum pugnantem pro aris et focis decet. Quare è favore nostro militario ipsum ordine condonavimus, et in Sigillum illius tria Turcia Capita designare et deprimere concessimus, quæ ipse gladio suo ad Urbem Regalem in singulari prœlio

vicit, mactavit, atque decollavit in Transilvaniæ Provincia: Sed fortuna cum variabilis ancepsque sit idem forte fortuito in Wallachia Provincia, Anno Domini 1602. die Mensis Novembris 18.* cum multis aliis etiam Nobilibus et aliis quibusdam militibus captus est à Domino Bascha electo ex Cambia regionis Tartariæ, cujus severitate adductus salutem quantam potuit quesivit, tantumque effecit, Deo omnipotente adjuvante, ut deliberavit se, et ad suos Commilitones revertit; ex quibus ipsum liberavimus, et hæc nobis testimonia habuit ut majori licentia frueretur qua dignus esset, jam tendet in patriam suam dulcissimam: Rogamus ergo omnes nostros charissimos, confinitimos, Duces, Principes,

* *Augusti* 8vo.

[P. 16] Comites, Barones, Gubernatores Urbium et Navium in eadem Regione et cœterarum Provinciarum in quibus ille residere conatus fuerit ut idem permittatur Capitaneus libere sine obstaculo omni versari. Hæc facientes pergraium nobis feceritis. Signatum Lesprizia in Misnia die Mensis Decembris 9. Anno Domini 1603.

Sigismundus Bathori.

Cum Privilegio propriæ Majestatis.

UNiversis, et singulis, cujuscunque loci, status, gradus, ordinis, ac conditionis ad quos hos præsens scriptum pervenerit, Guilielmus Segar Eques auratus alias dictus * Garterus Principalis Rex Armorum Anglicorum, Salutem. Sciatis, quod Ego prædictus Gerterus, notum, testatumque facio, quod Patentem suprascriptum,†, cum manu propria prædicti Ducis Transilvaniæ, subsignatum, et Sigillo suo affixum, Vidi: et Copiam veram ejusdem (in perpetuam rei memoriam) transcripsi, et recordavi in Archivis, et Registris Officii Armorum. Datum Londini 19. die Augusti, Anno Domini 1625. Annoque Regni Domini nostri Caroli Dei gratia Magnæ Britanniæ, Franciæ, et Hiberniæ Regis, Fidei Defensoris, &c. Primo.

*dominus.

† superaddem.

Guilielmus Segar, Garterus.

The same in English.

Sigismundus Bathor, by the Grace of God, Duke of Transilvania, Wallachia, and Moldavia, Earle of Anchard, Salford and Growenda; to whom this Writing may come or appeare. Know that We have given leave and licence to John Smith an English Gentleman, Captaine of 250. Souldiers, under the most Generous and Honourable Henry Volda, Earle of Meldritch, Salmaria, and [P. 17] Peldoia, Colonell of a thousand horse, and fifteene hundred foot, in the warres of Hungary and in the Provinces aforesaid under our authority; whose service doth deserve all praise and perpetuall memory towards us, as a man that did for God and his Country overcome his enemies: Wherefore out of Our love and favour, according to the law of Armes, We have ordained and given him in his shield of Armes, the figure and description of three Turks heads, which with his sword, before the towne of Regall, in single combat he did overcome, kill, and cut off, in the Province of Transilvania. But fortune, as she is very variable, so it chanced and happened to him in the Province of Wallachia, in the yeare of our Lord, 1602. the 18. day of November, with many others, as well Noble men, as also divers other Souldiers, were taken prisoners by the Lord Bashaw of Cambia, a Country of Tartaria: whose cruelty brought him such good fortune, by the helpe and power of Almighty God, that hee delivered himselfe, and returned againe to his company and fellow souldiers, of whom We doe discharge him, and this hee hath in witnesse thereof, being much more worthy of a better reward; and now intends to returne to his owne sweet Country. We desire therefore all our loving and kinde kinsmen, Dukes, Princes, Earles, Barons, Governours of Townes, Cities, or Ships, in this Kingdome, or any other Provinces he shall come in, that you freely let passe this the aforesaid Captaine, without any hinderance or molestation: and this doing, with all kindnesse we are alwayes ready to doe the like for you.

Sealed at Lipswick in Misenland, the ninth of December, in the yeare of our Lord, 1603.

SIGISMUNDUS BATHOR.

With the proper privilege of his Majestie.

TO all and singular, in what place, state, degree, order, or condition whatsoever, to whom this present writing shall come: I William Segar Knight, otherwise Garter, and principall King of Armes of England, wish health. Know that I the aforesaid Garter, do witnesse and approve, that this aforesaid Patent, I have seene,
[P. 18] signed and sealed under the proper hand and Seale Manual of the said Duke of Transilvania; and a true coppy of the same, as a thing for perpetuall memory, I have subscribed and recorded in the Register and office of the Heralds of Armes. Dated at London the nineteenth day of August, in the yeare of our Lord 1625. and in the first yeare of our Soveraigne Lord Charles by the grace of God, King of great Britaine, France, and Ireland, Defender of the faith, &c.

WILLIAM SEGAR.

Chapter IX.

Sigismundus sends Ambassadours unto the Emperour; the conditions re-assured, He yeeldeth up all to Busca, and returneth to Prague.

Usca having all this time beene raising new forces, was commanded from the Emperour againe to invade Transilvania, which being one of the fruitfullest and strongest Countries in those parts, was now rather a desart, or the very spectacle of desolation; their fruits and fields overgrowne with weeds, their Churches and battered Palaces and best buildings, as for feare, hid with Mosse and Ivy: being the very Bulwarke and Rampire of a great part of Europe, most fit by all Christians to have beene supplyed and maintained, was thus brought to ruine by them it most concerned to support it. But alas, what is it, when the power of Majestie pampered in all delights of pleasant vanity, neither knowing nor considering the labour of the Ploughman, the hazard of the Merchant, the oppression of Statesmen; nor feeling the piercing torments of broken limbes, and inveterated wounds, the toilsome marches, the bad lodging, the hungry diet, and the extreme misery that Souldiers endure to secure all those estates, and yet by the spight of malicious detraction, starves for want of their reward and recompences; whilst the politique Courtier, that commonly aimes more at his owne honors & ends than his Countries good, or his Princes glory, honour, or security, as this worthy Prince too well could testifie. But the Emperor being certified how weak and desperate his estate was, sent Busca againe with a great Army, to trie his fortune once more in Transilvania. The Prince considering how his Country & subjects were consumed; the small means he had any longer to defend his estate, both against the cruelty of the Turke, & the power of the Emperor, & the small care the Polanders had in supplying him, as they had promised, sent to Busca to have truce, till messengers might be sent to the Emperour for some better agreement, wherewith Busca was contented. The Ambassadours so prevailed, that the Emperour re-assured unto them the conditions he had promised the Prince at their confederacie, for the lands in Silesia, with 60000. ducats presently in hand, and 50000. ducats yearely as a pension. [P. 19] When this conclusion was knowne to Moyses his Lieftenant then in the field with the Army, that would doe anything rather than come in subjection to the Germans, he encouraged his Souldiers, and without any more adoe marched to encounter Busca, whom he found much better provided than he expected; so that betwixt them in six or seven houres, more than five or six thousand on both sides lay dead in the field. Moyses thus over-

Busca in Transilvania overthroweth Moyses.

throwne, fled to the Turks at Temesware, and his scattered troopes some one way, some another.

The Prince understanding of this so sudden and unexpected accident, onely accompanied with an hundred of his Gentry and Nobility, went into the campe to Busca, to let him know, how ignorant he was of his Lieftenants errour, that had done it without his direction or knowledge, freely offering to performe what was concluded by his Ambassadours with the Emperour; and so causing all his Garrisons to come out of their strong holds, he delivered all to Busca for the Emperour, and so went to Prague, where he was honourably received, and established in his possessions, as his Emperiall Majestie had promised. Busca assembling all the Nobility, tooke their oaths of allegeance and fidelity, and thus their Prince being gone, Transilvania became againe subject to the Emperour.

Sigismundus yeeldeth his country to Busca.

Busca assisteth Rodoll in Wallachia.

Now after the death of Michael, Vavoyd of Wallachia, the Turke sent one Jeremie to be their Vavoyd or Prince; whose insulting tyranny caused the people to take Armes against him, so that he was forced to flie into the confines of Moldavia; and Busca in the behalfe of the Emperour, proclaimed the Lord Rodoll in his stead. But Jeremy having assembled an Army of forty thousand Turks, Tartars, and Moldavians, returned into Wallachia. Rodoll not yet able to raise such a power, fled into Transilvania to Busca, his ancient friend; who considering well of the matter, and how good it would be for his owne security to have Wallachia subject to the Emperour, or at least such an employment for the remainders of the old Regiments of Sigismundus, (of whose greatnesse and true affection hee was very suspitious,) sent them with Rodoll to recover Wallachia, conducted by the valiant Captaines, the Earle Meldritch, Earle Veltus, Earle Nederspolt, Earle Zarvana, the Lord Bechlefield, the Lord Budendorfe, with their Regiments, and divers others of great ranke and quality, the greatest friends and alliances the Prince had; who with thirty thousand, marched along by the river Altus, to the streights of Rebrinke, where they entred Wallachia, encamping at Raza; Jeremie lying at Argish, drew his Army into his old campe, in the plaines of Peteske, and with his best diligence fortified it, intending to defend himselfe till more power came to him from the Crym-Tartar. Many small parties that came to his campe, Rodoll cut off; and in the nights would cause their heads to be throwne up and downe before the trenches. Seven of their Porters were taken, whom Jeremie commanded to be flayed quicke; and after hung their skinnes upon poles, and their carkasses and heads on stakes by them.

Chapter X. [P. 20]

The battell of Rotenton; a pretty stratagem of fire-works by Smith.

Odoll not knowing how to draw the enemie to battell, raised his Armie, burning and spoyling all where he came, and returned againe towards Rebrinke in the night, as if he had fled upon the generall rumour of the Crym-Tartars comming; which so inflamed the Turkes of a happy victory, they urged Jeremy against his will to follow them. Rodoll seeing his plot fell out as he desired, so ordered the matter, that having regained the streights, he put his Army in order, that had beene neere two dayes pursued, with continuall skirmishes in his Reare, which now making head against the enemie, that followed with their whole Armie in the best manner they could, was furiously charged with six thousand Hydukes, Wallachians, and Moldavians, led by three Colonells, Oversall, Dubras, and Calab, to entertaine the time till the rest came up; Veltus and Nederspolt with their Regiments, entertained them with the like courage, till the Zanzacke Hamesbeg, with six thousand more, came with a fresh charge, which Meldritch and Budendorfe.

A battell betwixt Rodoll and Jeremie.

rather like enraged lions, than men, so bravely encountred, as if in them only had consisted the victory; Meldritchs horse being slaine under him, the Turks pressed what they could to have taken him prisoner, but being remounted, it was thought with his owne hand he slew the valiant Zanzacke, whereupon his troopes retyring, the two proud Bashawes, Aladin and Zizimmus, brought up the front of the body of their battell. Veltus and Nederspolt having breathed, and joyning their troopes with Becklefield and Zarvana, with such an incredible courage charged the left flancke of Zizimmus, as put them all in disorder; where Zizimmus the Bashaw was taken prisoner, but died presently upon his wounds. Jeremie seeing now the maine battell of Rodoll advance, being thus constrained, like a valiant Prince in his front of the Vantgard, by his example so bravely encouraged his souldiers, that Rodoll found no great assurance of the victorie. Thus being joyned in this bloudy massacre, that there was scarce ground to stand upon, but upon the dead carkasses, which in lesse than an hower were so mingled, as if each Regiment had singled out other. The admired Aladin that day did leave behinde him a glorious name for his valour, whose death many of his enemies did lament after the victory, which at that instant fell to Rodoll. It was reported Jeremie was also slaine, but it was not so, but fled with the remainder of his Armie to Moldavia, leaving five and twenty thousand dead in the field, of both Armies.

Wallachia subjected to the Emperour.

And thus Rodoll was seated againe in his Soveraignty, and Wallachia became subject to the Emperour.

But long he rested not to settle his new estate, but there came newes, that certaine Regiments of stragling Tartars, were forraging those parts towards Moldavia. Meldritch with thirteene thousand men was sent against them, but when they heard it was the Crym-Tartar and [P. 21] his two sonnes, with an Armie of thirty thousand; and Jeremie, that had escaped with fourteene or fifteene thousand, lay in ambush for them about Langanaw, he retired towards Rottenton, a strong garrison for Rodoll: but they were so invironed with these hellish numbers, they could make no great haste, for skirmishing with their scouts, forragers, and small parties that still encountred them. But one night amongst the rest, having made a passage through a wood, with an incredible expedition, cutting trees thwart each other to hinder their passage, in a thicke fogge early in the morning, unexpectedly they met two thousand loaded with pillage, and two or three hundred horse and cattell; the most of them were slaine and taken prisoners, who told them where Jeremie lay in the passage, expecting the Crym-Tartar that was not farre from him. Meldritch intending to make his passage perforce, was advised of a pretty stratagem by the English Smith, which presently he thus accomplished; for having accommodated two or three hundred truncks with wilde fire, upon the heads of lances, and charging the enemie in the night, gave fire to the truncks, which blazed forth such flames and sparkles, that it so amazed not onely their horses, but their foot also; that by the meanes of this flaming encounter, their owne horses turned tailes with such fury, as by their violence overthrew Jeremy & his Army, without any losse at all to speak of to Meldritch. But of this victory long they triumphed not; for being within three leagues of Rottenton, the Tartar with neere forty thousand so beset them, that they must either fight, or be cut in peeces flying. Here Busca and the Emperour had their desire; for the Sunne no sooner displayed his beames, than the Tartar his colours; where at midday he stayed a while, to see the passage of a tyrannicall and treacherous imposture, till the earth did blush with the bloud of honesty, that the Sunne for shame did hide himselfe from so monstrous sight of a cowardly calamity. It was a most brave sight to see the banners and ensignes streaming in the aire, the glittering of Armour, the variety of colours, the motion of plumes, the forrests of lances, and the thicknesse of shorter weapons, till the silent expedition of the bloudy blast from the murdering Ordnance, whose roaring voice is not so soone heard as felt by the aymed at object, which made among them a most lamentable slaughter.

Chapter XI.

The names of the English that were slaine in the battell of Rottenton; and how Captaine Smith is taken prisoner; and sold for a slave.

The battell of Rottenton.

IN the valley of Veristhorne, betwixt the river of Altus, and the mountaine of Rottenton, was this bloudy encounter, where the most of the dearest friends of the noble Prince Sigismundus perished. Meldritch having ordered his eleven thousand in the best manner he could: at the foot of the mountaine upon his flancks, and before [P. 22] his front, he had pitched sharpe stakes, their heads hardned in the fire, and bent against the enemie, as three battalion of Pikes, amongst the which also there was digged many small holes. Amongst those stakes was ranged his footmen, that upon the charge was to retire, as there was occasion. The Tartar having ordered his 40000. for his best advantage, appointed Mustapha Bashaw to beginne the battell, with a generall shout, all their Ensignes displaying, Drummes beating, Trumpets and Howboyes sounding. Nederspolt and Mavazo with their Regiments of horse most valiantly encountred, and forced them to retire; the Tartar Begolgi with his Squadrons, darkening the skies with their flights of numberles arrowes, who was as bravely encountred by Veltus and Oberwin, which bloudie slaughter continued more than an houre, till the matchlesse multitude of the Tartars so increased, that they retired within their Squadrons of stakes, as was directed. The bloudy Tartar, as scorning he should stay so long for the victorie, with his massie troopes prosecuted the charge: but it was a wonder to see how horse and man came to the ground among the stakes, whose disordered troopes were there so mangled, that the Christians with a loud shout cryed Victoria; and with five or six field peeces, planted upon the rising of the mountaine, did much hurt to the enemy that still continued the battell with that furie, that Meldritch seeing there was no possibilitie long to prevaile, joyned his small troopes in one body, resolved directly to make his passage or die in the conclusion; and thus in grosse gave a generall charge, and for more than halfe an houre made his way plaine before him, till the maine battel of the Crym-Tartar with two Regiments of Turkes and Janizaries so overmatched them, that they were overthrowen. The night approaching, the Earle with some thirteene or foureteene hundred horse, swamme the River, some were drowned, all the rest slaine or taken prisoners: And thus in this bloudy field, neere 30000. lay, some headlesse, armlesse, and leglesse, all cut and mangled: where breathing their last, they gave this knowledge to the world, that for the lives of so few, the Crym-Tartar never paid dearer. But now the Countreyes of Transilvania and Wallachia, (subjected to the Emperour) and Sigismundus that brave Prince his Subject and Pensioner, the most of his Nobilitie, brave Captaines and Souldiers, became a prey to the cruell devouring Turke: where had the Emperor been as ready to have assisted him, and those three Armies led by three such worthy Captaines, as Michael, Busca, and Himselfe, and had those three Armies joyned together against the Turke, let all men judge, how happie it might have beene for all Christendome: and have either regained Bulgaria, or at least have beat him out of Hungaria, where hee hath taken much more from the Emperour, than hath the Emperour from Transilvania.

Extracted out of a Booke intituled, The warres of Hungary, Wallachia, and Moldavia, written by Francisco Ferneza, a learned Italian, the Princes Secretarie, and translated by Master Purchas.

The English men in this Battell.

In this dismall battell, where Nederspolt, Veltus, Zarvana, Mavazo, Bavell, and many other Earles, Barons, Colonels, Captaines, brave Gentlemen and Souldiers were slaine, Give mee leave to remember the names of our owne Country-men with him in those

exploits, that as resolutely as the best, in the defence of Christ and his Gospell, ended their dayes, as Baskerfield,
[P. 23] Hardwicke, Thomas Milemer, Robert Mullineux, Thomas Bishop, Francis Compton, George Davison, Nicholas Williams, and one John a Scot, did what men could doe, and when they could doe no more, left there their bodies, in testimonie of their mindes; only Ensigne Carleton, and Sergeant Robinson escaped: but Smith among the slaughtered dead bodies, and many a gasping soule, with toile and wounds lay groaning among the rest, till being found by the Pillagers hee was able to live, and perceiving by his armor & habit, his ransome might be better to them, than his death, they led him prisoner with many others; well they used him till his wounds were cured, and at Axopolis they were all sold for slaves, like beasts in a market-place, where everie Merchant, viewing their limbs and wounds, caused other slaves to struggle with them, to trie their strength, hee fell to the share of Bashaw Bogall, who sent him forthwith to Adrinopolis, so for Constantinople to his faire Mistresse for a slave. By twentie and twentie chained by the neckes, they marched in file to this great Citie, where they were delivered to their severall Masters, and he to the young Charatza Tragabigzanda.

Chapter XII.

How Captaine Smith was sent prisoner thorow the Blacke and Dissabacca Sea in Tartaria; the description of those Seas, and his usage.

THis Noble Gentlewoman tooke sometime occasion to shew him to some friends, or rather to speake with him, because shee could speake Italian, would feigne her selfe sick when she should goe to the Banians, or weepe over the graves, to know how Bogall tooke him prisoner; and if he were, as the Bashaw writ to her, a Bohemian

Lord conquered by his hand, as hee had many others, which ere long hee would present her, whose ransomes should adorne her with the glorie of his conquests.

But when she heard him protest he knew no such matter, nor ever saw Bogall till he bought him at Axopolis, and that hee was an English-man, onely by his adventures made a Captaine in those Countreyes. To trie the truth, shee found meanes to finde out many could speake English, French, Dutch, and Italian, to whom relating most part of these former passages he thought necessarie, which they so honestly reported to her, she tooke (as it seemed) much compassion on him; but having no use for him, lest her mother should sell him, she sent him to her brother, the Tymor Bashaw of Nalbrits, in the Countrey of Cambia, a Province in Tartaria.

How he was sent into Tartaria.

Here now let us remember his passing in this speculative course from Constantinople by Sander, Screwe, Panassa, Musa, Lastilla, to Varna, an ancient Citie upon the Blacke Sea. In all which journey, having little more libertie than his eyes judgement since his captivitie, he might see the Townes with their short Towers, and a most plaine, fertile, and delicate Countrey, especially that [P. 24] most admired place of Greece, now called Romania, but from Varna nothing but the Blacke Sea water, till he came to the two Capes of Taur and Pergilos, where hee passed the Straight of Niger, which (as he conjectured) is some ten leagues long, and three broad, betwixt two low lands, the Channell is deepe, but at the entrance of the Sea Dissabacca, their are many great Osie-shoulds, and many great blacke rockes, which the Turkes said were trees, weeds, and mud, throwen from the in-land Countryes, by the inundations and violence of the Current; and cast there by the Eddy. They sayled by many low Iles, and saw many more of those muddy rockes, and nothing else but salt water, till they came betwixt Susax and Curuske, only two white townes at the entrance of the river Bruapo appeared: In six or seven dayes saile, he saw foure or five seeming strong castles of stone, with flat tops and

The description of the Dissabacca Sea.

battlements about them, but arriving at Cambia, he was (according to their custome) well used. The river was there more than halfe a mile broad. The Castle was of a large circumference, fourteene or fifteene foot thicke, in the foundation some six foot from the wall, is a Paliizado, and then a Ditch of about fortie foot broad full of water. On the west side of it, is a Towne all of low flat houses; which as he conceived could bee of no great strength, yet it keepes all them barbarous Countreyes about it in admiration and subjection. After he had stayed there three dayes; it was two dayes more before his guides brought him to Nalbrits, where the Tymor then was resident, in a great vast stonie Castle with many great Courts about it, invironed with high stone wals, where was quartered their Armes, when they first subjected those Countreyes, which onely live to labour for those tyrannicall Turkes.

Smith his usage in Tartaria.

To her unkinde brother, this kinde Ladie writ so much for his good usage, that hee halfe suspected, as much as she intended; for shee told him, he should there but sojourne to learne the language, and what it was to be a Turke, till time made her Master of her selfe. But the Tymor, her brother, diverted all this to the worst of crueltie, for within an houre after his arrivall, he caused his Drub-man to strip him naked, and shave his head and beard so bare as his hand, a great ring of iron, with a long stalke bowed like a sickle, rivetted about his necke, and a coat made of Ulgries haire, guarded about with a peece of an undrest skinne. There were many more Christian slaves, and neere an hundred Forsados of Turkes and Moores; and he being the last, was slave of slaves to them all. Among these slavish fortunes there was no great choice; for the best was so bad, a dog could hardly have lived to endure: and yet for all their paines and labours no more regarded than a beast.

Chapter XIII.

The Turkes diet; the Slaves diet; the attire of the Tartars; and manner of Warres and Religions, &c.

The Tymors diet of Cambia is as the Turkes. [P. 25]

He Tymor and his friends fed upon Pillaw, which is boiled Rice and Garnances, with little bits of mutton or Buckones (which is rosted peeces of Horse, Bull, Ulgrie, or any beasts). Samboyses and Muselbits are great dainties, and yet but round pies, full of all sorts of flesh they can get chopped with varietie of herbs. Their best drinke is Coffa, of a graine they call Coava, boiled with water; and Sherbecke which is only honey and water; Mares milke, or the milke of any beast, they hold restorative; but all the Comminaltie drinke pure water. Their bread is made of this Coava, which is a kinde of blacke wheat, and Cuskus a small white seed like Millya in Biskay: but our common victuall, the entrailes of Horse and Ulgries. Of this, cut in small peeces, they will fill a great Cauldron, and being boiled with Cuskus, and put in great bowles in the forme of chaffing-dishes, they sit round about it on the ground, after they have raked it thorow so oft as they please with their foule fists, the remainder was for the Christian slaves. Some of this broth they would temper with Cuskus pounded, and putting the fire off from the hearth, powre there a bowle full, then cover it with coales till it be baked; which stewed with the remainder of the broth, and some small peeces of flesh, was an extraordinarie daintie.

The Slaves diet.

The Attire of those Tartars.

The better sort are attired like Turkes, but the plaine Tartar hath a blacke sheepe skinne over his backe, and two of the legs tied about his necke; the other two about his middle, with another over his belly, and the legs tied in the like manner behinde him: then two more made like a paire of bases, serveth him for breeches; with a little close cap to his skull, of blacke felt, and they use exceeding much of this felt, for carpets, for bedding, for Coats, and Idols. Their houses are much worse than your Irish, but the In-land Countreyes have none but Carts and Tents, which they ever remove from Countrey to Countrey, as they see occasion, driving with them infinite troopes of blacke sheepe, Cattell and Ulgries, eating all up before them as they goe.

The Tartars of Nagi and their manners.

For the Tartars of Nagi, they have neither Towne, nor house, corne, nor drinke; but flesh and milke. The milke they keepe in great skinnes like Burracho's, which though it be never so sower, it agreeth well with their strong stomackes. They live all in Hordias, as doth the Crim-Tartars, three or foure hundred in a company, in great Carts fifteene or sixteene foot broad, which is covered with small rods, wattled together in the forme of a birds nest turned upwards, and with the ashes of bones tempered with oile, Camels haire, and a clay they have: they lome them so well, that no weather will pierce them, and yet verie light.

Each Hordia hath a Murse, which they obey as their King. Their Gods are infinite. One or two thousand of those glittering white Carts drawen with Camels, Deere, Buls, and Ulgries, they bring round in a ring, where they pitch their Campe; and the Murse, with his chiefe alliances, are placed in the midst. They doe much hurt when they can get any Stroggs, which are great boats used upon the river Volga, (which they call Edle) to them that dwell in the Countrey of Perolog; and would doe much more, were it not for the Muscovites Garrisons that there inhabit.

Chapter XIIII. [P. 26]

The description of the Crym-Tartars; their houses and carts; their Idolatry in their lodgings.

The description of the Crym-Tartars Court.

Ow you are to understand, Tartary and Scythia are all one, but so large and spacious, few or none could ever perfectly describe it, nor all the severall kinds of those most barbarous people that inhabit it. Those we call the Crym-Tartars, border upon Moldavia, Podolia, Lituania, and Russia, are much more regular than the interior parts of Scythia. This great Tartarian Prince, that hath so troubled all his neighbours, they alwayes call Chan, which signifieth Emperour, but we, the Crym-Tartar. He liveth for most part in the best champion plaines of many Provinces; and his removing Court is like a great Citie of houses and tents, drawne on Carts, all so orderly placed East and West, on the right and left hand of the Prince· his house, which is alwayes in the midst towards the South, before which none may pitch their houses, every one knowing their order and quarter, as in an Armie. The Princes houses are very artificially wrought, both the foundation, sides, and roofe of wickers, ascending round to the top like a Dove-coat; this they cover with white felt, or white earth tempered with the powder of bones, that it may shine the whiter; sometimes with blacke felt, curiously painted with vines, trees, birds, and beasts; the breadth of the Carts are eighteene or twenty foot, but the house stretcheth foure or five foot over each side, and is drawne with ten or twelve, or for more state, twenty Camels and Oxen. They have also great baskets, made of smaller wickers like great chests, with a covering of the same, all covered over with blacke felt, rubbed over with tallow and sheeps milke to keepe out the raine: prettily bedecked with painting or feathers; in those they

His houses and carts.

Baskets.

put their household stuffe and treasure, drawne upon other carts for that purpose. When they take downe their houses, they set the doore alwayes towards the South, and their carts thirtie or fortie foot distant on each side, East and West, as if they were two walls: the women also have most curious carts; every one of his wives hath a great one for herselfe, and so many other for her attendants, that they seeme as many Courts, as he hath wives. One great Tartar or Nobleman, will have for his particular, more than an hundred of those houses and carts, for his severall offices and uses; but set so farre from each other, they will seeme like a great village.

Their idolatrie in their lodgings.

Having taken their houses from the carts, they place the Master alwayes towards the North; over whose head is alwayes an Image like a Puppet, made of felt, which they call his brother; the women on his left hand, and over the chiefe Mistris her head, such another brother; and betweene them a little one, which is the keeper of the house; at the good wives beds-feet is a kids skinne, stuffed with wooll, and neere it a Puppet looking towards the Maids; next the doore another, with a dried cowes udder, for the women that milke the kine, because only

[P. 27]

Cossmos is Mares milke.

the men milke mares; every morning, those Images in their orders they besprinkle with that they drinke, bee it Cossmos, or whatsoever, but all the white mares milke is reserved for the Prince. Then without the doore, thrice to the South, every one bowing his knee in honour of the fire; then the like to the East, in honour of the aire; then to the West, in honour of the water; and lastly to the North, in behalfe of the dead. After the servant hath done this duty to the foure quarters of the world, he returnes into the house; where his fellowes stand waiting, ready with two cups and two basons to give their master, and his wife that lay with him that night, to wash and drinke, who must keepe him company all the day following; and all his other wives come thither to drinke, where hee keepes his house that day; and all the gifts presented him till night, are laid up in her chests;

and at the doore a bench full of cups, and drinke for any of them to make merry.

Chapter XV.

Their feasts; common diet; Princes estate; buildings; tributes; lawes; slaves; entertainment of Ambassadours.

Their feasts.

Or their feasts they have all sorts of beasts, birds, fish, fruits, and hearbs they can get, but the more variety of wilde ones is the best; to which they have excellent drinke made of rice, millit, and honey, like wine; they have also wine, but in Summer they drinke most Cossmos, that standeth ready alwayes at the entrance of the doore, and by it a fidler; when the master of the house beginneth to drinke, they all cry, ha, ha, and the fidler playes, then they all clap their hands and dance, the men before their Masters, the women before their Mistresses; and ever when he drinks, they cry as before; then the fidler stayeth till they drinke all round; sometimes they will drinke for the victory; and to provoke one to drinke, they will pull him by the ears, and lugge and draw him, to stretch and heat him, clapping their hands, stamping with their feet, and dancing before the champions, offering them cups, then draw them backe againe to increase their appetite: and thus continue till they be drunke, or their drinke done, which they hold an honour, and no infirmity.

Their common diet.

Though the ground be fertile, they sow little corne, yet the Gentlemen have bread and hony-wine; grapes they have plenty, and wine privately, and good flesh and fish; but the common sort stamped millit, mingled with milke and water. They call Cassa for meat, and drinke any thing; also any beast unprofitable for service they kill, when they are like to die, or however they die, they will eat them, guts liver and all; but the most fleshy parts they cut in thinne slices, and hang it up in the

Sunne and wind without salting, where it will dry so hard, it will not putrifie in a long time. A Ramme they esteeme a great feast among forty or fiftie, which they cut in peeces boiled or roast, puts it in a great bowle with salt and water, for other sauce they have none; the master of the feast giveth every one a peece, which he eateth by himselfe, or carrieth away with him. Thus their hard fare makes them so infinite in Cattell; and their great number of captived women to breed upon, makes them so populous. But neere the Christian frontiers, the baser sort make little cottages of wood, called Ulusi, daubed over with durt and beasts dung, covered with sedge; yet in Summer they leave them, beginning their progresse in Aprill, with their wives, children, and slaves, in their carted houses, scarce convenient for foure or five persons; driving their flocks towards Perecopya, and sometimes into Taurica, or Osow, a towne upon the river Tanais, which is great and swift, where the Turke hath a garrison; and in October returne againe to their Cottages. Their Clothes are the skinnes of dogges, goats, and sheepe, lined with cotten cloath, made of their finest wooll, for of their worst they make their felt, which they use in aboundance, as well for shooes and caps, as houses, beds, and Idolls; also of the coarse wooll mingled with horse haire, they make all their cordage. Notwithstanding this wandring life, their Princes sit in great state upon beds, or carpits, and with great reverence are attended both by men and women, and richly served in plate, and great silver cups, delivered upon the knee, attired in rich furres, lined with plush, or taffity, or robes of tissue. These Tartars possesse many large and goodly plaines, wherein feed innumerable herds of horse and cattell, as well wilde as tame; which are Elkes, Bisones, Horses, Deere, Sheepe, Goates, Swine, Beares, and divers others.

[P. 28]

How they become populous.

Their Princes state.

Ancient buildings.

In those countries are the ruines of many faire Monasteries, Castles, and Cities, as Bacasaray, Salutium, Almassary, Perecopya, Cremum, Sedacom, Capha, and divers others by the Sea, but all kept with strong garrisons for the great Turke, who yearely by trade or trafficke, receiveth the chiefe commodities those fertile countries afford, as Bezer, Rice, Furres, Hides, Butter, Salt, Cattell, and Slaves; yet by the spoiles they get from the secure and idle Christians, they maintaine themselves in this Pompe. Also their wives, of whom they have as many as they will, very costly, yet in a constant custome with decency.

Commodities for tribute to the Turke.

They are Mahometans, as are the Turks, from whom also they have their Lawes, but no Lawyers, nor Attournies, onely Judges, and Justices in every Village, or Hordia: but capitall criminalls, or matters of moment, before the Chan himselfe, or Privie Counsells, of whom they are alwayes heard, and speedily discharged; for any may have accesse at any time to them, before whom they appeare with great reverence, adoring their Princes as Gods, and their spirituall Judges as Saints; for Justice is with such integrity and expedition executed, without covetousnesse, bribery, partiality, and brawling, that in six moneths they have sometimes scarce six causes to heare. About the Princes court none but his guard weares any weapon; but abroad they goe very strong, because there are many bandytos, and Theeves.

Good lawes yet no lawyers.

They use the Hungarians, Russians, Wallachians, and Moldavian slaves (whereof they have plenty) as beasts to every worke: and those Tartars that serve the Chan, or noblemen, have only victuall and apparell, the rest are generally nasty, and idle, naturally miserable, and in their warres, better theeves than souldiers.

Their slaves.

This Chan hath yeerely a Donative from the King of Poland, the Dukes of Lituania, Moldavia, and Nagagon Tartars; their Messengers commonly he useth bountifully, and verie nobly, but sometimes most cruelly; when any of them doth bring their Presents, by his houshold Officers they are entertained in a plaine field, with a moderate proportion of flesh, bread and wine, for once; but when they come before him, the Sultaines, Tuians,

[P. 29]

His entertainment of Ambassadours.

Ulans, Markies, his chiefe Officers and Councellors attend, one man only bringeth the Ambassadour to the Court gate, but to the Chan he is led betweene two Councellors; where saluting him upon their bended knees, declaring their message, are admitted to eat with him, and presented with a great silver cup full of Mead from his owne hand, but they drinke it upon their knees: when they are dispatched, he invites them againe, the feast ended, they go backe a little from the Palace doore, and rewarded with silke vestures wrought with gold downe to their anckles, with an horse or two, and sometimes a slave of their owne Nation.

In their robes presently they come to him againe, to give him thankes, take their leave, and so depart.

Chapter XVI.

How he levieth an Armie; their Armes and Provision; how he divideth the spoile; and his service to the Great Turke.

How he levieth an Armie.

Hen he intends any warres, he must first have leave of the Great Turke, whom hee is bound to assist when hee commandeth, receiving daily for himselfe and chiefe of his Nobilitie, pensions from the Turke, that holds all Kings but slaves that pay tribute or are subject to any: signifying his intent to all his subjects, within a moneth commonly he raiseth his Armie, and everie man is to furnish himselfe for three moneths victuals, which is parched Millit, or grownd to meale, which they ordinarily mingle with water (as is said), hard cheese or cruds dried and beaten to powder, a little will make much water like milke, and dried flesh, this they put also up in sackes: The Chan and his Nobles have some bread and Aquavitæ, and quicke cattell to kill when they please, wherewith verie sparingly they are contented. Being provided with expert Guides, and got into the Countrey he intends to invade, he sends forth his Scouts to bring in what prisoners they can, from whom he will wrest the utmost of their knowledge fit for his purpose: having advised with his Councell, what is most fit to be done, the Nobilitie, according to their antiquitie, doth march; then moves he with his whole Armie. If hee finde there is no enemie to oppose him, he adviseth how farre they shall invade: commanding everie man (upon paine of his life) to kill all the obvious Rusticks; but not to hurt any women, or children.

The manner of his warres.

Ten, or fifteene thousand, he commonly placeth, where hee findeth most convenient for his standing Campe; the rest of his Armie hee divides in several troops, bearing [P. 30] ten or twelve miles square before them, and ever within three or foure dayes returne to their Campe, putting all to fire and sword, but that they carrie with them backe to their Campe; and in this scattering manner he will invade a Countrey, and be gone with his prey, with an incredible expedition. But if he understand of an enemie, he will either fight in Ambuscado, or flie; for he will never fight any battel if he can chuse, but upon treble advantage; yet by his innumerable flights of arrowes, I have seene flie from his flying troopes, we could not well judge, whether his fighting or flying was most dangerous, so good is his horse, and so expert his bow-men; but if they be so intangled they must fight, there is none can bee more hardy, or resolute in their defences.

How he divides the spoile.

Regaining his owne borders, he takes the tenth of the principall captives, man, woman, childe, or beast (but his captaines that take them, will accept of some particular person they best like for themselves) the rest are divided amongst the whole Armie, according to every mans desert, and quality; that they keepe them, or sell them to who will give most; but they will not forget to use all the meanes they can, to know their estates, friends, and quality, and the better they finde you, the worse they will use you, till you doe agree to pay such a ransome, as they will impose upon you; therefore many great persons have endured much misery to conceale themselves, because their ransomes are so intolerable: their best hope is of some Christian Agent, that many times commeth to redeeme slaves, either with mony, or man for man: those Agents knowing so well the extreme covetousnesse of the Tartars, doe use to bribe some Jew or Merchant, that feigning they will sell them againe to some other nation, are oft redeemed for a very small ransome.

How the Chan doth serve the great Turke.

But to this Tartarian Armie, when the Turke commands, he goeth with some small artillery; and the Nagagians, Perecopens, Crimes, Osovens, and Cersessians, are his tributaries; but the Petigorves, Oczaconians, Byalogordens, and Dobrueen Tartars, the Turke by covenant commands to follow him; so that from all those Tartars he hath had an Army of an hundred and twenty thousand excellent, swift, stomackfull Tartarian horse, for foot they have none. Now the Chan, his Sultaines and nobility, use Turkish, Caramanian, Arabian, Parthian, and other strange Tartarian horses; the swiftest they esteeme the best; seldome they feede any more at home, than they have present use for; but upon their plaines is a short wodde like heath, in some countries like gaile, full of berries, farre much better than any grasse.

Their Armes.

Their Armes are such as they have surprised or got from the Christians or Persians, both brest-plates, swords, semiteres, and helmets; bowes and arrowes they make most themselves, also their bridles and saddles are indifferent, but the nobility are very handsome, and well armed like the Turkes, in whom consisteth their greatest glory; the ordinary sort have little armor, some a plaine young pole unshaven, headed with a peece of iron for a lance; some an old Christian pike, or a Turks cavatine: yet those tattertimallions will have two or three horses,
[P. 31] some foure, or five, as well for service, as for to eat; which makes their Armies seem thrice so many as there are souldiers. The Chan himselfe hath about his person ten thousand chosen Tartars and Janizaries, some small

Ordnance: and a white mares taile with a peece of greene taffity on a great Pike, is carried before him for a standard; because they hold no beast so precious as a white mare, whose milke is onely for the King & nobility, and to sacrifice to their Idolls; but the rest have ensignes of divers colours.

For all this miserable knowledge, furniture, and equipage, the mischiefe they doe in Christendome is wonderfull, by reason of their hardnesse of life and constitution, obedience, agilitie, and their Emperours bountie, honours, grace, and dignities he ever bestoweth upon those that have done him any memorable service in the face of his enemies.

A description of the Caspian Sea.

The Caspian Sea, most men agree that have passed it, to be in length about 200. leagues, and in breadth an hundred & fifty, environed to the East, with the great desarts of the Tartars of Turkamane; to the West, by the Circasses, and the mountaine Caucasus; to the North, by the river Volga, and the land of Nagay; and to the South, by Media, and Persia: this sea is fresh water in many places, in others as salt as the great Ocean; it hath many great rivers which fall into it, as the mighty river of Volga, which is like a sea, running neere two thousand miles, through many great and large Countries, that send into it many other great rivers; also out of Saberya, Yaick, and Yem, out of the great mountaine Caucasus, the river Sirus, Arash, and divers others, yet no Sea neerer it than the blacke Sea, which is at least an hundred leagues distant; in which Country live the Georgians, now part Armenians, part Nestorians; it is neither found to increase or diminish, or empty it selfe any way, except it be under ground, and in some places they can finde no ground at two hundred fadome.

Many other most strange and wonderfull things are in the land of Cathay towards the North-east, and Chyna towards the South-east, where are many of the most famous Kingdomes in the world; where most arts, plenty, and curiosities are in such abundance, as might seeme incredible, which hereafter I will relate, as I have briefly gathered from such authors as have lived there.

Chapter XVII.

How captaine Smith escaped his captivity; slew the Bashaw of Nalbrits in Cambia; his passage to Russia, Transilvania, and the middest of Europe to Affrica.

How Smith escaped his captivity.

ALl the hope he had ever to be delivered from this thraldome was only the love of Tragabigzanda, who surely was ignorant of his bad usage; for although he had often debated the matter with some Christians, that had beene there a long time slaves, they could not finde how to make an escape, by any reason or possibility; but God [P. 32] beyond mans expectation or imagination helpeth his servants, when they least thinke of helpe, as it hapned to him.

So long he lived in this miserable estate, as he became a thresher at a grange in a great field, more than a league from the Tymors house; the Bashaw as he oft used to visit his granges, visited him; and tooke occasion so to beat, spurne, and revile him, that forgetting all reason, he beat out the Tymors braines with his threshing bat, for they have no flailes; and seeing his estate could be no worse than it was, clothed himselfe in his clothes, hid his body under the straw, filled his knapsacke with corne, shut the doores, mounted his horse, and ranne into the desart at all adventure; two or three dayes thus fearfully wandring he knew not whither, and well it was he met not any to aske the way; being even as taking leave of this miserable world, God did direct him to the great way or Castragan, as they call it, which doth crosse these large territories, and generally knowne among them by these markes.

Their guides in those Countries.

In every crossing of this great way is planted a post,

and in it so many bobs with broad ends, as there be wayes, and every bob the figure painted on it, that demonstrateth to what part that way leadeth; as that which pointeth towards the Cryms Country, is marked with a halfe Moone, if towards the Georgians and Persia, a blacke man, full of white spots, if towards China, the picture of the Sunne, if towards Muscovia, the signe of a Crosse, if towards the habitation of any other Prince, the figure whereby his standard is knowne. To his dying spirits, thus God added some comfort in this melancholy journey: wherein if he had met any of that vilde generation, they had made him their slave, or knowing the figure engraven in the iron about his necke, (as all slaves have) he had beene sent backe againe to his master; sixteene dayes he travelled in this feare and torment, after the Crosse, till he arrived at Æcopolis, upon the river Don, a garrison of the Muscovites. The governour after due examination of those his hard events, tooke off his irons, and so kindly used him, he thought himselfe new risen from death, and the good Lady Callamata, largely supplied all his wants.

The description of Cambia and his passage to Russia.

This is as much as he could learne of those wilde Countries, that the Country of Cambia is two dayes journy from the head of the great river Bruapo, which springeth from many places of the mountaines of Innagachi, that joyne themselves together in the Poole Kerkas; which they account for the head, and falleth into the Sea Dissabacca, called by some the lake Meotis, which receiveth also the river Tanais, and all the rivers that fall from the great Countries of the Circassi, the Cartaches, and many from the Tauricaes, Precopes, Cummani, Cossunka, and the Cryme; through which Sea he sailed, and up the river Bruapo to Nalbrits, and thence through the desarts of Circassi to Æcoplis, as is related; where he stayed with the Governour, till the Convoy went to Coragnaw; then with his certificate how hee found him, and had examined, with his friendly letters sent him by Zumalacke to Caragnaw, whose Governour in like manner

so kindly use him, that by this meanes he went with a safe conduct to Letch, and Donka, in Cologoske, and thence to Berniske, and Newgrod in Seberia, by Rezechica,
[P. 33] upon the river Niper in the confines of Littuania. From whence with as much kindnesse he was convoyed in like manner by Coroski, Duberesko, Duzihell, Drohobus, and Ostroge in Volonia; Saslaw and Lasco in Podolia; Halico and Collonia in Polonia; and so to Hermonstat in Transilvania. In all his life he seldome met with more respect, mirth, content, and entertainment; and not any Governour where he came, but gave him somewhat as a present, besides his charges; seeing themselves as subject to the like calamity. Through those poore continually forraged Countries there is no passage, but with the Carravans or Convoyes; for they are Countries rather to be pitied, than envied; and it is a wonder any should make warres for them. The Villages are onely here and there a few houses of straight Firre trees, laid heads and points above one another, made fast by notches at the ends more than a mans height, and with broad split boards, pinned together with woodden pinnes, as thatched for coverture. In ten Villages you shall scarce finde ten iron nailes, except it be in some extraordinary mans house. For their Townes, Æcopolis, Letch, and Donko, have rampiers made of that woodden walled fashion, double, and betwixt them earth and stones, but so latched with crosse timber, they are very strong against any thing but fire; and about them a deepe ditch, and a Palizado of young Firre trees: but most of the rest have only a great ditch cast about them, and the ditches earth is all their rampier; but round well environed with Palizadoes. Some have some few small peeces of small Ordnance, and slings, calievers, and muskets; but their generallest weapons are the Russe bowes and arrowes; you shall find pavements over bogges, onely of young Firre trees laid crosse one over another, for two or three houres journey, or as the passage requires: and yet in two dayes travell you shall scarce see six habitations. Notwith-

His observations in his journey to Transilvania, through the midst of Europe.

Part of the Trauels of Capt IOH
TARTARS and others extracted
Capt SMITH throwne into the Sea ... to Shore, and was releeued Chap
The Coast of Barbarie
Tunis
BARBARIE
Bugia
The Coast of SAVOY
Nice
Tallown
How hee releeued OLYMPAGH by
His three single Combats Chap. 7.
His Encounter with TVRBASHAW Chap. 7.
His Combat with GRVALGO. Cap
Chap. 7
Capt SMITH led Captiue to the BASHAW of NALBRITS in TARTARIA. Chap. 12.
Drub. man
Smith
Bashaw
Three TVRKS heads in a banne
P. Sigismundus
P. Moyses
MRten Dr. sculptor
How he was presented to Prince

N SMITH, a mongst TVRKES,
out of the HISTORY by IOHN PAYN
ratagem of Lights Chap. 4
The Siege of REGALL in Transilvania Chap. 7
t of threehundred horsmen.
How he slew BONNY:MVLGRO. Chap. 7.
giuen him for Armes. Chap. 8.
Capt SMITH Killeth the BASHAW of Nalbrits and on his horse escapeth. Chap. 17.
IGISMVNDVS. Chap. 8.
London Printed by Iames Reeue

standing, to see how their Lords, Governours, and Captaines are civilized, well attired and acoutred with Jewells, Sables, and Horses, and after their manner with curious furniture, it is wonderfull: but they are all Lords or slaves, which makes them so subject to every invasion.

In Transilvania he found so many good friends, that but to see and rejoyce himselfe (after all those encounters) in his native Country, he would ever hardly have left them; though the mirrour of vertue, their Prince, was absent. Being thus glutted with content, and neere drowned with joy, he passed high Hungaria by Fileck, Tocka, Cassovia, and Underoroway, by Ulmicht, in Moravia, to Prague in Bohemia: at last he found the most gracious Prince Sigismundus, with his Colonell, at Lipswick in Misenland: who gave him his Passe, intimating the service he had done, and the honours he had received, with fifteene hundred ducats of gold to repaire his losses: with this, he spent some time to visit the faire Cities and Countries of Drasdon in Saxonie, Magdaburg and Brunswicke; Cassell in Hessen; Wittenberg, Ullum, and Minikin in Bavaria; Aughsbrough, and her Universities; Hama, Franckford, Mentz, the Palatinate; Wormes, Speyre, and Strausborough; passing Nancie in Loraine, and France by Paris to Orleans, hee went down the river of Loyer, to Angiers, and imbarked himselfe at Nantz in Britanny, for Bilbao in Biskay, to see Burgos, Valiadolid, the admired monasterie of the [P. 34]
Escuriall, Madrill, Toledo, Cordua, Cuedyriall, Civill, Cheryes, Cales, and Saint Lucas in Spaine.

[Chapter XVIII.

Chapter XVIII.

The observations of Captaine Smith, Mr. Henrie Archer and others in Barbarie.

The three golden Bals of Affrica.

The description of Morocco.

BEing thus satisfied with Europe and Asia; understanding of the warres in Barbarie, hee went from Gibralter to Guta and Tanger, thence to Saffee, where growing into acquaintance with a French man of warre, the Captaine and some twelve more went to Morocco, to see the ancient monuments of that large renowned Citie: it was once the principall Citie in Barbarie, situated in a goodly plaine Countrey, 14 miles from the great Mount Atlas, and sixtie miles from the Atlanticke Sea; but now little remaining, but the Kings Palace, which is like a Citie of it selfe, and the Christian Church, on whose flat square steeple is a great brouch of iron, whereon is placed the three golden Bals of Affrica: the first is neere three Ells in circumference, the next above it somewhat lesse, the uppermost the least over them, as it were an halfe Ball, and over all a prettie guilded Pyramides. Against those golden Bals hath been shot many a shot. Their weight is recorded 700. weight of pure gold, hollow within, yet no shot did ever hit them, nor could ever any Conspirator attaine that honor as to get them downe. They report the Prince of Morocco betrothed himselfe to the Kings Daughter of Æthiopia, he dying before their marriage, she caused those three golden Balls to be set up for his Monument, and vowed virginitie all her life. The Alfantica is also a place of note, because it is invironed with a great wall, wherein lye the goods of all the Merchants securely guarded. The Juderea is also (as it were) a Citie of it selfe, where dwell the Jewes: the rest for the most part is defaced: but by the many pinnacles and towers, with Balls on their tops, hath much appearance of much sumptuousnesse and curiositie.

There have been many famous Universities, which are now but stables for Fowles & Beasts, & the houses in most parts lye tumbled one above another; the walls of Earth are with the great fresh flouds washed to the ground; nor is there any village in it, but tents for Strangers, Larbes & Moores. Strange tales they will tell of a great Garden, wherein were all sorts of Birds, Fishes, Beasts, Fruits & Fountaines, which for beautie, Art, and pleasure, exceeded any place knowne in the world, though now nothing but dung-hils, Pigeon-houses, shrubs and bushes. There are yet many excellent fountaines adorned with marble, and many arches, pillers, towers, ports and Temples; but most only reliques of lamentable ruines and sad desolation.

A bloudie Empresse.

When Mully Hamet reigned in Barbarie, he had three sonnes, Mully Shecke, Mully Sidan, and Mully Befferres. He was a most good and noble King, that governed well with peace and plentie, till his Empresse, more cruell than any beast in Affrica, poysoned him, her owne [P. 35] daughter, Mully Shecke his eldest sonne borne of a Portugall Ladie, and his daughter, to bring Mully Sidan to the Crowne now reigning, which was the cause of all those brawles and warres that followed betwixt those Brothers, their children, and a Saint that start up but he played the Devill.

King Mully Hamet, or the Great Zerff of Barbarie.

King Mully Hamet was not blacke, as many suppose, but Molata, or tawnie, as are the most of his subjects; everie way noble, kinde and friendly, verie rich and pompous in State and Majestie, though hee sitteth not upon a Throne nor Chaire of Estate, but crosse legged upon a rich Carpet, as doth the Turke, whose Religion of Mahomet, with an incredible miserable curiositie they observe. His Ordinarie Guard is at least 5000 but in progresse he goeth not with lesse than 20000. horsemen, himselfe as rich in all his Equipage, as any Prince in Christendome, and yet a Contributor to the Turke. In all his Kingdome were so few good Artificers, that hee entertained from England, Gold-smiths, Plummers,

His great love to Englishmen.

Carvers, and Polishers of stone, and Watch-makers, so much hee delighted in the reformation of workmanship, hee allowed each of them ten shillings a day standing fee, linnen, woollen, silkes, and what they would for diet and apparell, and custome-free to transport, or import what they would; for there were scarce any of those qualities in his Kingdomes but those, of which there are divers of them living at this present in London. Amongst the rest, one Mr. Henry Archer, a Watch-maker, walking in Morocco, from the Alfantica to the Juderea, the way being verie foule, met a great Priest, or a Sante (as they call all great Clergy-men) who would have thrust him into the durt for the way; but Archer, not knowing what he was, gave him a box on the eare, presently he was apprehended, and condemned to have his tongue cut out, and his hand cut off; but no sooner it was knowen at the Kings Court, but 300. of his Guard came, and broke open the Prison, and delivered him, although the fact was next degree to Treason.

The strange love of a Lyon.

Concerning this Archer, there is one thing more worth noting: Not farre from Mount Atlas, a great Lionesse in the heat of the day, did use to bathe her selfe, and teach her young Puppies to swimme in the river Cauzeff, of a good bredth; yet she would carrie them one after another over the river: which some Moores perceiving watched their opportunitie, and when the river was betweene her and them, stole foure of her whelps, which she perceiving, with all the speed shee could passed the river, and comming neere them they let fall a whelpe (and fled with the rest) which she tooke in her mouth, and so returned to the rest: A Male and a Female of those they gave Mr. Archer, who kept them in the Kings Garden, till the Male killed the Female, then he brought it up as a Puppy-dog lying upon his bed, till it grew so great as a Mastiffe, and no dog more tame or gentle to them hee knew: but being to returne for England, at Saffee he gave him to a Merchant of Marsellis, that presented him to the French King, who sent him to King

James, where it was kept in the Tower seven yeeres: After one Mr. John Bull, then servant to Mr. Archer, with divers of his friends, went to see the Lyons, not knowing any thing at all of him; yet this rare beast smelled him before hee saw him, whining, groaning, and [P. 36] tumbling, with such an expression of acquaintance, that being informed by the Keepers how hee came thither; Mr. Bull so prevailed, the Keeper opened the grate, and Bull went in: But no Dogge could fawne more on his Master, than the Lyon on him, licking his feet, hands, and face, skipping and tumbling to and fro, to the wonder of all the beholders; being satisfied with his acquaintance, he made shift to get out of the grate. But when the Lyon saw his friend gone, no beast by bellowing, roaring, scratching, and howling, could expresse more rage and sorrow, nor in foure dayes after would he either eat or drinke.

Another kinde Lyon in Morocco.

In Morocco, the Kings Lyons are all together in a Court, invironed with a great high wall; to those they put a young Puppy-dogge: the greatest Lyon had a sore upon his necke, which this Dogge so licked that he was healed: the Lyon defended him from the furie of all the rest, nor durst they eat till the Dogge and he had fed; this Dog grew great, and lived amongst them many yeeres after.

The description of Fez.

Fez also is a most large and plentifull Countrey, the chiefe Citie is called Fez, divided into two parts; old Fez containing about 80. thousand housholds, the other 4000. pleasantly situated upon a River in the heart of Barbarie, part upon hils, part upon plaines, full of people, and all sorts of Merchandise. The great Temple is called Carucen, in bredth seventeene Arches, in length 120. borne up with 2500. white marble pillars: under the chiefe Arch, where the Tribunall is kept, hangeth a most huge lampe, compassed with 110. lesser, under the other also hang great lamps, and about some are burning fifteene hundred lights. They say they were all made of the bels the Arabians brought from Spaine. It hath three gates of notable height, Priests and Officers so many, that the circuit of the Church, the Yard, and other houses, is little lesse than a mile and an halfe in compasse; there are in this Citie 200. Schooles, 200. Innes, 400. water-mils, 600. water-Conduits; 700. Temples and Oratories; but fiftie of them most stately and richly furnished. Their Alcazar or Burse is walled about, it hath twelve gates, and fifteen walks covered with tents to keepe the Sun from the Merchants, and them that come there. The Kings Palace, both for strength and beautie is excellent, and the Citizens have many great privileges. Those two Countreyes of Fez and Morocco, are the best part of all Barbarie, abounding with people, cattell, and all good necessaries for mans use. For the rest, as the Larbes or Mountainers, the Kingdomes of Cocow, Algier, Tripoly, Tunis, and Ægypt; there are many large histories of them in divers languages, especially that writ by that most excellent Statesman, John de Leo, who afterward turned Christian. The unknowen Countries of Ginny and Binne, this six and twentie yeeres have beene frequented with a few English ships only to trade, especially the river of Senega, by Captaine Brimstead, Captaine Brockit, Mr. Crump, and divers others. Also the great river of Gambra, by Captaine Jobson, who is returned in thither againe in the yeere 1626. with Mr. William Grent, and thirteene or fourteene others, to stay in the Countrey, to discover some way to those rich mines of Gago or Tumbatu, from whence is supposed the Moores of Barbarie have their gold, and the certaintie of those supposed descriptions and relations of those interiour parts, which daily the more they are sought into, the more they are corrected. For surely, those interiour parts of Affrica are little knowen to either English, French, or Dutch, though they use much the Coast; therefore wee will make a little bold with the observations of the Portugalls.

A briefe description of the most unknowen parts of Affrica.

[P. 37]

Chapter XIX.

The strange discoveries and observations of the Portugalls in Affrica.

He Portugalls on those parts have the glorie, who first coasting along this Westerne shore of Affrica, to finde passage to the East Indies, within this hundred and fiftie yeeres, even from the Streights of Gibralter, about the Cape of Bone Esperance to the Persian Gulfe, and thence all along the Asian Coast to the Moluccas, have subjected many great Kingdomes, erected many Common-wealths, built many great and strong Cities; and where is it they have not beene by trade or force? no not so much as Cape de Verd, and Sermleone; but most Bayes or Rivers, where there is any trade to bee had, especially gold, or conveniencie for refreshment, but they are scattered; living so amongst those Blacks, by time and cunning they seeme to bee naturalized amongst them. As for the Isles of the Canaries, they have faire Townes, many Villages, and many thousands of people rich in commodities.

How the Portugalls coasted to the East Indies.

Ordoardo Lopez, a noble Portugall, Anno Dom 1578. imbarquing himselfe for Congo to trade, where he found such entertainment, finding the King much oppressed with enemies, hee found meanes to bring in the Portugalls to assist him, whereby he planted there Christian Religion, and spent most of his life to bring those Countreyes to the Crowne of Portugall, which he describeth in this manner.

Or Edward.

The Kingdome of Congo is about 600. miles diameter any way, the chiefe Citie called St. Savadore, seated upon an exceeding high mountaine, 150. miles from the Sea, verie fertile, and inhabited with more than 100000. persons, where is an excellent prospect over all the plaine Countreyes about it, well watered, lying (as it were) in

The Kingdome of Congo.

the Center of this Kingdome, over all which the Portugalls now command, though but an handfull in comparison of Negroes. They have flesh and fruits verie plentifull of divers sorts.

This Kingdom is divided into five Provinces, viz. Bamba, Sundi, Pango, Bacca, and Pembo; but Bamba is the principall, and can affoord 400000. men of warre. Elephants are bred over all those Provinces, and of wonderfull greatnesse; though some report they cannot kneele, nor lye downe, they can doe both, and have their joynts as other creatures for use: with their fore-feet they will leape upon trees to pull downe the boughes, and are of that strength, they will shake a great Cocar tree for the nuts, and pull downe a good tree with their tuskes, to get the leaves to eat, as well as sedge and long grasse, Cocar nuts and berries, &c. which with their trunke they put in their mouth, and chew it with their smaller teeth; in most of those Provinces, are many rich mines, but the Negars opposed the Portugalls for working in them.

Wilde Elephants.

[P. 38]

The Kingdome of Angola.

The Kingdome of Angola is wonderfull populous, and rich in mines of silver, copper, and most other mettalls; fruitfull in all manner of food, and sundry sorts of cattell, but dogges flesh they love better than any other meat: they use few clothes, and no Armour; bowes, arrowes, and clubs, are their weapons. But the Portugalls are well armed against those engines; and doe buy yearely of those Blacks more than five thousand slaves, and many are people exceeding well proportioned.

The Kingdome of Anchicos.

The Anchicos are a most valiant nation, but most strange to all about them. Their Armes are Bowes, short and small, wrapped about with serpents skinnes, of divers colours, but so smooth you would thinke them all one with the wood, and it makes them very strong; their strings little twigs, but exceeding tough and flexible; their arrowes short, which they shoot with an incredible quicknesse. They have short axes of brasse and copper for swords; wonderfull loyall and faithfull, and exceeding simple, yet so active, they skip amongst the rockes like goats. They trade with them of Nubea, and Congo, for Lamache, which is a small kinde of shell fish, of an excellent azure colour, male and female, but the female they hold most pure; they value them at divers prices, because they are of divers sorts, and those they use for coine, to buy and sell, as we doe gold and silver; nor will they have any other money in all those Countries, for which they give Elephants teeth; and slaves for salt, silke, linnen cloth, glasse-beads, and such like Portugall commodities. *A strange mony.*

They circumcise themselves, and marke their faces with sundry slashes from their infancie. They keepe a shambles of mans flesh, as if it were beefe or other victuall: for when they cannot have a good market for their slaves; or their enemies they take, they kill and sell them in this manner; some are so resolute in shewing how much they scorne death, they will offer themselves and slaves to this butchery to their Prince and friends; and though there be many nations will eat their enemies, in America and Asia, yet none but those are knowne to be so mad, as to eat their slaves and friends also. *A shambles of mans flesh.*

Religions and idolls they have as many, as nations and humours; but the devill hath the greatest part of their devotions, whom all those Blacks doe say is white; for there are no Saints but Blacks. *Their Religions and Idols.*

But besides those great Kingdomes of Congo, Angola, and Azichi in those unfrequented parts are the Kingdomes of Lango, Matania, Buttua, Sofola, Mozambeche, Quivola, the Isle of Saint Lawrence, Mombaza, Melinda, the Empires of Monomatopa, Monemugi, and Presbiter John, with whom they have a kinde of trade; and their rites, customes, climates, temperatures, and commodities by relation. *Divers nations yet unknowne, and the wonders of Affrica.*

Also of great Lakes, that deserve the names of Seas, and huge mountaines of divers sorts, as some scorched [P. 39]
with heat, some covered with snow; the mountaines of

the Sunne, also of the Moone, some of crystall, some of iron, some of silver, and mountaines of gold, with the originall of Nilus; likewise sundry sorts of cattell, fishes, Fowles, strange beasts, and monstrous serpents; for Affrica was alwayes noted to be a fruitfull mother of such terrible creatures; who meeting at their watering places, which are but Ponds in desart places, in regard of the heat of the Country, and their extremities of nature, make strange copulations, and so ingender those extraordinary monsters. Of all these you may reade in the history of this Edward Lopez, translated into English by Abraham Hartwell, and dedicated to John Lord Archbishop of Canterbury, 1597. But because the particulars are most concerning the conversion of those Pagans, by a good poore Priest that first converted a Noble man, to convert the King, and the rest of the Nobility; sent for so many Priests and ornaments into Portugall, to solemnize their baptismes with such magnificence, which was performed with such strange curiosities, that those poore Negros adored them as Gods, till the Priests grew to that wealth, a Bishop was sent to rule over them, which they would not endure, which endangered to spoile all before they could bee reconciled. But not to trouble you too long with those rarities of uncertainties; let us returne againe to Barbary, where the warres being ended, and Befferres possessed of Morocco, and his fathers treasure; a new bruit arose amongst them, that Muly Sidan, was raising an Armie against him, who after tooke his brother Befferres prisoner; but by reason of the uncertainty, and the perfidious, treacherous, bloudy murthers rather than warre, amongst those perfidious, barbarous Moores, Smith returned with Merham, and the rest to Saffe, and so aboard his Ship, to try some other conclusions at Sea.

Chapter XX.

A brave Sea fight betwixt two Spanish men of warre, and Captaine Merham with Smith.

Erham a captaine of a man of war then in the Road, invited captaine Smith, and two or three more of them aboord with him, where he spared not any thing he had to expresse his kindnesse, to bid them welcome, till it was too late to goe on shore, so that necessitie constrained them to stay aboord; a fairer Evening could not bee, yet ere midnight such a storme did arise, they were forced to let slip Cable and Anchor, and put to Sea; spooning before the wind, till they were driven to the Canaries; in the calmes they accommodated themselves, hoping this strange accident might yet produce some good event; not long it was before they tooke a small Barke comming from Teneryf, loaded with Wine; three or foure more they chased, two they tooke, but found little in them, save a few passengers, that told them of five Dutch men of warre, about the Isles, so that they stood for Boyadora, upon the Affrican shore, betwixt which and Cape Noa, [P. 40] they descried to saile. Merham intending to know what they were, hailed them; very civilly they dansed their topsailes, and desired the man of warre to come aboord them, and take what he would, for they were but two poore distressed Biskiners. But Merham, the old fox, seeing himselfe in the lions pawes, sprung his loufe, the other tacked after him, and came close up to his nether quarter, gave his broad side, and so loufed up to windward; the Vice-Admirall did the like; and at the next bout, the Admirall with a noise of Trumpets, and all his Ordnance, murtherers, and muskets, boorded him on his broad side; the other in like manner on his ley quarter, that it was so darke, there was little light, but fire and smoake; long he stayed not, before he fell off, leaving

4. or 5. of his men sprawling over the grating; after they had battered Merham about an houre, they boorded him againe as before; and threw foure kedgers or grapnalls in iron chaines, then shearing off they thought so to have torne downe the grating; but the Admiralls yard was so intangled in their shrouds, Merham had time to discharge two crosse barre shot amongst them, and divers bolts of iron made for that purpose, against his bow, that made such a breach, he feared they both should have sunke for company; so that the Spaniard was as yare in slipping his chained Grapnalls, as Merham was in cutting the tackling, kept fast their yards in his shrouds; the Vice-admirall presently cleared himselfe, but spared neither his Ordnance nor Muskets to keepe Merham from getting away, till the Admirall had repaired his leake; from twelve at noone, till six at night, they thus interchanged one volly for another; then the Vice-admirall fell on starne, staying for the Admirall that came up againe to him, and all that night stood after Merham, that shaped his course for Mamora, but such small way they made, the next morning they were not three leagues off from Cape Noa. The two Spanish men of warre, for so they were, and well appointed, taking it in scorne as it seemed, with their chase, broad side, and starne, the one after the other, within Musket shot, plying their ordnance; and after an houres worke commanded Merham a maine for the King of Spaine upon faire quarter; Merham dranke to them, and so discharged his quarter peeces: which pride the Spaniard to revenge, boorded him againe, and many of them were got to the top to unsling the maine saile, which the Master and some others from the round house, caused to their cost to come tumbling downe; about the round house the Spaniards so pestered, that they were forced to the great Cabben and blew it up; the smoake and fire was so vehement, as they thought the Ship on fire; they in the fore castle were no lesse assaulted, that blew up a peece of the grating, with a great many of Spaniards more; then they

cleared themselves with all speed, and Merham with as much expedition to quench the fire with wet clothes and water, which beganne to grow too fast. The Spaniard still playing upon him with all the shot they could; the open places presently they covered with old sailes, and prepared themselves to fight to the last man. The angry Spaniard seeing the fire quenched, hung out a flagge of truce to have but a parley; but that desperate Merham [P. 41] knew there was but one way with him, and would have none, but the report of his Ordnance, which hee did know well how to use for his best advantage. Thus they spent the next after-noone, and halfe that night; when the Spaniards either lost them, or left them. Seven and twentie men Merham had slaine, and sixteene wounded, and could finde they had received 140. great shot. A wounded Spanyard they kept alive, confessed they had lost 100. men in the Admirall, which they did feare would sinke, ere she could recover a Port. Thus reaccommodating their sailes, they sailed for Sancta Cruse, Cape Goa, and Magadore, till they came againe to Saffee; and then he returned into England.

Chapter XXI.

The continuation of the generall Historie of Virginia; the Summer Iles; and New England; with their present estate from 1624. to this present 1629.

Oncerning these Countreyes, I would be sorrie to trouble you with repeating one thing twice, as with their Maps, Commodities, People, Government & Religion yet knowen, the beginning of those plantations, their numbers and names, with the names of the Adventurers, the yeerely proceedings of everie Governour both here and there. As for the misprisions, neglect, grievances, and the causes of all those rumours, losses and crosses that

have happened; I referre you to the Generall Historie, where you shall finde all this at large; especially to those pages, where you may read my letter of advice to the Councell and Company, what of necessitie must be done, or lose all and leave the Countrey, pag. 70. what commodities I sent home, pag. 163. my opinion and offer to the Company, to feed and defend the Colonies, pag. 150. my account to them here of my actions there, pag. 163. my seven answers to his Majesties Commissioners: seven questions what hath hindered Virginia, and the remedie, pag. 165. How those noble Gentlemen spent neere two yeares in perusing all letters came from thence; and the differences betwixt many factions, both here and there, with their complaints; especially about the Sallerie, which should have beene a new office in London, for the well ordering the sale of Tobacco, that 2500. pounds should yearely have beene raised out of it, to pay foure or five hundred pounds yearly to the Governor of that Companie; two or three hundred to his Deputie; the rest into stipends of thirtie or fiftie pounds yearely for their Clerks and under Officers which were never there, pag. 153, but not one hundred pounds for all them in Virginia, or any thing for the most part of the Adventurers in England, except the undertakers for the Lotteries, Setters out of ships, Adventurers of commodities, also their Factors and many other Officers, there imployed only by friendship to raise their fortunes out of the labours of the true industrious planters by the title of their office,
[P. 42] who under the colour of sinceritie, did pillage and deceive all the rest most cunningly: For more than 150000. pounds have beene spent out of the common stocke, besides many thousands have beene there consumed, and neere 7000. people that there died, only for want of good order and government, otherwise long ere this there would have beene more than 20000. people, where after twentie yeeres spent onely in complement, and trying new conclusions, was remaining scarce 1500. with some few cattell.

Then the Company dissolved, but no account of any

thing; so that his Majestie appointed Commissioners to oversee, and give order for their proceedings. Being thus in a manner left to themselves, since then within these foure yeeres, you shall see how wonderfully they have increased beyond expectation; but so exactly as I desired, I cannot relate unto you. For although I have tired my selfe in seeking and discoursing with those returned thence, more than would a voyage to Virginia; few can tell me any thing, but of that place or places they have inhabited, and he is a great traveller that hath gone up & downe the river of James Towne, been at Pamaunke, Smiths Isles, or Accomack; wherein for the most part they keepe one tune of their now particular abundance, and their former wants, having beene there, some sixteene yeeres, some twelve, some six, some neere twentie, &c. But of their generall estate, or any thing of worth, the most of them doth know verie little to any purpose.

Now the most I could understand in generall, was from the relation of Mr. Nathaniel Cawsey, that lived there with mee, and returned Anno Dom. 1627. and some others affirme; Sir George Yerley was Governour, Captaine Francis West, Doctor John Poot, Captaine Roger Smith, Captaine Matthewes, Captaine Tucker, Mr. Clabourne and Master Farrer of the Councell: their habitations many. The Governour, with two or three of the Councell, are for most part at James Towne, the rest repaire thither as there is occasion; but everie three moneths they have a generall meeting, to consider of their publike affaires. *Their estate.* 1627.

Their numbers then were about 1500. some say rather 2000. divided into seventeene or eighteene severall Plantations; the greatest part thereof towards the falls, are so inclosed with Pallizadoes they regard not the Salvages; and amongst those Plantations above James Towne, they have now found meanes to take plentie of fish, as well with lines, as nets, and where the waters are the largest; having meanes, they need not want. *Their numbers.*

Their condition with the Salvages. Upon this River they seldome see any Salvages; but in the woods, many times their fires: yet some few there are, that upon their opportunitie have slaine some few stragglers, which have beene revenged with the death of so many of themselves; but no other attempt hath beene made upon them this two or three yeares.

Their increase of Cattle and Poultrie. Their Cattle, namely Oxen, Kine, Buls, they imagine to be about 2000. Goats great store and great increase; the wilde Hogs, which were infinite, are destroyed and eaten by the Salvages: but no family is so poore, that hath not tame Swine sufficient; and for Poultrie, he is [P. 43] a verie bad husband breedeth not an hundred in a yeere, and the richer sort doth daily feed on them.

Plenty of Corne. For bread they have plentie, and so good, that those that make it well, better cannot be: divers have much English corne, especially Mr. Abraham Perce, which prepared this yeere to sow two hundred acres of English wheat, and as much with barley, feeding daily about the number of sixtie persons at his owne charges.

Their drinke. For drinke, some malt the Indian corne, others barley, of which they make good Ale, both strong and small, and such plentie thereof, few of the upper Planters drinke any water: but the better sort are well furnished with Sacke, Aquavitæ, and good English Beere.

Their servants diet. Their servants commonly feed upon Milke Homini, which is bruized Indian corne pounded, and boiled thicke, and milke for the sauce; but boiled with milke the best of all will oft feed on it, and leave their flesh; with milke, butter and cheese; with fish, Bulls flesh, for they seldome kill any other, &c. And everie one is so applyed to his labour about Tobacco and Corne, which doth yeeld them such profit, they never regard any food from the Salvages, nor have they any trade or conference with them, but upon meere accidents and defiances: and now the Merchants have left it, there have gone so many voluntarie ships within this two yeeres, as have furnished them with Apparell, Sacke, Aquavitæ, and all necessaries, much better than ever before.

For Armes, there is scarce any man but he is furnished with a Peece, a Jacke, a Coat of Maile, a Sword, or Rapier; and everie Holy-day, everie Plantation doth exercise their men in Armes, by which meanes, hunting and fowling, the most part of them are most excellent markmen. *Their Armes and exercise.*

For Discoveries they have made none, nor any other commoditie than Tobacco doe they apply themselves unto, though never any was planted at first. And whereas the Countrey was heretofore held most intemperate and contagious by many, now they have houses, lodgings and victuall, and the Sunne hath power to exhale up the moyst vapours of the earth, where they have cut downe the wood, which before it could not, being covered with spreading tops of high trees; they finde it much more healthfull than before; nor for their numbers, few Countreyes are lesse troubled with death, sicknesse, or any other disease, nor where overgrowne women become more fruitfull. *Their health and discoveries.*

Since this, Sir George Yerley died 1628. Captaine West succeeded him; but about a yeere after returned for England: Now Doctor Poot is Governour, and the rest of the Councell as before: James Towne is yet their chiefe seat, most of the wood destroyed, little corne there planted, but all converted into pasture and gardens, wherein doth grow all manner of herbs and roots we have in England in abundance, and as good grasse as can be. Here most of their Cattle doe feed, their Owners being most some one way, some another, about their plantations, and returne againe when they please, or any shipping comes into trade. Here in winter they have hay for their Cattell: but in other places they browze upon wood, and the great huskes of their corne, with some corne in them, doth keepe them well. Mr. Hutchins saith, they have 2000 Cattle, and about 5000. people; but Master Floud, John Davis, William Emerson, and divers others, say, about five thousand people, and five thousand kine, calves, oxen, and bulls; for goats, *The present estate of Virginia, 1629.* [P. 44] *Master Hutchins. Five thousand people. Five thousand cattell.*

Goats, Hogs, and Poultry, infinite.

hogs, and poultry; corne, fish, deere, and many sorts of other wilde beasts; and fowle in their season, they have so much more than they spend, they are able to feed three or foure hundred men more than they have; and doe oft much releeve many ships, both there, and for their returne; and this last yeare was there at least two or three and twenty saile. They have oft much salt fish from New England; but fresh fish enough, when they will take it; Peaches in abundance at Kecoughtan; Apples, Peares, Apricocks, Vines, figges, and other fruits some have planted, that prospered exceedingly, but their diligence about Tobacco left them to be spoiled by the cattell, yet now they beginne to revive; Mistresse Pearce, an honest industrious woman, hath beene there neere twentie yeares, and now returned, saith, shee hath a Garden at James towne, containing three or foure acres, where in one yeare shee hath gathered neere an hundred bushels of excellent figges; and that of her owne provision she can keepe a better house in Virginia, than here in London for 3. or 400. pounds a yeare; yet went thither with little or nothing. They have some tame geese, ducks, and turkies. The masters now do so traine up their servants and youth in shooting deere, and fowle, that the youths will kill them as well as their Masters. They have two brew-houses, but they finde the Indian corne so much better than ours, they beginne to leave sowing it. Their Cities and Townes are onely scattered houses, they call plantations, as are our Country Villages, but no Ordnance mounted. The Forts Captaine Smith left a building, so ruined, there is scarce mention where they were; no discoveries of any thing more, than the curing of Tobacco, by which hitherto, being so present a commodity of gaine, it hath brought them to this abundance; but that they are so disjoynted, and every one commander of himselfe, to plant what he will: they are now so well provided that they are able to subsist; and if they would joine together now to worke upon Sope-ashes, Iron, Rape-oile, Mader, Pitch and Tarre,

Good Hospitality.

Commodities worth making, Blacke Walnut, Ash for Pikes, Oke for planks, knees for Ships, Cipresse for Chests, &c.

Flax and Hempe; as for their Tobacco, there comes from many places such abundance, and the charge so great, it is not worth the bringing home.

There is gone, and now a going, divers Ships, as Captaine Perse, Captaine Prine, and Sir John Harvy to be their governour, with two or three hundred people: there is also some from Bristow, and other parts of the West Country a preparing, which I heartily pray to God to blesse, and send them a happy and prosperous voyage.

Nathaniel Causie, Master Hutchins, Master Floud, John Davis, William Emerson, Master William Barnet, Master Cooper, and others.

Chapter XXII. [P. 45]

The proceedings and present estate of the Summer Iles, from An. Dom. 1624 to this present 1629.

FRom the Summer Iles, Master Ireland, and divers others report, their Forts, Ordnance, and proceedings, are much as they were in the yeare 1622. as you may read in the generall History, page 199. Captaine Woodhouse governour. There are few sorts of any fruits in the West Indies, but they grow there in abundance; yet the fertility of the soile in many places decayeth, being planted every yeare; for their Plantaines, which is a most delicate fruit, they have lately found a way by pickling or drying them, to bring them over into England, there being no such fruit in Europe, & wonderfull for increase. For fish, flesh, figs, wine, and all sorts of most excellent hearbs, fruits, and rootes they have in abundance. In this Governours time, a kinde of Whale, or rather a Jubarta, was driven on shore in Southampton tribe from the west, over an infinite number of rocks, so bruised, that the water in the Bay where she lay, was all oily, and the rocks about it all bedasht with Parmacitty, congealed like ice, a good quantity we gathered, with which we commonly cured any byle, hurt, or bruise; some burnt it in their lamps, which blowing out, the very snuffe will burne, so long as there is any of the oile remaining, for two or three dayes together.

The next Governour, was Captaine Philip Bell, whose time being expired, Captaine Roger Wood possessed his place, a worthy Gentleman of good desert, and hath lived a long time in the Country; their numbers are about two or three thousand, men, women, and children, who increase there exceedingly; their greatest complaint, is want of apparell, and too much custome, and too many officers; the pity is, there are more men than women, yet no great mischiefe, because there is so much lesse pride: the cattell they have increase exceedingly; their forts are well maintained by the Merchants here, and Planters there; to be briefe, this isle is an excellent bit, to rule a great horse.

The present estate of the Summer Isles. 1629.

All the Cohow birds and Egbirds are gone; seldome any wilde cats seene; no Rats to speake of; but the wormes are yet very troublesome; the people very healthfull; and the Ravens gone; fish enough but not so neere the shore as it used, by the much beating it; it is an Ile that hath such a rampire and a ditch, and for the quantity so manned, victualled, and fortified, as few in the world doe exceed it, or is like it.

An evill mischance.

The 22. of March, two ships came from thence; the Peter Bonaventure, neere two hundred tunnes, and sixteene peeces of Ordnance; the Captaine, Thomas Sherwin; the Master, Master Edward Some, like him in condition, a goodly, lusty, proper, valiant man: the Lydia, wherein was Master Anthony Thorne, a smaller ship; were chased by eleven ships of Dunkerk; being thus overmatched, Captaine Sherwin was taken by them in Turbay, only his valiant Master was slaine; the ship
[P. 46] with about seventy English men, they carried betwixt Dover and Callis, to Dunkerk; but the Lydia safely recovered Dartmouth.

These noble adventurers for all those losses, patiently doe beare them; but they hope the King and state will understand it is worth keeping, though it afford nothing but Tobacco, and that now worth little or nothing, custome and fraught payed, yet it is worth keeping, and not supplanting; though great men feele not those losses, yet Gardiners, Carpenters, and Smiths doe pay for it.

From the relation of Robert Chesteven, and others.

Chapter XXIII.

The proceedings and present estate of New England, since 1624. to this present 1629.

WHen I went first to the North part of Virginia, where the Westerly Colony had beene planted, it had dissolved it selfe within a yeare, and there was not one Christian in all the land. I was set forth at the sole charge of foure Merchants of London; the Country being then reputed by your westerlings, a most rockie, barren, desolate desart; but the good returne I brought from thence, with the maps and relations I made of the Country, which I made so manifest, some of them did beleeve me, and they were well embraced, both by the Londoners, and Westerlings, for whom I had promised to undertake it, thinking to have joined them all together, but that might well have beene a worke for Hercules. Betwixt them long there was much contention; the Londoners indeed went bravely forward; but in three or foure yeares, I and my friends consumed many hundred pounds amongst the Plimothians, who only fed me with delayes, promises, and excuses, but no performance of any thing to any purpose. In the interim, many particular ships went thither, and finding my relations true, and that I had not taken that I brought home from the French men, as had beene reported; yet further for my

Considerations about the losse of time.

paines to discredit me, and my calling it New England, they obscured it, and shadowed it, with the title of Canada, till at my humble suit, it pleased our most Royall King Charles, whom God long keepe, blesse, and preserve, then Prince of Wales, to confirme it with my map and booke, by the title of New England; the gaine thence returning did make the fame thereof so increase, that thirty, forty, or fifty saile went yearly only to trade and fish; but nothing would bee done for a plantation, till about some hundred of your Brownists of England, Amsterdam, and Leyden, went to New Plimouth, whose humorous ignorances, caused them for more than a yeare, to endure a wonderfull deale of misery, with an infinite patience; saying my books and maps were much better cheape to teach them, than my selfe; many other have used the like good husbandry, that have payed soundly in trying their selfe-willed conclusions; but those in time doing well, divers others have in small handfulls undertaken to goe there, to be severall Lords and Kings of themselves, but most vanished to nothing; notwithstanding the fishing ships, made such good returnes, at last it was ingrossed by twenty Pattenties, that divided my map into twenty parts, and cast lots for their shares; but money not comming in as they expected, procured a Proclamation, none should goe thither without their licences to fish; but for every thirty tunnes of shipping, to pay them five pounds; besides, upon great penalties, neither to trade with the natives, cut downe wood for their stages, without giving satisfaction, though all the Country is nothing but wood, and none to make use of it, with many such other pretences, for to make this Country plant it selfe, by its owne wealth: hereupon most men grew so discontented, that few or none would goe; so that the Pattenties, who never one of them had beene there, seeing those projects would not prevaile, have since not hindred any to goe that would, that within these few last yeares, more have gone thither than ever.

The effect of niggardlinesse.

[P. 47]

A new plantation. 1629.

Now this yeare 1629. a great company of people of

good ranke, zeale, meanes, and quality, have made a great stocke, and with six good ships in the moneths of Aprill and May, they set saile from Thames, for the Bay of the Massachusetts, otherwise called Charles River; viz. the George Bonaventure, of twenty peeces of Ordnance, the Talbot nineteene, the Lions-whelpe eight, the May-flower fourteene, the Foure Sisters, foureteene, the Pilgrim foure, with three hundred and fifty, men, women, and children; also an hundred and fifteene head of Cattell, as horse, mares, and neat beast; one and forty goats, some Conies, with all provision for houshold, and apparell; six peeces of great Ordnance for a Fort, with Muskets, Pikes, Corselets, Drums, Colours, with all provisions necessary for a plantation, for the good of man; other particulars I understand of no more, than is writ in the generall historie of those Countries.

But you are to understand, that the noble Lord chiefe Justice Popham, Judge Doderege; the Right Honourable Earles of Pembroke, Southampton, Salesbury, and the rest, as I take it, they did all thinke, as I and them went with me did; That had those two Countries beene planted, as it was intended, that no other nation should come plant betwixt us. If ever the King of Spaine and we should fall foule, those Countries being so capable of all materialls for shipping, by this might have beene owners of a good Fleet of ships, and to have releeved a whole Navy from England upon occasion; yea, and to have furnished England with the most Easterly commodities; and now since, seeing how conveniently the Summer Iles fell to our shares, so neere the West Indies, wee might with much more facility than the Dutchmen have invaded the West Indies, that doth now put in practice, what so long hath beene advised on, by many an honest English States-man.

Notes of inconveniencie.

Those Countries Captaine Smith oft times used to call his children that never had mother; & well he might, for few fathers ever payed dearer for so little content; and for those that would truly understand, how many [P. 48] strange accidents hath befallen them and him; how oft up, how oft downe, sometimes neere desperate, and ere long flourishing, cannot but conceive Gods infinite mercies and favours towards them. Had his designes beene to have perswaded men to a mine of gold, though few doth conceive either the charge or paines in refining it, nor the power nor care to defend it; or some new Invention to passe to the South Sea; or some strange plot to invade some strange Monastery: or some portable Countrie; or some chargeable Fleet to take some rich Carocks in the East Indies; or Letters of Mart to rob some poore Merchants; what multitudes of both people and mony, would contend to be first imployed: but in those noble endevours (now) how few of quality, unlesse it be to beg some Monopolie; and those seldome seeke the common good, but the commons goods; as you may reade at large in his generall history, page 217, 218, 219. his generall observations and reasons for this plantation; For yet those Countries are not so forward but they may become as miserable as ever, if better courses be not taken than is; as this Smith will plainly demonstrate to his Majesty; or any other noble person of ability, liable generously to undertake it; how within a short time to make Virginia able to resist any enemy, that as yet lieth open to all; and yeeld the King more custome within these few yeares, in certaine staple commodities, than ever it did in Tobacco; which now not being worth bringing home, the custome will bee as uncertaine to the King, as dangerous to the plantations.

Chapter XXIIII.

A briefe discourse of divers voyages made unto the goodly Countrey of Guiana, and the great River of the Amazons; relating also the present Plantation there.

T is not unknowen how that most industrious & honourable Knight Sir Walter Rauleigh, in the yeare of our Lord 1595. taking the Ile of Trinidado, fell with the Coast of Guiana Northward of the Line ten degrees, and coasted the Coast; and searched up the River Oranoca; where understanding that twentie severall voyages had beene made by the Spanyards, in discovering this Coast and River; to finde a passage to the great Citie of Mano, called by them the Eldorado, or the Golden Citie: he did his utmost to have found some better satisfaction than relations: But meanes failing him, hee left his trustie servant Francis Sparrow to seeke it, who wandring up and downe those Countreyes, some foureteene or fifteene yeares unexpectedly returned: I have heard him say, he was led blinded into this Citie by Indians; but little discourse of any purpose touching the largenesse of the report of it; his body seeming as a man of an uncurable consumption, shortly dyed hereafter in England. There are above thirtie faire rivers that fall into the Sea, betweene the River of Amazons and Oranoca, which are some nine degrees asunder.

Sparrow left to seeke the great Citie of Mano.

[P. 49]

In the yeare 1605. Captaine Ley, brother to that noble Knight Sir Oliver Ley, with divers others, planted himselfe in the River Weapoco, wherein I should have beene a partie; but hee dyed, and there lyes buried, and the supply miscarrying, the rest escaped as they could.

Captaine Charles Ley.

Sir Thomas Roe, well knowen to be a most noble Gentlemen, before he went Lord Ambassadour to the Great Mogoll, or the great Turke, spent a yeare or two

Sir Thomas Roe.

upon this Coast, and about the River of the Amazones, wherein he most imployed Captaine Matthew Morton, an expert Sea-man in the discoverie of this famous River, a Gentleman that was the first shot and mortally supposed wounded to death with me, in Virginia, yet since hath beene twice with command in the East Indies; Also Captaine William White, and divers others worthy and industrious Gentlemen, both before and since, hath spent much time and charge to discover it more perfitly; but nothing more effected for a Plantation, till it was undertaken by Captaine Robert Harcote, 1609.

Captain Morton.

Captaine White.

This worthy Gentleman, after he had by Commission made a discoverie to his minde, left his brother Michael Harcote, with some fiftie or sixtie men in the River Weapoco, and so presently returned to England, where he obtained by the favour of Prince Henrie, a large Patent for all that Coast called Guiana, together with the famous River of Amazones, to him and his heires: but so many troubles here surprized him, though he did his best to supply them, he was not able, only some few hee sent over as passengers with certaine Dutch-men, but to small purpose. Thus this businesse lay dead for divers yeeres, till Sir Walter Rauleigh, accompanied with many valiant Souldiers and brave Gentlemen, went his last voyage to Guiana, amongst the which was Captaine Roger North, brother to the Right Honourable the Lord Dudley North, who upon this voyage having stayed and seene divers Rivers upon this Coast, tooke such a liking to those Countreyes, having had before this voyage more perfect and particular information of the excellencie of the great River of the Amazones, above any of the rest, by certaine Englishmen returned so rich from thence in good commodities, they would not goe with Sir Walter Rauleigh in search of gold; that after his returne for England, he endevoured by his best abilities to interest his Countrey and state in those faire Regions, which by the way of Letters Patents unto divers Noblemen and Gentlemen of qualitie, erected into a company and perpetuitie for trade

Captain Harcote.

and plantation, not knowing of the Interest of Captaine Harcote.

Whereupon accompanied with 120. Gentlemen and others, with a ship, a pinnace, and two shallops, to remaine in the Countrey, hee set saile from Plimouth the last of April 1620; and within seven weekes after hee arrived well in the Amazones, only with the losse of one old man: some hundred leagues they ran up the River to settle his men, where the sight of the Countrey and people so contented them, that never men thought themselves more happie: Some English and Irish that had lived there some eight yeeres, only supplyed by the Dutch, hee reduced to his company and to leave the Dutch: having made a good voyage, to the value of more than the charge, he returned to England with divers good commodities, besides Tobacco: So that it may well be conceived, that if this action had not beene thus crossed, the Generalitie of England had by this time beene wonne and encouraged therein. But the time was not yet come, that God would have this great businesse effected, by reason of the great power the Lord Gundamore, Ambassadour for the King of Spaine, had in England, to crosse and ruine those proceedings, and so unfortunate Captaine North was in this businesse, hee was twice committed prisoner to the Tower, and the goods detained, till they were spoiled, who beyond all others was by much the greatest Adventurer and Loser.

Captaine Roger North.

[P. 50]

Notwithstanding all this, those that he had left in the Amazons would not abandon the Countrey. Captaine Thomas Painton, a worthy Gentleman, his Lieutenant, dead: Captaine Charles Parker, brother to the Right Honourable the Lord Morley, lived there six yeares after: Mr. John Christmas, five yeares, so well, they would not returne, although they might, with divers other Gentlemen of qualitie and others: all thus destitute of any supplyes from England. But all authoritie being dissolved, want of government did more wrong their proceedings, than all other crosses whatsoever. Some

Nota bene.

releefe they had sometime from the Dutch, who knowing their estates, gave what they pleased and tooke what they list. Two brothers Gentlemen, Thomas and William Hixon, who stayed three yeares there, are now gone to stay in the Amazons, in the ships lately sent thither.

The businesse thus remaining in this sort, three private men left of that Company, named Mr. Thomas Warriner, John Rhodes, and Robert Bims, having lived there about two yeares, came for England, and to be free from the disorders that did grow in the Amazons for want of Government amongst their Countrey-men, and to be quiet amongst themselves, made meanes to set themselves out for St. Christophers; their whole number being but fifteene persons, that payed for their passage in a ship going for Virginia, where they remained a yeare before they were supplyed, and then that was but foure or five men.

Thus this Ile, by this small beginning, having no interruption by their owne Countrey, hath now got the start of the Continent and maine Land of Guiana, which hath beene layd apart and let alone untill that Captaine North, ever watching his best opportunitie and advantage of time in the state, hath now againe pursued and set on foot his former designe. Captaine Harcote being now willing to surrender his grant, and to joyne with Captaine North in passing a new Patent, and to erect a company for trade and plantation in the Amazons, and all the Coast and Countrey of Guiana for ever.

Whereupon they have sent this present yeare in Januarie, and since 1628. foure ships with neere two hundred persons; the first ship with 112 men, not one miscarried; the rest went since, not yet heard of, and are preparing another with their best expedition: and since Januarie is gone from Holland, 100. English and Irish, conducted by the old Planters.

This great River lieth under the Line, the two chiefe head lands North and South, are about three degrees
[P. 51] asunder, the mouth of it is so full of many great and

small Iles, it is an easie matter for an unexperienced Pilot to lose his way. It is held one of the greatest rivers in America, and as most men thinke, in the world: and commeth downe with such a fresh, it maketh the Sea fresh more than thirtie miles from the shore. Captaine North having seated his men about an hundred leagues in the Maine, sent Captaine William White, with thirtie Gentlemen and others, in a pinnace of thirtie tun, to discover further; which they did some two hundred leagues, where they found the River to divide it selfe in two parts, till then all full of Ilands, and a Countrey most healthfull, pleasant and fruitful; for they found food enough, and all returned safe & in good health: In this discoverie, they saw many Townes well inhabited, some with three hundred people, some with five, six, or seven hundred; and of some they understood to be of so many thousands, most differing verie much, especially in their languages: whereof they suppose by those Indians, they understand are many hundreds more, unfrequented till then by any Christian, most of them starke naked, both men, women and children, but they saw not any such giant-like women as the Rivers name importeth. But for those where Captaine North hath seated his company, it is not knowen where Indians were ever so kinde to any Nation, not sparing any paines, danger or labour, to feed and maintaine them. The English following their buildings, fortifications and sugar-workes; for which they have sent most expert men, and with them all things necessarie for that purpose; to effect which, they want not the helpe of those kinde Indians to produce; and many other good commodities, which (God willing) will ere long make plaine and apparent to this Kingdome, and all the Adventurers and Well-willers to this Plantation, to bee well worthy the cherishing and following with all alacritie.

[Chapter XXV.

1623.

Chapter XXV.

The beginning and proceedings of the new plantation of St. Christopher by Captaine Warner.

Aster Ralfe Merifield and others, having furnished this worthy industrious Gentleman, hee arrived at St. Christophers, as is said, with fifteene men, the 28. of Januarie, 1623. viz. William Tested, John Rhodes, Robert Bims, Mr. Benifield, Sergeant Jones, Mr. Ware, William Royle, Rowland Grascocke, Mr. Bond, Mr. Langley, Mr. Weaver, Edward Warner their Captaines sonne (and now Deputy-Governour till his fathers returne), Sergeant Aplon, one Sailor and a Cooke: At their arrivall they found three French-men, who sought to oppose Captaine Warner, and to set the Indians upon us; but at last we all became friends, and lived with the Indians a moneth. Then we built a Fort, and a house: and planting fruits, by September we made a crop of Tobacco; but upon
A Hericano. the nineteenth of September came a Hericano and blew it away: all this while wee lived upon Cassada bread,
[P. 52] Potatoes, Plantines, Pines, Turtels, Guanes, and fish plentie; for drinke wee had Nicnobbie.

1624. The 18. of March 1624. arrived Captaine Jefferson with three men passengers in the Hope-well of London, with some trade for the Indians, and then we had another crop of Tobacco, in the meane time the French had planted themselves in the other end of the Ile; with this crop Captaine Warner returned for England in September, 1625.

1625. In his absence came in a French pinnace, under the command of Monsieur de Nombe, that told us the Indians had slaine some French-men in other of the Charybes Iles, and that there were six Peryagoes, which are huge great trees formed as your Canowes, but so laid out on the sides with boords, they will seeme like a little Gally: six of those, with about foure or five hundred strange Indians, came unto us, we bade them be gone, but they would not; whereupon we and the French joyned together, and upon the fifth of November set upon them, and put them to flight: upon New-yeares Even they came againe, found three English going about the Ile, whom they slue. Untill the fourth of August, we stood upon our guard, living upon the spoile and did nothing. But now Captaine Warner arriving againe with neere an hundred people, then we fell to worke and planting as before; but upon the fourth of September, came such a Hericano, as blewe downe all our houses, Tobacco, and two Drums into the aire we know not whither, drove two ships on shore that were both split; all our provision thus lost, we were very miserable, living onely on what we could get in the wilde woods, we made a small party of French and English to goe aboord for provision, but in their returning home, eight French men were slaine in the harbour.

Their fight with the Indians.

1626.

A Hericano.

Eight French slaine.

Thus wee continued till neere June that the Tortels came in, 1627. but the French being like to starve, sought to surprize us, and all the Cassado, Potatos, and Tobacco we had planted, but we did prevent them. The 26. of October, came in Captaine William Smith, in the Hopewell, with some Ordnance, shot and powder, from the Earle of Carlile; with Captaine Pelham and thirty men, about that time also came the Plow; also a small ship of Bristow, with Captaine Warners wife, and six or seven women more.

1627.

Upon the 25. of November, the Indians set upon the French, for some injury about their women, and slew six and twentie French men, five English, and three Indians. Their weapons are bowes and arrowes; their bowes are never bent, but the string lies flat to the bow; their arrowes a small reed, foure or five foot long, headed some with the poysoned sting of the taile of a Stingray,

Three Indians slaine.

some with iron, some with wood, but all so poysoned, that if they draw but bloud, the hurt is incurable.

The arrivall of many English ships. The next day came in Captaine Charles Saltonstall, a young Gentleman, son of Sir Samuell Saltonstall, who brought with him good store of all commodities to releeve the plantation; but by reason some Hollanders, and others, had bin there lately before him, who carried away with them all the Tobacco, he was forced to put away all his commodities upon trust till the next crop; in the meane time hee resolved there to stay, and imploy him-
[P. 53] selfe & his company in planting Tobacco, hoping thereby to make a voyage, but before he could be ready to returne for England, a Hericano hapning, his ship was split, to his great losse, being sole Merchant and owner himselfe, notwithstanding forced to pay to the Governour, the fift part of his Tobacco, and for fraught to England, three pence a pound, and nine pence a pound custome, which amounts together to more than threescore pound in the hundred pound, to the great discouragement of him and many others, that intended well to those plantations. Neverthelesse he is gone againe this present yeare 1629. with a ship of about three hundred tunnes, and very neere two hundred people, with Sir William Tuffton Governour for the Barbados, and divers gentlemen, and all manner of commodities fit for a plantation.

Captaine Prinne, Captaine Stone, and divers others, came in about Christmas; so that this last yeare there hath beene about thirtie saile of English, French, and Dutch ships, and all the Indians forced out of the Ile, for they had done much mischiefe amongst the French in cutting their throats, burning their houses, and spoyling their Tobacco; Amongst the rest Tegramund, a little childe the Kings sonne, his parents being slaine or fled, was by great chance saved, and carefully brought to England by Master Merifield, who brought him from thence, and bringeth him up as his owne children.

The description of the Ile. It lyeth seventeene degrees Northward of the line, about an hundred and twenty leagues from the Cape de tres Puntas, the neerest maine land in America. It is about eight leagues in length, and foure in bredth; an Iland amongst 100. Iles in the West Indies, called the Caribes, where ordinarily all them that frequent the West Indies, refresh themselves; those most of them are rocky, little, and mountainous, yet frequented with the Canibals; many of them inhabited, as Saint Domingo, Saint Mattalin, Saint Lucia, Saint Vincent, Granada and Margarita, to the Southward; Northward, none but Saint Christophers, and it but lately, yet they will be ranging Marigalanta, Guardalupo, Deceado, Monserat, Antigua, Mevis, Bernardo, Saint Martin, Saint Bartholomew, but the worst of the foure Iles possessed by the Spanyard, as Portorico, or Jamica, is better than them all; as for Hispaniola, and Cuba, they are worthy the title of two rich Kingdomes, the rest not respected by the Spanyards, for want of harbors, and their better choice of good land, and profit in the maine. But Captaine Warner, having beene very familiar with Captain Painton, in the Amazon, hearing his information of this St. Christophers; and having made a yeares tryall, as it is said, returned for England, joyning with Master Merifield, and his friends, got Letters Pattents, from King James, to plant and possesse it. Since then, the Right Honourable the Earle of Carlile, hath got Letters Pattents also, not only of that, but all the Caribes Iles about it, who is now chiefe Lord of them, and the English his tenants, that doe possesse them; over whom he appointeth such Governours and Officers, as their affaires require; and although there be a great custome imposed upon them, considering their other charges, both to feed and maintaine themselves; yet there is there, and now a going, neere upon the number of three thousand people; where by reason of the rockinesse and thicknesse of the woods in the Ile, it is difficult to passe, and such a snuffe [P. 54] of the Sea goeth on the shore, ten may better defend than fifty assault. In this Ile are many springs, but yet water is scarce againe in many places; the valleyes and

The springs, temper, and seasons.

sides of the hills very fertile, but the mountaines harsh, and of a sulphurous composition; all overgrowne with Palmetas, Cotten trees, Lignum vitæ, and divers other sorts, but none like any in Christendome, except those carried thither; the aire very pleasant and healthfull, but exceeding hot, yet so tempered with coole breaths, it seemes very temperate to them that are a little used to it; the trees being alwaies greene, the daies and nights alwayes very neere equall in length, alwayes Summer; only they have in their seasons great gusts and raines, and sometimes a Hericano, which is an overgrowne, and a most violent storme.

A strange hatching of egges for beasts.

In some of those Iles, are cattell, goats, and hogges, but here none but what they must carry; Gwanes they have, which is a little harmlesse beast, like a Crokadell, or Aligator, very fat and good meat, she layes egges in the sand, as doth the land Crabs, which live here in abundance, like Conies in Boroughs, unlesse about May, when they come downe to the Sea side, to lay in the sand, as the other; and all their egges are hatched by the heat of the Sunne.

From May to September they have good store of Tortasses, that come out of the Sea to lay their egges in the sand, and are hatched as the other; they will lay halfe a pecke at a time, and neere a bushell ere they have done; and are round like Tenis-balls: this fish is like veale in taste, the fat of a brownish colour very good and wholsome. We seeke them in the nights, where we finde them on shore, we turne them upon their backs, till the next day we fetch them home. For they can never returne themselves, being so hard a cart may goe over them; and so bigge, one will suffice forty or fifty men to dinner. Divers sorts of other fish they have in abundance, and Prawnes most great and excellent, but none will keepe sweet scarce twelve houres.

Birds.

The best and greatest is a Passer Flaminga, which walking at her length is as tall as a man; Pigeons and Turtle Doves in abundance; some Parrots, wilde Hawkes, but divers other sorts of good Sea fowle, whose names we know not.

Cassado is a root planted in the ground, of a wonderfull increase, and will make very good white bread, but the Juyce ranke poyson, yet boyled, better than wine; Potatos, Cabbages, and Radish plenty. *Roots.*

Mayes, like the Virginia wheat; we have Pine-apples, neere so bigge as an Hartichocke, but the most daintiest taste of any fruit; Plantains, an excellent, and a most increasing fruit; Apples, Prickell Peares, and Pease but differing all from ours. There is Pepper that groweth in a little red huske, as bigge as a Walnut, about foure inches in length, but the long cods are small, and much stronger, and better for use, than that from the East Indies. *Fruits.*

There is two sorts of Cotten, the silke Cotten as in the East Indies, groweth upon a small stalke, as good for beds as downe; the other upon a shrub, and beareth a cod bigger than a Walnut, full of Cotten wooll: Anotto also groweth upon a shrub, with a cod like the other, and nine or ten on a bunch, full of Anotto, very good [P. 55] for Dyers, though wilde; Sugar Canes, not tame, 4. or 5. foot high; also Masticke, and Locus trees; great and hard timber, Gourds, Muske Melons, Water Melons, Lettice, Parsly; all places naturally beare purslaine of it selfe; Sope-berries like a Musket-bullet, that washeth as white as Sope; in the middle of the root is a thing like a sedge, a very good fruit, we call Pengromes; a Pappaw is as great as an apple, coloured like an Orange, and good to eat; a small hard nut, like a hazell nut, growes close to the ground, and like this growes on the Palmetas, which we call a Mucca nut; Mustard-seed will grow to a great tree, but beares no seed, yet the leaves will make good mustard; the Mancinell tree the fruit is poyson; good figs in abundance; but the Palmeta serveth to build Forts and houses, the leaves to cover them, and many other uses; the juyce we draw from them till we sucke them to death (is held restorative), and the top for meat doth serve us as Cabbage; but oft we want poudered Beefe, and Bacon, and many other needfull necessaries.

By Thomas Simons, Rowland Grascocke, Nicholas Burgh, and others.

Chapter XXVI.

The first planting of the Barbados.

He Barbados lies South-west and by South, an hundred leagues from Saint Christophers, threescore leagues West and South from Trinidado, and some fourescore leagues from Cape de Salinos, the next part of the maine. The first planters brought thither by Captaine Henry Powel, were forty English with seven or eight Negros; then he went to Disacuba in the maine, where he got thirty Indians, men, women, and children, of the Arawacos, enemies both to the Caribes, and the Spaniards. The Ile is most like a triangle, each side forty or fifty miles square, some exceeding great rocks, but the most part exceeding good ground; abounding with an infinite number of Swine, some Turtles, and many sorts of excellent fish; many great ponds wherein is Ducke and Mallard; excellent clay for pots, wood and stone for building, and a spring neere the middest of the Ile, of Bitume, which is a liquid mixture like Tarre, that by the great raines falls from the tops of the mountaines, it floats upon the water in such abundance, that drying up, it remaines like great rocks of pitch, and as good as pitch for any use.

A description of the Ile.

The Mancinell apple, is of a most pleasant sweet smell, of the bignesse of a Crab, but ranke poyson, yet the Swine and Birds have wit to shun it; great store of exceeding great Locus trees, two or three fadome about, of a great height, that beareth a cod full of meale, will make bread in time of necessity. A tree like a Pine,

Fruits and trees.

beareth a fruit so great as a Muske Melon, which hath alwayes ripe fruit, flowers, or greene fruit, which will refresh two or three men, and very comfortable; Plumb trees many, the fruit great and yellow, which but strained [P. 56] into water in foure and twenty houres will be very good drinke; wilde figge trees there are many; all those fruits doe fat the hogges; yet at some times of the yeare they are so leane, as carrion; Gwane trees beare a fruit so bigge as a Peare, good and wholsome; Palmetaes of three severall sorts; Papawes, Prickle Peares good to eat or make drinke; Cedar trees very tall and great; Fusticke trees are very great and the wood yellow, good for dying; sope berries, the kernell so bigge as a sloe, and good to eat; Pumpeons in abundance; Goads so great as will make good great bottles, and, cut in two peeces, good dishes and platters; many small brooks of very good water; Ginni wheat, Cassado, Pines and Plantaines; all things we there plant doe grow exceedingly, so well as Tobacco; The corne, pease, and beanes, cut but away the stalke, young sprigs will grow, and so beare fruit for many yeares together, without any more planting; the Ile is overgrowne with wod or great reeds, those wods which are soft are exceeding light and full of pitch, and those that are hard, are so hard and great, they are as hard to cut as stone.

Their numbers.

Master John Powell came thither the fourth of August 1627. with forty five men, where we stayed three weeks, and then returning, left behind us about an hundred people, and his sonne John Powell for his Deputy, as Governour; but there have beene so many factions amongst them, I cannot from so many variable relations give you any certainty for their orderly Government: for all those plenties, much misery they have endured, in regard of their weaknesse at their landing, and long stay without supplies; therefore those that goe thither, it were good they carry good provision with them; but the Ile is most healthfull, and all things planted doe increase abundantly: and by this time there is, and now a going, about the number of fifteene or sixteene hundred people.

Sir William Curtine, and Captaine John Powell, were the first and chiefe adventurers to the planting this fortunate Ile; which had beene oft frequented by men of Warre to refresh themselves, and set up their shallops; being so farre remote from the rest of the Iles, they never were troubled with any of the Indies. Harbours they have none, but exceeding good Rodes, which with a small charge might bee very well fortified; It doth ebbe and flow foure or five foot, and they cannot perceive there hath ever beene any Hericano in that Ile.

From the relations of Captaine John White, and Captaine Wolverstone.

Chapter XXVII.

The first plantation of the Ile of Mevis.

The description of the Ile.

Ecause I have ranged and lived amongst those Ilands, what my authours cannot tell me, I think it no great errour in helping them to tell it my selfe. In this little Ile of Mevis, more than twenty [P. 57] yeares agoe, I have remained a good time together, to wod, and water and refresh my men; it is all woddy, but by the Sea side Southward there are sands like downes, where a thousand men may quarter themselves conveniently; but in most places the wod groweth close to the water side, at a high water marke, and in some places so thicke of a soft spungy wood like a wilde figge tree, you cannot get through it, but by making your way with hatchets, or fauchions: whether it was the dew of those trees, or of some others, I am not certaine, but many of our men became so tormented with a burning swelling all over their bodies, they seemed like scalded men, and neere mad with paine;

The Bath.

Here we found a great Poole, wherein bathing themselves, they found much ease; and finding it fed with a pleasant small streame that came out of the woods, we found the head halfe a mile within the land, distilling from a many of rocks, by which they were well cured in two or three dayes. Such factions here we had, as commonly attend such voyages, that a paire of gallowes was made, but Captaine Smith, for whom they were intended, could not be perswaded to use them; but not any one of the inventers but their lives by justice fell into his power, to determine of at his pleasure, whom with much mercy he favoured, that most basely and unjustly would have betrayed him.

A great misprison.

The last yeare, 1628., Master Littleton, with some others got a Pattent of the Earle of Carlile, to plant the Ile called the Barbados, thirty leagues Northward of Saint Christophers; which by report of their informers, and undertakers, for the excellencie and pleasantnesse thereof, they called Dulcina, but when they came there, they found it such a barren rocke, they left it; although they were told as much before, they would not beleeve it, perswading themselves, those contradicters would get it for themselves, was thus by their cunning opinion, the deceiver of themselves; for seeing it lie conveniently for their purpose in a map, they had not patience to know the goodnesse or badnesse, the inconvenience nor probabilities of the quality, nor quantity; which errour doth predominate in most of our homebred adventurers, that will have all things as they conceit and would have it; and the more they are contradicted, the more hot they are; but you may see, by many examples in the generall history, how difficult a matter it is, to gather the truth from amongst so many forren and severall relations, except you have exceeding good experience both of the Countries, people, and their conditions; and those ignorant undertakings, have beene the greatest hinderance of all those plantations.

Their numbers.

At last because they would be absolute, they came to Mevis, a little Ile by Saint Christophers; where they seated themselves, well furnished with all necessaries, being about the number of an hundred, and since increased to an hundred and fifty persons, whereof many were old planters of Saint Christophers, especially Master Anthony Hinton, and Master Edward Thompson. But because all those Iles for most part are so capable to produce, and in nature like each other, let this discourse serve for the description of them all. Thus much concerning those plantations, which now after all this time, losse, and charge, should they be abandoned, suppressed, and dissolved, were most lamentable; and surely seeing they all strive so much about this Tobacco, and that the fraught thereof, and other charges are so great, and so open to any enemie, by that commodity they cannot long subsist.

And it is a wonder to me to see such miracles of
[P. 58] mischiefes in men; how greedily they persue to dispossesse the planters of the Name of Christ Jesus, yet say they are Christians, when so much of the world is unpossessed; yea, and better land than they so much strive for, murthering so many Christians, burning and spoiling so many cities, villages, and Countries, and subverting so many kingdomes, when so much lieth vast, or only possessed by a few poore Savages, that more serve the Devill for feare, than God for love; whose ignorance we pretend to reforme, but covetousnesse, humours, ambition, faction, and pride, hath so many instruments, we performe very little to any purpose; nor is there either honour or profit to be got by any that are so vile, to undertake the subversion, or hinderance of any honest intended christian plantation.

Certaine exploits of Captaine Smith.

Now to conclude the travels and adventures of Captaine Smith; how first he planted Virginia, and was set ashore with about an hundred men in the wilde woods; how he was taken prisoner by the Savages, by the King of Pamaunke tied to a tree to be shot to death, led up and downe their Country to be shewed for a wonder; fatted as he thought, for a sacrifice for their Idoll, before whom they conjured him three dayes, with strange dances and invocations, then brought him before their Emperor

Powhatan, that commanded him to be slaine, how his daughter Pocahontas saved his life, returned him to James towne, releeved him and his famished company, which was but eight and thirty to possesse those large dominions; how he discovered all the severall nations upon the rivers falling into the Bay of Chisapeacke; stung neere to death with a most poysoned taile of a fish called Stingray: how Powhatan out of his Country, tooke the Kings of Pamaunke and Paspahegh prisoners, forced thirty nine of those Kings to pay him contribution, subjected all the Savages: how Smith was blowne up with gunpowder, and returned for England to be cured:

Also how hee brought our new England to the subjection of the Kingdome of great Britaine; his fights with the Pirats, left alone amongst a many French men of Warre, and his ship ran from him; his Sea-fights for the French against the Spaniards; their bad usage of him; how in France in a little boat he escaped them; was adrift all such a stormy night at Sea by himselfe, when thirteene French ships were split, or driven on shore by the Ile of Ree, the generall and most of his men drowned, when God to whom be all honour and praise, brought him safe on shore to all their admirations that escaped; you may read at large in his generall history of Virginia, the Summer Iles, and New England.

[Chapter XXVIII.

Chapter XXVIII.

The bad life, qualities and conditions of Pyrats; and how they taught the Turks and Moores to become men of warre.

AS in all lands where there are many people, there are some theeves, so in all Seas much frequented, there are some pyrats; the most ancient within the memory of threescore yeares was one Callis, who most refreshed himselfe upon the Coast of Wales; Clinton and Pursser his companions, who grew famous, till Queene Elizabeth of [P. 59] blessed memory, hanged them at Wapping; Flemming was as expert and as much sought for as they, yet such a friend to his Country, that discovering the Spanish Armado, he voluntarily came to Plimouth, yeelded himselfe freely to my Lord Admirall, and gave him notice of the Spaniards comming; which good warning came so happily and unexpectedly, that he had his pardon, & a good reward; some few Pirats there then remained; notwithstanding it is incredible how many great and rich prizes the little barques of the West Country daily brought home, in regard of their small charge; for there are so many difficulties in a great Navy, by wind and weather, victuall, sicknesse, losing and finding one another, they seldome defray halfe the charge: but for the grace, state, and defence of the Coast and narrow Seas, a great Navy is most necessary, but not to attempt any farre voyage, except there be such a competent stocke, the want not wherewith to furnish and supply all things with expedition; But to the purpose.

The difficulties of a great Navie.

After the death of our most gracious Queene Elizabeth, of blessed memory, our Royall King James, who from his infancie had reigned in peace with all Nations; had no imployment for those men of warre, so that those that were rich rested with that they had; those that were

What occasioneth Pirats.

poore and had nothing but from hand to mouth, turned Pirats; some, because they became sleighted of those for whom they had got much wealth; some, for that they could not get their due; some, that had lived bravely, would not abase themselves to poverty; some vainly, only to get a name; others for revenge, covetousnesse, or as ill; and as they found themselves more and more oppressed, their passions increasing with discontent, made them turne Pirats.

Now because they grew hatefull to all Christian Princes, they retired to Barbary, where although there be not many good Harbours but Tunis, Argier, Sally, Mamora, and Tituane, there are many convenient Rodes, or the open Sea, which is theire chiefe Lordship: For their best harbours Massalqueber, the townes of Oran, Mellila, Tanger, and Cuta, within the Streights, are possessed by the Spaniards; without the Streights they have also Arzella, and Mazagan; Mamora likewise they have lately taken, and fortified. Ward, a poore English sailer, and Dansker a Dutchman, made first here their Marts, when the Moores knew scarce how to saile a ship; Bishop was Ancient, and did little hurt; but Easton got so much, as made himselfe a Marquesse in Savoy; and Ward lived like a Bashaw in Barbary; those were the first that taught the Moores to be men of warre. Gennings, Harris, Tompson, and divers others, were taken in Ireland, a Coast they much frequented, and died at Wapping. Hewes, Bough, Smith, Walsingam, Ellis, Collins, Sawkwell, Wollistone, Barrow, Wilson, Sayres, and divers others, all these were Captaines amongst the Pirats, whom King James mercifully pardoned; and was it not strange, a few of these should command the Seas. Notwithstanding the Malteses, the Pope, Florentines, Genoeses, Dutch, and English, Gallies, and Men of Warre, they would rob before their faces, and even at their owne Ports, yet seldome more than three, foure, five or six in a Fleet: many times they had very good ships, and well manned, but commonly in such factions amongst

Their chiefe randevouz.

Their conditions.

themselves, and so riotous, quarrellous, treacherous, blasphemous, and villanous, it is more than a wonder they could so long continue, to doe so much mischiefe; and all they got, they basely consumed it amongst Jewes, Turks, Moores, and whores.

[P. 60] The best was, they would seldome goe to Sea, so long as they could possibly live on shore, being compiled of English, French, Dutch, and Moores, (but very few Spanyards, or Italians) commonly running one from another, till they became so disjoynted, disordered, debawched, and miserable, that the Turks and Moores beganne to command them as slaves, and force them to instruct them in their best skill, which many an accursed runnagado or Christian turned Turke, did, till they have made those Sally men, or Moores of Barbary so powerfull as they be, to the terror of all the Straights, and many times they take purchase in the maine Ocean, yea sometimes even in the narrow Seas in England, and those are the most cruell villaines in Turkie, or Barbarie; whose natives are very noble, and of good natures, in comparison of them.

Runnagados.

Advertisements for wilde heads.

To conclude, the misery of a Pirate (although many are as sufficient Sea-men as any) yet in regard of his superfluity, you shall finde it such, that any wise man would rather live amongst wilde beasts than them; therefore let all unadvised persons take heed, how they entertaine that quality; and I could wish Merchants, Gentlemen, and all setters forth of ships, not to bee sparing of a competent pay, nor true payment; for neither Souldiers nor Sea-men can live without meanes, but necessity will force them to steale; and when they are once entered into that trade, they are hardly reclaimed. Those titles of Sea-men and Souldiers, have beene most worthily honoured and esteemed, but now regarded for most part, but as the scumme of the world; regaine therefore your wonted reputations, and endevour rather to adventure to those faire plantations of our English Nation; which however in the beginning were scorned and contemned, yet now you see how many rich and gallant people come from thence, who went thither as poore as any Souldier or Sailer, and gets more in one yeare, than you by Piracie in seven. I intreat you therefore to consider, how many thousands yearely goe thither; also how many Ships and Sailers are imployed to transport them, and what custome they yearely pay to our most Royall King Charles, whose prosperity and his Kingdomes good, I humbly beseech the immortall God ever to preserve and increase.

FINIS.

A Sea Grammar

A SEA GRAMMAR

With the Plaine Exposition of
Smiths Accidence for
young Sea-men,
enlarged.

Divided into fifteene Chapters: what they are you may partly conceive by the Contents.

Written by Captaine John Smith, sometimes Governour of Virginia, and Admirall of New-England.

LONDON,
Printed by John Haviland, 1627.

To all the Right Honourable, and most generous Lords in England, especially those of his Majesties Privy Councell, and Councell of Warre.

Great Lords,

Ulius Cæsar wrote his owne Commentaries, holding it no lesse honour to write, than fight; much hath bin writ concerning the art of war by land, yet nothing concerning the same at Sea. Many others might better than my selfe have done this, but since I found none endevourd it, I have adventured, encouraged by the good entertainment of my late printed Accidence. This I suppose will be much bettered by men in these things better experienced, others ignorance may fault it: I have beene a miserable Practitioner in this Schoole of Warre by Sea and Land more than thirty yeeres, however chance or occasion have kept me from your Lordships knowledge or imployment. Yet I humbly entreat your Lordships to accept and patronize this little Pamphlet, as the best testimony I can present your Honours, of my true duty to my King and Country. Thus humbly craving your Honours pardons, and favourable construction of my good intent, I remaine

Your Honours in all duty
to be commanded,

John Smith.

To the Reader
and all worthy Adventurers by Sea, and well-wishers to Navigation.

Honest Readers,

F my desire to doe good hath transported mee beyond my selfe, I intreat you excuse me, and take for requitall this rude bundle of many ages observations; although they be not so punctually compiled as I could wish, and it may bee you expect; At this present I cannot much amend them; if any will bestow that paines, I shall thinke him my friend, and honour his endevours. In the interim accept them as they are, and ponder errours in the balance of goodwill,

Your friend,

John Smith.

PANEGYRICK VERSES.

To his well deserving friend Captaine John Smith.

REader within this little worke thou hast
The view of things present, to come, and past,
Of consequence and benefit to such
As know but little, thinking they know much;
And in thy quiet chamber safely read,
Th' experience of the living and the dead,
Who with great paine and perill oft have tride
When they on angry Neptunes backe did ride.
He having with his Trident strucke the maine,
To hoise them up and throw them downe againe
Deare friend I'le cease and leave it to thy Booke.
To praise thy labour. Reader over-looke.

EDW. INGHAM.

To the much deserving Captaine, John Smith.

I Hate to flatter thee, but in my heart
I honour thy faire worth and high desert;
And thus much I must say, thy merits claime
Much praise & honor, both from Truth & Fame.
What Judge so e're thy Actions over-looke,
Thou need'st not feare a triall by thy Booke.

GEOR. BUCKE.

To his worthily-deserving friend Captaine John Smith.

THe Lighter Hippias of Troy disclos'd,
Germans in India Cannowes now in trade,
The Barge by grave Amocles was compos'd,
The Argozees first the Illyrians made,
The Galley Jason built that Græcian sparke,
The Cyprians first did crosse the Seas with Barke.

The Keele by the Phænicians first was nam'd,
The Tyrrhens first made anchors, Plateans oares;
The Rhodians for the Brigandine are fam'd,
Cyrenians found the Craer, and Creet adores
Dædal for Masts, and Saile-yards; Typhis wife
(With triple honour) did the sterne devise.

The Tackle famous Anacharsis wrought,
Noble Pyseus did the Stem first frame,
To light the Copians first the Rudder brought,
Young Icarus for Sailes acquir'd great fame,
Thou, with the best of these mai'st glory share,
Thou hast devis'd, compil'd a worke so rare.

For what long travels observations true
On Seas, (where waves doe seeme to wash the skies)
Have made thee know, thou (willing) do'st unscrew
To those that want like knowledge; each man cries
Live worthy Smith; England for this endevour
Will (if not stupid) give thee thanks for ever.

NICOLAS BURLEY.

In laudem Nobilissimi viri Johannis Smith.

MOney, the worlds soule, that both formes and fames her,
Is her bad Genius to, it damnes, and shames her.
If merit and desert were truly weighed
In Justice Scales, not all by money swey'd;

111

A Sea Grammar,

WITH

THE PLAINE EXPOSITION of SMITHS Accidence for young Sea-men, enlarged.

Diuided into fifteene Chapters: what they are you may partly conceiue by the Contents.

Written by Captaine IOHN SMITH, sometimes Gouernour of VIRGINIA, and Admirall of NEW-ENGLAND.

LONDON,
Printed by IOHN HAVILAND,
1627.

Smith should not want reward, with many moe,
  Whom sad oblivion now doth over-flow.
For now no good things gotten without money,
  Except tis got, as Beares from thornes licke honey,
With danger to themselves. For poore mens words
  Are wind, and aire : Great mens are pickes and swords.
Greatnesse more safe may act lust, theft, or treason,
  Than poore John Smith or I may steale two peason,
Or drinke a harmelesse cup, to chase away
  Sad cares and griefes that haunt us every day.
Who saw thy Virgin limbd by thee so truly,
  Would sweare thou hadst beene one that sawest her newly,
One of her latest lovers. But to tell
  The truth, I thinke they know her not so well.
And this Sea Grammar learn'd long since by thee,
  Thou now hast form'd so artificiallie,
That many a beardlesse boy, and Artlesse foole,
Preferr'd before thee, may come to thy schoole.

JOHN HAGTHORPE.

To his Friend Captaine Smith, on his Grammar.

MUch traveld Captaine, I have heard thy worth
  By Indians, in America set forth ;
Mee silence best seemes to keepe, and then
Thy better praise be sung by better men,
Who feele thy vertues worthinesse : Who can
Derive thy words, is more Grammarian,
Than Camden, Clenard, Ramus, Lilly were ;
Here's language would have non-plust Scaliger.
These and thy travels may in time be seene
By those which stand at Helme, and prime ones beene.

EDW. JORDEN.

In Authorem.

Techno-logicall, a Greeke word compounded of two Greeke words, τεχνὴ-λογὸς, signifies words of Art.

*Pr. 5. Genus. Species. *Differentia. Propriam. Accidens.*

EAch Science termes of Art hath wherewithall
To expresse themselves, calld Technologicall.
Logicke doth teach what Prædicables bee,
Genus and Species,* with the other three.
Philosophie, purblind in the first Creation,
Talks of first Matters forme, and void Privation.
Geographie teaches how for to define
Tropicks, Meridians, and the Æquators line.
So words of Art belong to Navigation
And ships, which here from thee receive translation;
That now th' untraveld land-man may with ease
Here know the language both of ships and Seas.
I have no Art of words due praise to impart
To thee that thus expound'st the words of Art.

W. S.

In Authorem.

THou which in Sea-learning would'st Clerk commence,
First learne to reade, and after reade to learne,
For words to sound, and not to know their sense,
Is for to saile a ship without a Sterne.
By this Sea Grammar thou mayst distinguish
And understand the Latine by the English.

Here mayst thou learne the names of all ships geere,
And with their names, their natures, and their use;
To hoise the Sailes, and at the Helme to steere;
To know each Shroud, each Rope, each Knot, each Noose,
And by their names to call them every one,
'Tis such a Booke as may be call'd Such none.

And yet a Smith thereof the Authour is,
And from his Forge alone we have the same,
Who, for his skill in such a worke as this,
Doth farre excell all others of his name:
He's neither Lock-Smith, Gold-Smith, nor Black-Smith,
But (to give him his right name) he's Jack Smith.

S. S.

The Contents.

A SEA GRAMMAR

THE CONTENTS

THE Expositions of all the most difficult words seldome used but amongst sea men: where you finde the word in the Margent in that breake against it: you shall find the exposition so plainly and briefly, that any willing capacity may easily understand them.

A Sea Grammar

Chap. I.

Of Dockes, and their definitions.

Docke is a great pit or pond, or creeke by a harbour side, made convenient to worke in, with two great floud-gates built so strong and close, that the Docke may be dry till the ship be built or repaired, and then being opened, let in the water to float and lanch her, and this is called a dry Docke. A wet Docke is any place, where you may hale in a ship into the oze out of the tides way, where shee may docke her selfe. A cradel is a frame of timber, made along a ship, or the side of a gally by her billidge, for the more ease and safty in lanching, much used in Turkie, Spaine, and Italy. And the stockes are certaine framed posts, much of the same nature upon the shore to build a Pinnace, a Catch, a Frigot, or Boat, &c. To those Dockes for building belongs their wood-yards, with saw-pits, and all sorts of timber, but the masts and yards are chained together in some great water to keepe them [P. 2] from rotting, and in season; Also a crab is necessary, which is an engine of wood of three clawes, placed on the ground in the nature of a Capsterne, for the lanching of ships, or heaving them into the Docke.

A dry Docke. *A wet Docke.* *A Cradle.* *The stockes.*

[Chap. II.

Chap. II.

How to build a ship with the definitions of all the principall names of every part of her principall timbers, also how they are fixed one to another, and the reasons of their use.

The Keele. THe first and lowest timber in a ship is the keele, to which is fastened all the rest; this is a great tree or more, hewen to the proportion of her burden, laid by a right line in the bottome of the docke, or stockes. At the one end is skarfed *The Stem.* into it, the Stem, which is a great timber wrought compassing, and all the butt-ends of the planks *The Sterne.* forwards are fixed to it. The Sterne post is another great timber, which is let into the keele at the other end some- *The fashion peeces.* what sloping, & from it doth rise the two fashion peeces, like a paire of great hornes, to those are fastened all the plankes that reach to the after end of the ship, but before *The Rungs.* you use any plankes, they lay the Rungs, called floore timbers, or ground timbers, thwart the keele; thorow *The Limberholes.* those you cut your Limberholes to bring the water to the well for the pumpe, the use of them is when the ship is built to draw in them a long haire rope, by pulling it from sterne to stem, to scowre them, and keepe them cleane from choaking.

The Floore. Those ground timbers doe give the floore of the ship, being straight, saving at the ends they begin to compasse, *Rungheads.* and there they are called the Rungheads, and doth direct [P. 3] the Sweepe or Mould of the Foot-hookes and Navell *Sweepe. Mould.* timbers, for there doth begin the compasse and bearing of the ship, those are skarfed into the ground timbers, *Skarfing.* which is one peece of wood let into another, or so much wood cut away from the one as from the other, for when any of those timbers are not long enough of themselves, they are skarfed in this manner, to make two or three as one: those next the keele are called the ground Foot-hookes, the other the upper Foot-hookes; but first lay your keeleson over your floore timbers, which is another long tree like the keele, and this lying within as the other without, must be fast bound together with strong iron bolts thorow the timbers and all, and on those are all the upper workes raised, when the Foot-hookes are skarfed, as is said, and well bolted, when they are planked up to the Orlop they make the ships Howle, and those timbers in generall are called the ships ribs, because they represent the carkasse of any thing hath ribs. The sleepers run before and after on each side the keeleson, on the floore well bolted to the Foot-hookes, which being thus bound doe strengthen each other. The Spurkits are the spaces betwixt the timbers alongst the ship side in all parts, but them in Howle below the Sleepers, are broad boords, which they take up to cleare the Spurkits, if any thing get betwixt the timbers.

Foot-hookes. *Keeleson.* *Howle.* *Ribs.* *Sleepers.* *Spurkits.*

The Garbord is the first planke next the keele on the outside, the Garbord strake is the first seame next the keele, your rising timbers are the hookes, or ground timbers and foot-hookes placed on the keele, and as they rise by little and little, so doth the run of the ship from the floore, which is that part of the ship under water which comes narrower by degrees from the floore timbers along to the sterne post, called the ships way aftward, for according to her run she will steare well or ill, by reason of the quicknesse or slownesse of the water comming to the rudder: now all those plankes under water, as they rise and are joyned one end to another, the fore end is called the Butt-end in all ships, but in great ships they are commonly most carefully bolted, for if one [P. 4] of those ends should spring, or give way it would be a great troublesome danger to stop such a leake, the other parts of those plankes are made fast with good Treenailes

The Garbord. *Garbord strake.* *Rising timbers.* *The Run.* *Plankes.* *Butt-ends.* *Treenailes.*

Trunnions. and Trunnions of well seasoned timber, thorow the timbers or ribs, but those plankes that are fastened into *Whoodings.* the ships stem are called whoodings.

The gathering of those workes upon the ships quarter *The Tucke.* under water is called the Tucke, if it lie too low it makes her have a fat quarter, and hinders the quicke passage of the water to the rudder; if too high she must be laid out in that part, else she will want bearing for her after *Transome.* workes. The Transome is a timber lies thwart the sterne, betwixt the two fashion peeces, and doth lay out the *Buttocks.* breadth of the ship at the buttockes, which is her breadth from the Tucke upwards, and according there to her breadth or narrownesse, we say she hath a narrow or broad buttocke, the fashion peeces, before spoke of, are the two outmost timbers, on either side the sterne, excepting the *Rake.* counters. The ships Rake is so much of her hull as hangs over both ends of the keele, so much as is forward is said, she rakes so much forward, and so in like manner *The Hull.* aftward: by the hull is meant, the full bulke or body of a ship without masts or any rigging from the stem to the sterne: The Rake forward is neere halfe the length of the keele, and for the Rake aftward about the forepart of her Rake forward, but the fore Rake is that which gives the ship good way, and makes her keep a good wind, but if she have not a full Bow, it will make her pitch her head much into the Sea; if but a small Rake forward, the sea will meet her so fast upon the Bowes, she will make small way, and if her sterne be upright as it were, *Bluffe.* she is called Bluffe, or Bluffe-headed. A ships Billage *Bluffeheaded.* *Billage.* is the breadth of the floore when she doth lie aground, & Billage water is that which cannot come to the pumpe, we say also she is bilged, when she strikes on a rocke, an anchors flooke or any thing that breakes her plankes or timbers, to spring a leake.

Plankes. [P. 5] When you have berthed or brought her up to the planks, which are those thicke timbers which goeth fore *Beames.* and aft on each side, whereon doth lie the beames of the *Orlop.* first Orlop, which is the first floore to support the plankes doth cover the Howle, those are great crosse timbers, that keepes the ship sides asunder, the maine beame is ever next the maine mast, where is the ships greatest breadth, the rest from this is called the first, second, third, fourth, &c. forward or aftward beames. Great ships have a tier of beames under the Orlop whereon lies no decke, and great posts and binders called Riders from them to the keele in howle only to strengthen all. But the beames of the Orlop is to be bound at each end with sufficient Knees, which is a crooked peece of wood bowed like a knee, that bindes the beames and foot-hookes, being bolted together, some stand right up and downe, some a long the ship, and are used about all the deckes, some sawed or hewed to that proportion, but them which grow naturally to that fashion are the best.

Riders.

Knees.

Lay the Orlop with good planke according to her proportion, so levell as may be is the best in a man of Warre, because all the Ports may be of such equall height, so that every peece may serve any Port, without making any beds or platformes to raise them, but first bring up your worke as before to the second decke or Orlop, and by the way you may cut your number of port holes according to the greatnesse of your ship; by them fasten your Ringbolts for the tackles of your Ordnances, you use Ringbolts also for bringing the plankes and wailes to the ship side, and Set bolts for forcing the workes and plankes together, Clinch bolts are clinched with a riveting hammer for drawing out. But Rag bolts are so jaggered that they cannot be drawne out. Fore locke bolts hath an eye at the end, whereinto a fore locke of iron is driven to keepe it from starting backe. Fend bolts are beat into the outside of a ship with the long head to save her sides from galling against other ships. Drive bolts is a long piece of iron to drive out a treenaile, or any such thing, besides divers others so usefull that without them [P. 6] and long iron spikes and nailes, nothing can be well done; yet I have knowne a ship built, hath sailed to and againe over the maine Ocean, which had not so

Ports.

Beds.

Ringbolts.

Set bolts.

Clinch bolts.

Rag bolts.

Fore locke bolts.

Fend bolts.

Drive bolts.

She was built of Cedar.

much as a naile of iron in her but onely one bolt in her keele.

Clamps. Now your risings are above the first Orlop as the Clamps are under it, which is long thicke plankes like them, fore and aft on both sides, under the ends of the Beames and timbers of the second Decke or Orlop, or the third Decke or Orlop, or the third Decke which is never called by the name of Orlop, and yet they are all but Decks; also the halfe Decke and quarter Decke, whereon the beames, and timbers beare are called risings. A Flush Decke is when from stem to sterne, it lies upon a right line fore and aft which is the best for a man of Warre, both for the men to helpe and succour one another, as for the using of their armes, or remounting any dismounted peece, because all the Ports on that Decke are on equall height, which cannot be without beds and much trouble, where the Decke doth camber or lie compassing. To sinke a Decke is to lay it lower, to raise a Decke to put it higher, but have a care you so cut your Port holes, one peece lie not right over another for the better bringing them to your marke.

Decks. A halfe Decke. A quarter Decke. A Flush Decke. A cambered Decke. To sinke a Deck. To raise a Deck.

The halfe Decke is from the maine mast to the steareage, & the quarter Decke from that to the Masters Cabin called the round house, which is the utmost of all; but you must understand all those workes are brought up together, as neere equally as may bee from bend to bend, or waile to waile, which are the outmost timbers on the ship sides, and are the chiefe strength of her sides, to which the foot-hookes, beames, & knees, are bolted, and are called the first, second, and third Bend; but the chaine waile is a broad timber set out amongst them, a little above where the chaines and shrouds are fastened together to spread the shrouds the wider the better to succour the masts. Thus the sides and Deckes are wrought till you come at the Gunwaile, which is the upmost waile goeth about the upmost strake or seame of the upmost Decke about the ships waste, and the ships quarter is from the maine mast aftward.

Bend, or waile. Chaine waile. Gun waile. [P. 7] *The ships quarters.*

Culvertailed is letting one timber into another in such sort that they cannot slip out, as the Carling ends are fixed in the beames, and Carlings are certaine timbers lieth along the ship from beame to beame, on those the ledges doe rest whereunto the plankes of the Deckes are fastened. The Carling knees are also timbers comes thwart the ship from the sides of the Hatches way, betwixt the two masts, and beares up the Decke on both sides, and on their ends lieth the commings of the hatches, which are those timbers and plankes which beares them up higher than the Deckes, to keepe the water from running downe at the hatches; also they fit Loopholes in them for the close fights, and they are likewise a great ease for men to stand upright if the Deckes be low. The Hatches way is when they are open where the goods are lowered that way right downe into the howle, and the hatches are like trap doores in the middest of the Deckes, before the maine mast, by certaine rings, to take up or lay downe at your pleasure.

Culvertailed *Carlings.* *Carling knees.* *Commings.* *Loopholes.* *Hatches way.*

A scuttle-hatch is a little hatch doth cover a little square hole we call the Scuttle, where but one man alone can goe downe into the ship, there are in divers places of the ship whereby men passe from Decke to Decke, and there is also small Scuttles grated, to give light to them betwixt Deckes, and for the smoke of Ordnances to passe away by. The Ramshead is a great blocke wherein is three shivers into which are passed the halyards, and at the end of it in a hole is reved the ties, and this is onely belonging to the fore and maine halyards; to this belong the fore Knight, and the maine Knight, upon the second Decke fast bolted to the Beames. They are two short thicke peeces of wood, commonly carved with the head of a man upon them, in those are foure shivers apeece, three for the halyards and one for the top rope to run in, and Knevels are small pieces of wood nailed to the inside of the ship, to belay the sheats and tackes unto.

A Scuttle. *Ramshead.* *The fore Knight.* *The main Knight.* *Knevels.*

The Capstaine is a great peece of wood stands upright upon the Decke, abaft the maine mast, the foot standing

Capstaine. [P. 8]

in a step upon the lower decke, and is in the nature of a windis, to winde, or weigh up the anchors, sailes, top masts, ordnances, or any thing; it is framed in divers squares, with holes thorow them, thorow which you put *Capstaine bars.* your Capstaine barres, for as many men as can stand at them to thrust it about, and is called manning the *The Spindle.* Capstaine. The maine body of it is called the Spindle. *Whelps.* The Whelps are short peeces of wood made fast to it, to keepe the Cable from comming too high in the turning *Paul.* about; The Paul is a short piece of iron made fast to the Decke, resting upon the whelps to keepe the Capstaine from recoiling which is dangerous, but in great ships they have two, the other standing in the same manner betwixt the fore mast and the maine, to heave upon the *Jeare Capstaine.* Jeare rope, and is called the Jeare Capstaine, to straine any rope, or hold off by, when we way Anchor, to heave a head, or upon the violl, which is when an Anchor is in stiffe ground wee cannot weigh it, or the Sea goeth so high the maine Capstaine cannot purchase in the Cable, then we take a Hawser opening one end, and so puts into it Nippers some seven or eight fadome distant from each other wherewith wee binde the Hawser to the Cable, and so brings it to the Jeare Capstaine to heave upon it, and this will purchase more than the maine Capstaine *The violl.* can. The violl is fastened together at both ends with an eye or two, with a wall knot and seased together. A *A windas.* windas is a square peece of timber, like a Role before the fore Castle in small ships, and forced about with hand-spikes for the same use as is the Capstaine.

The Pumpe. What are the parts of a pumpe you may see in every *The Brake.* place, the handle we call the brake, the pumpes can, is *The Can.* a great can we power water into pumps to make it pumpe. *The Daile.* The daile is a trough wherein the water doth runne over *Chained Pumps.* the Deckes; But in great ships they use chained pumps which will goe with more ease, and deliver more water. *A Bur Pump.* The Dutch men use a Burre pumpe by the ship side, wherein is onely a long staffe with a Burre at the end, like a Gunners spunge, to pumpe up the Billage water that by reason of the bredth of the ships floore cannot come to the well: In pumping they use to take spels, that is, fresh men to releeve them, and count how many strokes they pumpe each watch, whereby they know if the ship be stanch, or tight, or how her leakes increase. The Pumpe sucks, is when the water being out, it drawes up nothing but froth and winde. They have also a little Pumpe made of a Cane, a little peece of hollow wood or Latten like an Elder gun, to pumpe the Beere or Water out of the Caske, for at Sea wee use no Taps, and then stave the Caske to make more roome, and packeth the Pipe-staves or boords up as close as may be in other Caske till they use them. [P. 9] *The Pumpe sucks.* *A beere Pumpe.*

The Skuppers are little holes close to all the Decks thorow the Ships sides, whereat the water doth runne out when you pumpe or wash the Decks; the Skupper-leathers are nailed over those holes upon the lower Decke to keepe out the Sea from comming in, yet give they way for it to runne out: Skupper nailes are little short ones with broad heads, made purposely to naile the Skupper-leathers, and the cotes of Masts and Pumps. The Waist is that part of the Ship betwixt the maine Mast and the fore-castle, and the Waist boords are set up in the Ships waist, betwixt the Gun-waile and the waist trees, but they are most used in Boats, set up alongst their sides to keepe the Sea from breaking in. *The Skuppers.* *Skupper-leathers.* *Skupper-nailes.* *The Waist.* *Waist boords.* *Waist trees.*

There are usually three Ladders in a Ship; the entering Ladder is in the Waist, made formally of wood, and another out of the Gallery made of Ropes to goe into the boat by in foule weather, and the third at the Beak-head, made fast over the Boulspret to get upon it, onely used in great Ships. *The entering Ladder.* *Gallery Ladder.* *Boultspret Ladder.*

It were not amisse now to remember the Fore-castle, being as usefull a place as the rest, this is the forepart of the Ship above the Decks over the Bow; there is a broad Bow & a narrow Bow, so called according to the broadnes or the thinnesse: the Bow is the broadest part of the Ship before, compassing the Stem to the Loufe, which *The Fore-castle.* *Bow.* *Loufe.*

[P. 10] reacheth so farre as the Bulk-head of the Fore-castle extendeth. Against the Bow is the first breach of the Sea, if the Bow be too broad, she will seldome carry a *Cut a feather.* Bone in her mouth or cut a feather, that is, to make a fome before her: where a well bowed Ship so swiftly presseth the water, as that it foameth, and in the darke night sparkleth like fire. If the Bow bee too narrow, as before is said, she pitcheth her head into the Sea, so that the meane is the best if her after way be answerable. *Hauses.* The Hauses are those great round holes before, under the Beak-head, where commonly is used the Cables when you come to an Anchor, the bold or high Hause is the best, for when they lie low in any great sea, they will take in very much water, the which to keepe out, they build a circle of planke either abaft or before the maine *Manger.* Mast called the Manger: and a Hause plug at Sea, now the Fore-castle doth cover all those being built up like a halfe decke, to which is fixed the Beake-head, and the *Prow.* Prow is the Decke abaft the Fore-castle, whereon lyeth the Prow peeces.

The Beak-head. The Beak-head is without the ship before the fore Castle, supported by the maine knee, fastened into the stem, all painted and carved as the sterne, and of great use, as well for the grace and countenance of the ship, as a place for men to ease themselves in. To it is fastened the coller of the maine stay, and the fore tacks there brought aboord; also the standing for rigging and trimming the spretesaile geare, under the midest of it *Combe.* is the Combe, which is a little peece of wood with two *Bits.* holes in it to bring the fore tacks aboord. The Bits are *Crosspeece.* two great peeces of timber, and the Crospeece goeth thorow them, they are ordinarily placed abaft the Manger in the ships loofe, to belay the Cable thereto when you ride at Anchor: Their lower parts are fastened to the Riders, but the middle part in great ships are bolted to two great beames crosse to the Bowes, and yet in extraordinary stormes we are glad to make fast the Cable to the maine Mast for strengthning of the Bits and safety of the Bowes, which have in great stormes beene torne from the ships. The David is a short peece of timber, at the end whereof in a notch they hang a blocke in a strap called the Fish-block, by which they hale up the flook of the Anchor to the Ships bow, it is put out betwixt the Cat and the Loufe, and to be removed when you please. The Cat is also a short peece of timber aloft right over the Hawse; in the end it hath two shivers in a blocke, wherein is reeved a Rope, to which is fastned a great hooke of Iron, to trice up the Anchor from the Hawse to the top of the fore-castle. *David.* [P. 11] *Fish-block.* *Cat.*

A Bulks head is like a seeling or a wall of boords thwart the Ship, as the Gunroome, the great Cabin, the bread roome, the quarter Decke, or any other such division: but them which doth make close the fore-castle, and the halfe Decke, the Mariners call the Cubbridge heads, wherein are placed murtherers, and abaft Falcons, Falconets, or Rabinits to cleare the Decks fore and aft so well as upon the ships sides, to defend the ship and offend an enemy. Sockets are the holes wherein the pintels of the murderers or fowlers goe into. The hollow arching betwixt the lower part of the Gallery and the Transome, is called the lower Counter; the upper Counter is from the Gallery to the arch of the round house, and the Brackets are little carved knees to support the Galleries. *A Bulkes head.* *Cubbridge head.* *Sockets.* *Low Counter.* *Upper Counter.* *Brackets.*

The Stearage roome, is before the great Cabin, where he that steareth the Ship doth alwaies stand, before him is a square box nailed together with woodden pinnes, called a Bittacle, because iron nailes would attract the Compasse; this is built so close, that the Lampe or Candle only sheweth light to the stearage, and in it alwaies stands the Compasse, which every one knowes is a round box, and in the midst of the bottome a sharpe pin called a Center whereon the Fly doth play, which is a round peece of pace-boord, with a small wyer under it touched with the Load-stone, in the midst of it is a little brasse Cap that doth keepe it levell upon the Center. On the *The Stearage.* *Great Cabin.* *Bittacle.* *The Compasse.*

upper part is painted 32. points of the Compasse covered with glasse to keepe it from dust, breaking, or the wind; [P. 12] this Box doth hang in two or three brasse circles, so fixed they give such way to the moving of the Ship that still the Box will stand steady: there is also a darke Compasse, and a Compasse for the variation, yet they are but as the other, onely the darke Compasse hath the points blacke and white, and the other onely touched for the true North and South. Upon the Bittacle is also the Travas, which is a little round boord full of holes upon lines like the Compasse, upon which by the removing of a little sticke they keepe an account, how many glasses (which are but halfe houres) they steare upon every point. The Whip-staffe is that peece of wood like a strong staffe the Stearsman or Helmesman hath alwaies in his hand, going thorow the Rowle, and then made fast to the Tiller with a Ring.

A darke Compasse. *A Compasse for Variation.* *The Travas.* *The Whip-staffe.* *The Rowle.*

The Tiller is a strong peece of wood made fast to the Rudder, which is a great timber somewhat like a Planke, made according to the burthen of the ship, and hung at the sterne upon hookes and hinges, they call Pintels and Gudgions, or Rudder-irons. The Tiller playeth in the Gunroome over the Ordnances by the Whip-staffe; whereby the Rudder is so turned to and fro as the Helmesman pleaseth, and the Cat holes are over the Ports, right with the Capstaine as they can, to heave the Ship a sterne by a Cable or a Hauser called a sterne-fast. On each side the Stearage roome are divers Cabins, as also in the great Cabin, the quarter Decke, and the round house, with many convenient seates or Lockers to put any thing in, as in little Cupberts.

The Tiller. *Rudder.* *Pintels.* *Gudgions or Rudder-Irons.* *The Gun-roome.* *Cat holes.* *Lockers.*

The Bread-roome is commonly under the Gun-roome, well dried or plated. The Cook-roome where they dresse their victuall may bee placed in divers places of the Ship, as sometimes in the Hould, but that oft spoileth the victuall by reason of the heat, but commonly in Merchantmen it is in the Fore-castle, especially being contrived in Fornaces; besides in a chase their Sterne is that part of the ship they most use in fight, but in a man of warre

The bread-roome. *Cooke-roome.* *Sterne.*

they fight most with their Prow, and it is very troublesome to the use of his Ordnance, and very dangerous lying [P. 13] over the Powder-roome, some doe place it over the Hatches way, but that as the Stewards roome are ever to be contrived according to the Ships imploiment, &c. Calking is beating Okum into every seame or betwixt *Calking.* planke and planke, and Okum is old Ropes torne in *Okum.* peeces like Towze Match, or Hurds of Flax, which being close beat into every seame with a calking Iron and a *Calking-Iron.* Mallet, which is a hammer of wood and an iron chissell, being well payed over with hot pitch, doth make her more *Paying.* tight than it is possible by joyning Planke to Planke. Graving is onely under water, a white mixture of Tallow, *Graving.* Sope and Brimstone; or Train-oile, Rosin, and Brimstone boiled together, is the best to preserve her calking and make her glib or slippery to passe the water; and when it is decayed by weeds, or Barnacles, which is a *Barnacles, or* kinde of fish like a long red worme, will eat thorow all *Wormes.* the Plankes if she be not sheathed, which is as casing the Hull under water with Tar, and Haire, close covered over with thin boords fast nailed to the Hull, which though the Worme pierce, shee cannot endure the Tar. Breaming her, is but washing or burning of all the filth *Broming or* with reeds or broome, either in a dry dock or upon her *Breaming.* Careene; which is, to make her so light as you may *Careene.* bring her to lye on the one side so much as may be in the calmest water you can, but take heed you overset her not; and this is the best way to Breame Ships of great burthen, or those have but 4. sharpe Flores for feare of brusing or oversetting. Parsling is most used *Parsling.* upon the Decks and halfe Decks; which is, to take a list of Canvas so long as the seame is you would parsell, being first well calked, then powre hot pitch upon it, and it will keepe out the water from passing the seames. There remaines nothing now as I can remember to the building the Hull of a Ship, nor the definition of her most proper tearmes, but onely seeling the Cabins and such other parts as you please, and to bind an end with all things fitting for the Sea, as you may reade in the Covenants betwixt the Carpenter and the Owner, which are thus.

[P. 14]

Notes for a Covenant betweene the Carpenter and the Owner.

If you would have a Ship built of 400. Tuns, she requires a planke of 4. inches: if 300. Tuns, 3. inches: small Ships 2. inches, but none lesse. For clamps, middle bands and sleepers, they be all of six inch planke for binding within. The rest for the sparring up of the workes of square three inch planke. Lay the beames of the Orlope, if she be 400. Tuns at ten foot deepe in howle, and all the beames to be bound with two knees at each end, and a standard knee at every beames end upon the Orlope, all the Orlope to be laid with square three inch planke, and all the plankes to be treenailed to the beames.

Six foot would be betweene the beames of the Deck and Orlope, and ten ports on each side upon the lower Orlope, all the binding betweene them should bee with three inch or two inch planke, and the upper Decke should bee laid with so many beames as are fitting with knees to bind them; laying that Decke with spruce Deale of thirty foot long, the sap cut off, and two inches thicke, for it is better than any other.

Then for the Captaines Cabben or great Cabben, the Stearage, the halfe Decke, the Round house, the Fore-castle, and to binde an end with the Capsterne and all things fitting for the Sea, the Smiths worke, the carving, joyning, and painting excepted, are the principall things I remember to be observed, for a Charter-party betwixt the Merchant, the Master, and the Owner, you have Presidents of all sorts in most Scriveners shops.

Chap. III. [P. 15]

How to proportion the Masts and Yards for a Ship, by her Beame and Keele.

Hen a ship is built, she should be masted, wherein is a great deale of experience to be used so well as art; for if you overmast her, either in length or bignesse, she will lie too much downe by a wind, and labour too much a hull, and that is called a Taunt-mast, but if either too small or too short, she is under masted or low masted, and cannot beare so great a saile as should give her her true way. For a man of warre, a well ordered Taunt-mast is best, but for a long voyage, a short Mast will beare more Canvasse, and is lesse subject to beare by the boord: Their Rules are divers, because no Artist can build a Ship so truly to proportion, neither set her Masts, but by the triall of her condition, they may bee impayred or amended: suppose a Ship of 300. Tunnes be 29 foot at the Beame, if her maine Mast be 24. inches diameter, the length of it must be 24. yards, for every inch in thicknesse is allowed a yard in length, and the fore Mast 22. inches in thicknesse, must bee 22. yards in length; your Bowle spret both in length and thicknesse must bee equall to the fore Mast, the Misen 17. yards in length, and 17. inches diameter.

A Ship over-masted.

Taunt-masted.

Under-masted.

An example.

But the Rule most used is to take the 4-5th parts of the bredth of the Ship, and multiply that by three, will give you so many foot as your maine Mast should bee in length, the bignesse or thicknesse will beare it also, allowing an inch for a yard; but if it be a made Mast, that is greater than one Tree, it must be more: for

The rule most used.

A made Mast, or an arme Mast.

[P. 16] example, suppose the Ships bredth 30. foot, foure fifts of 30. foot are 24. foot, so you finde the maine Mast must be 24. yards long, for every yard is 3. foot and 24. inches thorow, allowing an inch to every yard. The fore Mast is to be in length 4-5ths of the maine Mast, which will be 20. yards wanting one 4-5ths part of a yard, and 20. inches thorow. The Boulspret must ever bee equall with the fore Mast. The misen Mast halfe the length of the maine Mast, which will be 12. yards long, and 12. inches diameter. Now as you take the proportion of the Masts from the Beame or bredth of the Ship, so doe you the length of the yards from the Keele.

The Steps. *Partners.* These Masts have each their steps in the Ship, and their partners at every Decke where thorow they passe to the Keele, being strong timbers bolted to the Beams in circling the Masts, to keep them steady in their steps fast wedged for rowling; yet some ships will not saile so wel as when it doth play a little, but that is very dangerous in foule weather. *Cotes.* *Tarpawling.* Their Cotes are peeces of tarred Canvas, or a Tarpawling put about them and the Rudder to keepe the water out. *Cheeks.* At the top of the fore Mast and maine Mast are spliced cheeks, or thicke clamps of wood, thorow which are in each two holes called the *The Hounds.* Hounds, wherein the Tyes doe runne to hoise the yards, but the top Mast hath but one hole or hound, and one *The Cap.* tye. Every Mast also hath a Cap if a top; which is a peece of square timber with a round hole in it to receive the top Masts or Flag-staffe, to keepe them steady and strong, lest they be borne by the boord in a stiffe gale. *Crosse-trees.* The Crosse-trees are also at the head of the Masts, one let into another crosse, and strongly bolted with the *Tressel-trees.* Tressell trees, to keepe up the top Masts which are fastened in them, and those are at the tops of each Mast; all the Masts stand upright but the Boulspret which lyeth along over the Beak-head, and that timber it resteth on *Pillow.* is called the Pillow.

An example of the Yards by the Keele. Now for the yards, suppose the ship be 76. foot at the Keele, her maine yard must be 21. yards in length, and in thickness but 17. inches. The fore Yard 19. yards long, and 15. inches diameter or thick. The spret-saile Yard 16. yards long, and but nine inches thicke, and your [P. 17] Misen-yard so long as the Mast, the top yards beares halfe proportion to the maine, and fore yard, and the top gallants, the halfe to them, but this rule is not absolute; for if your Masts be taunt, your yards must be the shorter; if a low Mast, the longer, but this is supposed the best. To have the maine Yard 5-6ths parts of her Keele in length: the top Yard 3-7ths of the maine Yard, and the maine Yard for bignesse 3-4ths parts of an inch, for a yard in length. The length of the fore Yard 4-5ths of the maine Yard; the Crossejacke Yard and Spretsaile Yard to be of a length; but you must allow the Misen Yard and Spretsaile Yard ½ inch of thicknesse to a yard in length. But to give a true Arithmeticall and Geometricall proportion for the building of all sorts of Ships, were they all built after one mould, as also of their Masts, Yards, Cables, Cordage, and Sailes, were all the stuffe of like goodnesse, a methodicall rule as you see might bee projected: but their lengths, bredths, depths, rakes and burthens are so variable and different, that nothing but experience can possibly teach it.

[Chap. IIII.

Chap. IIII.

The names of all the Masts, Tops, and Yards belonging to a Ship.

THe Boul-spret, the Spretsaile yard, the Spretsaile top-mast; the Spretsaile top saile yard; the fore Mast, the fore yard, the fore top mast, the fore top-saile yard, the fore top gallant Mast, the fore top gallant saile yard, Cotes, Wouldings, Gromits, and Staples for all yards. The maine Mast, the maine Yard, the maine Top. The
[P. 18] maine top Mast, the maine top-saile Yard. The top gallant Mast, the maine top gallant saile Yard. The Trucke is a square peece of wood at the top wherein you put the Flag-staffe. The Misen, the Misen Yard, the Misen top mast, the Misen top saile yard. The Crosse Jacke. In great ships they have two Misens, the latter is called the Bonaventure Misen. A Jury Mast, that is, when a Mast is borne by the boord, with Yards, Roofes, Trees, or what they can, spliced or fished together they make a Jury-mast, woulding or binding them with ropes fast triced together with hand-spikes, as they use to would or binde any Mast or Yard.

Chap. V.

How all the Tackling and Rigging of a Ship is made fast one to another, with their names, and the reasons of their use.

He rigging a Ship, is all the Ropes or Cordage belonging to the Masts and Yards; and it is proper to say, The Mast is well rigged, or the Yard is well rigged, that is, when all the Ropes are well sised to a true proportion of her burthen. We say also, when they are too many or too great, shee is over-rigged, and doth much wrong a Ship in her sailing; for a small waight aloft, is much more in that nature than a much greater below, and the more upright any Ship goeth, the better she saileth.

Riggage or Cordage. *A Mast well rigged.* *A Yard well rigged.* *Over rigged.*

All the Masts, Top-masts, and Flag-staves have staies, excepting the Spret saile-top Mast, the maine Masts stay is made fast by a Lannier to a Coller, which is a great Rope that comes about the head and Boulspret, the other end to the head of the maine Mast. The maine top-Masts stay is fastened to the head of the fore Mast by [P. 19] a strop and a dead mans eye. The maine top-gallant Masts stay in like manner to the head of the fore top-Mast. The fore Masts and stayes belonging to them in like manner are fastened to the Boulspret, and Spretsaile top-Mast, and those staies doe helpe to stay the Boulspret. The Misen staies doe come to the maine Mast, and the Misen top Mast staies to the shrouds with Crowes-feet: the use of those staies are to keepe the Masts from falling aftwards, or too much forwards. Those Lanniers are many small Ropes reeved into the dead mens eyes of all shrouds, either to slaken them or set them taught;

All Masts have staies except one. *A Coller.* *A Lannier.* *Dead mens eyes.* *Crowes-feet.*

also all the staies have their blocks, and dead mens eyes have Lanniers. Dead mens eyes are blocks, some small, some great, with many holes but no shivers, the Crowes-feet reeved thorow them are a many of small lines, sometimes 6. 8. or 10. but of small use more than for fashion to make the Ship shew full of small Ropes.

Blocks or Pullies. Shivers. A Cocke. Running ropes.

Blocks or Pullies are thick peeces of wood having shivers in them, which is a little Wheele fixed in the middest with a Cocke or Pin, some are Brasse, but the most of Wood, whereon all the running Ropes doe runne, some are little, some great, with 3. 4. or 5. shivers in them, and are called by the names of the Ropes whereto

Double blocks.

they serve. There are also double blocks, that where there is use of much strength will purchase with much ease, but not so fast as the other, and when wee hale any Tackle or Haleyard to which two blocks doe belong, when

Block and block.

they meet, we call that blocke and blocke.

All Masts have Shrouds, &c.

The Shrouds are great Ropes which goe up either sides of all Masts. The Misen maine Mast and fore Mast shrouds have at their lower ends dead mens eyes seased into them, and are set up taught by Lanniers to the chaines; at the other end, over the heads of those Masts are pendants, for Tackels and Swifters under them. The top-Masts shrouds in like manner are fastened with Lanniers and dead mens eyes to the Puttocks or plats of iron belonging to them, aloft over the head of the Mast

Chaines.

as the other: and the Chaines are strong plates of iron

[P. 20]

fast bolted into the Ships side by the Chaine-waile. When

To Ease.

the Shrouds are too stiffe, we say, ease them, when too

Taught.

slacke, we say, set Taught the Shrouds, but the Boulspret hath no Shrouds, and all those small ropes doe crosse the

Ratlings. Puttocks.

Shrouds like steps are called Ratlings. The Puttocks goe from the Shrouds of the fore Mast, maine Mast or Misen, to goe off from the Shrouds into the Top, Cap, or Bowle, which is a round thing at the head of either Mast for men to stand in, for when the Shrouds come neere the top of the Mast, they fall in so much, that without the Puttocks you could not get into the Top, and in a manner they are a kinde of a Shroud. A Pendant is a short rope made fast at one end to the head of the Mast or the Yards arme, having at the other end a blocke with a shiver to reeve some running rope in, as the Pendants of the backe staies and Tackles hang a little downe on the inside of the Shrouds: all Yards-armes have them but the Misen, into which the Braces are reeved, and also there are Pendants or Streamers hang from the yards armes, made of Taffaty, or coloured flanell cloth to beautifie the Ship onely: Parrels are little round Balls called Trucks, and little peeces of wood called ribs, and ropes which doe incircle the Masts, and so made fast to the Yards, that the Yards may slip up and downe easily upon the Masts, and with the helpe of the Brest-rope doth keepe the Yard close to the Mast. The standing ropes are the shrouds and staies, because they are not removed, except it be to be eased or set taughter. *Pendants.* *Parrels.* *Ribs.* *Brest-ropes.* *Standing ropes.*

The Tackles or ropes runne in three parts, having a Pendant with a blocke at the one end, and a blocke with a hooke at the other, to heave any thing in or out of the ship; they are of divers sorts, as the Botes tackles made fast the one to the fore shrouds, the other to the maine, to hoise the Bote in or out: also the tackles that keepe firme the Masts from straying. The Gunners tackles for haling in or out the Ordnances: but the winding tackle is the greatest, which is a great double blocke with three shivers to the end of a small Cable about the head of the Mast, and serveth as a Pendant. To which is made fast a Guy, which is a rope brought to it from the fore mast, to keepe the weight upon it steady, or from swinging to and againe: Into the blocke is reeved a hawser, which is also reeved thorow another double blocke, having a strop at the end of it; which put thorow the eye of the slings is locked into it with a fid, and so hoise the goods in or out by the helpe of the Snap-blocke. *The Tackles are of divers sorts, &c.* *A Guy.* [P. 21]

Cat harpings are small ropes runne in little blockes from one side of the ship to the other, neere the upper decke to keepe the shrouds tight for the more safety of *Cat harpings.*

Halyards. the mast from rowling. The Halyards belong to all masts, for by them wee hoise the yards to their height, *The Ties.* and the Ties are the ropes by which the yards doe hang, and doe carry up the yards when wee straine the Halyards; the maine yard and fore yard ties are first reeved thorow the Rams head, then thorow the Hounds, with a turne in the eye of the slings which are made fast to the yard; the missen yard and top yard have but single Ties, that is, one doth but run in one part, but the Spretsaile yard hath none, for it is made fast with a paire of slings to the *A Horse.* boltspret. A Horse is a rope made fast to the fore mast shrouds, and the Spretsaile sheats, to keepe those sheats cleare of the anchor flookes.

To Sling. *Slings.* To sling is to make fast any caske, yard, ordnances, or the like in a paire of Slings, and Slings are made of a rope spliced at either end into it selfe with one eye at either end, so long as to bee sufficient to receive the caske, the middle part of the rope also they seaze together, and so maketh another eye to hitch the hooke of the tackle, another sort are made much longer for the hoising of ordnances, another is a chaine of iron to Sling or binde the yards fast aloft to the crosse trees in a fight, lest the *Canhookes.* ties should bee cut, and so the mast must fall. The Canhookes are two hookes fastened to the end of a rope with a noose, like this the Brewers use to sling or carry their barrels on, and those serve also to take in or out hogs- *A Parbunkell.* heads, or any other commodities. A Parbunkel is two ropes that have at each end a noose or lumpe that being [P. 22] crossed, you may set any vessell that hath but one head upon them, bringing but the loopes over the upper end of the caske, fix but the tackle to them, and then the vessell will stand strait in the middest to heave out, or take in without spilling.

Puddings. Puddings are ropes nailed round to the yards armes close to the end, a pretty distance one from another, to save the Robbins from galling upon the yards, or to serve the anchors ring to save the clinch of the cable from *Robbins.* galling. And the Robbins are little lines reeved into the eylet holes of the saile under the head ropes, to make fast the saile to the yard, for in stead of tying, sea men alwayes say, make fast. Head lines, are the ropes that make all the sailes fast to the yard. *Head lines.*

Furling lines are small lines made fast to the top saile, top gallant saile, and the missen yards armes. The missen hath but one called the smiting line, the other on each side one, and by these we farthell or binde up the sailes. The Brales are small ropes reeved thorow Blockes seased on each side the ties, and come down before the saile, and at the very skirt are fastened to the Creengles, with them we furle or farthell our sailes acrosse, and they belong onely to the two courses and the missen: to hale up the Brales, or brale up the saile, is all one; Creengles are little ropes spliced into the Bolt-ropes of all sailes belonging to the maine and fore mast, to which the bolings bridles are made fast, and to hold by when we shake off a Bonnet. *Furling lines.* *A smiting line.* *Brales.* *Creengles.*

Boltropes is that rope is sowed about every saile, soft and gently twisted, for the better sowing and handling the sailes. Bunt lines is but a small rope made fast to the middest of the Boltrope to a creengle reeved thorow a small blocke which is seased to the yard, to trice or draw up the Bunt of the saile, when you farthell or make it up. The Clew garnet is a rope made fast to the clew of the saile, and from thence runnes in a blocke seased to the middle of the yard, which in furling doth hale up the clew of the saile close to the middle of the yard, and the clew line is the same to the top sailes top gallant and [P. 23] spret sailes, as the Clew garnet is to the maine and fore-sailes. The Clew of a saile is the lowest corner next the Sheat and Tackes, and stretcheth somewhat goaring or sloping from the square of the saile, and according to the Goaring she is said to spread a great or a little clew. Tackes are great ropes which having a wall-knot at one end seased into the clew of the saile, and so reeved first thorow the chestres, and then commeth in at a hole in the ships sides, this doth carry forward the clew of the saile *Bolt ropes.* *Bunt lines.* *Clew Garnet.* *Clew line.* *A Clew.* *Goaring.* *Tackes.*

Sheats. to make it stand close by a wind. The Sheats are bent to the clews of all sailes, in the low sailes they hale aft the clew of the sailes, but in top sailes they serve to hale them home, that is, to bring the clew close to the yards arme. *Braces.* The Braces belong to all yards but the missen, every yard hath two reeved at their ends thorow two pendants, and those are to square the yards, or travasse them as you please. *Boling.* The Boling is made fast to the leech of the saile about the middest to make it stand the sharper or closer by a wind, it is fastened by two, three, or foure ropes like a crows foot to as many parts of the saile which is called *Boling bridles.* the Boling bridles, onely the missen Boling is fastened to the lower end of the yard, this rope belongs to all sailes except the Spret-saile, and Spret-saile Top-saile, which not having any place to hale it forward by, they cannot *Sharp the Boling.* use those sailes by a wind: sharp the maine Boling is to hall it taught: hale up the Boling is to pull it harder *Checke the Boling.* forward on: checke or ease the Boling is to let it be more slacke.

Lee fanngs. Lee fanngs is a rope reeved into the creengles of the courses, when wee would hale in the bottome of the saile, *Reeving.* to lash on a bonnet or take in the saile; and Reeving is but drawing a rope thorow a blocke or oylet to runne up *Leech lines.* and down. Leech lines are small ropes made fast to the *Leech of a saile.* Leech of the top-sailes, for they belong to no other; and are reeved into a blocke at the yard close by the top-saile ties, to hale in the Leech of the saile when you take them in. The Leech of a saile is the outward side of a skirt *Earings.* of a saile, from the earing to the clew; and the Earing is [P. 24] that part of the bunt rope which at all the foure corners of the saile is left open as it were a ring. The two upmost parts are put over the ends of the yards armes, and so made fast to the yards, and the lowermost are seased or *Bent.* Bent to the sheats, and tackes into the clew. *Lifts.* The Lifts are two ropes which belong to all yards armes, to top the yards; that is, to make them hang higher or lower at your pleasure. But the top-saile Lifts doe serve for sheats to the top gallant yards, the haling them is called the Topping the Lifts, as top a starboard, or top a port. *Topping the Lifts.*

Legs are small ropes put thorow the bolt ropes of the maine and fore saile, neere to a foot in length, spliced each end into the other in the leech of the saile, having a little eye whereunto the martnets are fastened by two hitches, and the end seased into the standing parts of the martnets, which are also small lines like crow feet reeved thorow a blocke at the top mast head, and so comes downe by the mast to the decke; but the top-saile martnets are made fast to the head of the top gallant mast, and commeth but to the top, where it is haled and called the top martnets, they serve to bring that part of the leech next the yards arme up close to the yard. Latchets are small lines sowed in the Bonnets and Drablers like loops to lash or make fast the Bonnet to the course, or the course to the Drabler, which we call lashing the Bonnet to the course, or the Drabler to the Bonnet. The Loofe hooke is a tackle with two hookes, one to hitch into a cringle of the maine, or fore saile, in the bolt rope in the leech of the saile by the clew, and the other to strap spliced to the chestres to bouse or pull downe the saile to succour the tackes in a stiffe gale of wind, or take off or put on a Bonnet or a Drabler, which are two short sailes to take off or put to the fore course or the maine, which is the fore saile, or maine saile. *Legs.* *Martnet.* *Latchets.* *Lashing.* *The Loofe hook.* *Bouse.* *A Bonnet.* *A Drabler.* *A Course.*

The Knave-line is a rope hath one end fastened to the crosse trees, and so comes downe by the ties to the Rams head, to which is seased a small peece of wood some two foot long with a hole in the end, whereunto the line is reeved, and brought to the ships side, and haled taught to the Railes to keepe the ties and Halyards from turning about one another when they are new. Knettels are two rope yarnes twisted together, and a knot at each end, whereunto to sease a blocke, a rope, or the like. Rope yarnes are the yarnes of any rope untwisted, they serve to sarve small ropes, or make Sinnet, Mats, Plats, or Caburnes, and make up the at the sailes yards armes. *A Knave line.* [P. 25] *Knettels.* *Rope yarnes.*

Sinnet. Sinnet is a string made of rope yarne commonly of two, foure, six, eight or nine strings platted in three parts, which being beat flat they use it to sarve ropes or *Mats or Panch.* Mats. That which we call a Panch, are broad clouts, woven of Thrums and Sinnet together, to save things from galling about the maine and fore yards at the ties, and also from the masts, and upon the Boltspret, Loufe, Beakehead or Gunwaile to save the clewes of the sailes *Caburne.* from galling or fretting. Caburne is a small line made of spun yarne to make a bend of two Cables, or to sease the *Seasing.* Tackels, or the like. Seasing is to binde fast any ropes together, with some small rope yarne. Marline is any line, to a blocke, or any tackell, Pendant, Garnet, or the like. There is also a rope by which the Boat doth ride *Seasen.* by the ships side, which we cal a Seasen. To sarve any *Sarve or Sirvis.* rope with plats or Sinnet, is but to lay Sinnet, Spun yarne, Rope yarne, or a peece of Canvas upon the rope, and then rowle it fast to keepe the rope from galling about the shrowds at the head of the masts, the Cable in the Hawse, the flooke of the Anchor, the Boat rope or any thing. *Spunyarne.* Spun yarne is nothing but rope yarne made small at the ends, and so spun one to another so long as you will with *Caskets.* a winch. Also Caskets are but small ropes of Sinnet made fast to the gromits or rings upon the yards, the longest are in the midst of the yards betwixt the ties, and are called the brest Caskets, hanging on each side the yard in small lengths, only to binde up the saile when it is furled.

Marling. Marling is a small line of untwisted hemp, very pliant and well tarred, to sease the ends of Ropes from raveling out, or the sides of the blockes at their arses, or if the saile [P. 26] rent out of the Boltrope, they will make it fast with marlin *Marling spike.* till they have leisure to mend it. The marling spike, is but a small peece of iron to splice ropes together, or open *Splicing.* the bolt rope when you sew the saile. Splicing is so to *A round Splice.* let one ropes end into another they shall be as firme as if they were but one rope, and this is called a round Splice; *A cut Splice.* but the cut Splice is to let one into another with as much distance as you will, and yet bee strong, and undoe when you will. Now to make an end of this discourse with a knot, you are to know, Sea-men use three, the first is called the Wall knot, which is a round knob, so made with the strouds or layes of a rope, it cannot slip; the Sheates, Takes, and Stoppers use this knot. The Boling knot is also so firmely made and fastened by the bridles into the creengles of the sailes, they will breake, or the saile split before it will slip. The last is the Shepshanke, which is a knot they cast upon a Runner or Tackle when it is too long to take in the goods, and by this knot they can shorten a rope without cutting it, as much as they list, and presently undoe it againe, and yet never the worse.

A Knot.

A Wall knot.

A Boling knot.

Sheepshanks Knot.

[Chap. VI.

Chap. VI.

What doth belong to the Boats and Skiffe with the definition of all those thirteene Ropes which are onely properly called Ropes belonging to a ship and the Boat and their use.

A long Boat. OF Boats there are divers sorts, but those belonging to ships, are called either the long Boat or ships Boat, which should bee able to weigh her sheat anchor, those will live in any reasonable sea, especially the long Boat; great ships have also other small Boats called Shallops and Skiffes, which are with more ease and lesse trouble rowed to and againe upon any small occasion. To a Boat belongs a mast and saile, a stay sheat & Halyard, Rudder & Rudder irons, as to a ship, also in any discovery they use a Tarpawling, which is a good peece of Canvas washed over with Tar, to cover the Bailes or hoopes over the sterne of their Boat, where they lodge in an harbor which is that you call a Tilt covered with wadmall in your Wherries; or else an Awning, which is but the boats saile, or some peece of an old saile brought over the yard and stay, and boumed out with the boat hooke, so spread over their heads, which is also much used, as well a shore as in a ship, especially in hot countreys to keepe men from the extremity of heat or wet which is very oft infectious. Thoughts are the seats whereon the Rowers sit; and Thowles small pins put into little holes in the Gunwaile or upon the Boats side, against which they beare the oares when they row, they have also a Daved, and also in long Boats a windlesse to weigh the anchor by, which is with more ease than the ship can. The two arching timbers

A Shallop. *A Skiffe.* [P. 27] *Tarpawling.* *Bailes.* *Awning.* *Thoughts.* *Thowles.*

against the Boat head are called Carlings. Man the Boat is to put a Gang of men, which is a company into her, they are commonly called the Coxswaine Gang who hath the charge of her. Free the Boat is to baile or cast out the water. Trim the Boat is to keepe her straight. Winde the Boat is to bring her head the other way. Hold water is to stay her. Forbeare is to hold still any oare you are commanded, or on the broad, or whole side. A fresh Spell is to releeve the Rowers with another Gang, give the Boat more way for a dram of the bottell, who saies Amends, one and all, Vea, vea, vea, vea, vea, that is, they pull all strongly together.

A Gang. *Free or Baile.* *Trim Boat.* *Winde Boat.* *Holde water.* *Forbeare.* *A Spell.* *Vea, vea, vea.*

The Entering rope is tied by the ships side, to hold by as you goe up the Entering ladder, cleats, or wailes. *The Entering rope.*

The Bucket rope that is tied to the Bucket by which you hale and draw water up by the ships side. *Bucket rope.*

The Bolt ropes are those wherein the sailes are sowed. *Bolt ropes.*

The Port ropes hale up the Ports of the Ordnances. *Port ropes.*

The Jeare rope is a peece of a hawser made fast to the maine yard, another to the fore yard close to the ties, reeved thorow a blocke which is seased close to the top, and so comes downe by the mast, and is reeved thorow another blocke at the bottome of the mast close by the decke; great ships have on each side the ties one, but small ships none: the use is to helpe to hoise up the yard to succour the ties, which though they breake yet they would hold up the mast. *Jeare rope.* [P. 28]

The Preventer rope is a little one seased crosse over the ties, that if one part of them should breake, yet the other should not runne thorow the Rams head to indanger the yard. *Preventer rope.*

The Top ropes are those wherewith we set or strike the maine or fore Top masts, it is reeved thorow a great blocke seased under the Cap, reeved thorow the heele of the Top mast thwart ships, and then made fast to a ring with a clinch on the other side the Cap, the other part comes downe by the ties, reeved into the Knights, and so brought to the Capstaine when they set the Top masts. *Top ropes.*

Keele ropes. The Keele rope, you have read in the building, is of haire in the Keele to scower the Limber holes.

Rudder rope. The Rudder rope is reeved thorow the stem post, and goeth thorow the head of the Rudder, and then both ends spliced together, serves to save the Rudder if it should bee strucke off the irons.

Cat rope. The Cat rope is to hale up the Cat.

Boy rope. The Boy rope is that which is tied to the boy by the one end, and the anchors flooke by the other.

Boat rope. The Boat rope is that which the ship doth tow her Boat by, at her sterne.

Ghest rope. *Shearing.* The Ghest rope is added to the Boat rope when shee is towed at the ships sterne, to keepe her from shearing, that is, from swinging to and againe; for in a stiffe gale she will make such yawes, and have such girds, it would indanger her to bee torne in peeces, but that they use to *Swifting.* swift her, that is, to incircle the Gunwaile with a good rope, and to that make fast the Ghest rope.

Chap. VII. [P. 29]

The names of all sorts of Anchors, Cables, and Sailes, and how they beare their proportions, with their use. Also how the Ordnances should bee placed, and the goods stowed in a ship.

He proper tearmes belonging to Anchors are many: the least are called Kedgers, to use in calme weather in a slow streame, or to kedg up and downe a narrow River, which is when they feare the winde or tide may drive them on shore; they row by her with an Anchor in a boat, and in the middest of the streame, or where they finde most fit if the Ship come too neere the shore, and so by a Hawser winde her head about, then waigh it againe till the like occasion, and this is kedging. There is also a streame Anchor not much bigger, to stemme an easie stream or tide. Then there is the first, second, and third Anchor, yet all such as a Ship in faire weather may ride by, and are called Bow Anchors. The greatest is the sheat Anchor, and never used but in great necessity. They are commonly made according to the burthen of the Ship by proportion, for that the sheat Anchor of a small ship will not serve for a Kedger to a great ship. Also it beareth a proportion in it selfe, as the one flooke, which is that doth sticke in the ground, is but the third part of the shanke in length; at the head of the Shanke there is a hole called an Eye, and in it a Ring, wherein is the Nut to which there is fast fixed a Stocke of wood crossing the Flookes, and the length is taken from the length of the Shanke. These differ not in shape but in waight, from

A Kedger. *Streame Anchor.* *The first. Second. Third Anchor. Sheat Anchor.* *An Anchors shanke. Flook. Shoulder. Beame or Nut. Eye. Ring. Stocke.* [P. 30]

two hundred, to three or foure thousand waight. Grapells, or Graplings, are the least of all, and have foure flookes but no stock; for a boat to ride by, or to throw into a ship in a fight, to pull downe the gratings or hold fast.

A Cable, the first, second, and third. The Cables also carry a proportion to the Anchors, but if it be not three stroud, it is accounted but a Hawser, yet a great ships Hawser may be a Cable to the sheat Anchor for a small ship: and there is the first, second, and third *Sheat Anchor Cable.* Cable, besides the Sheat Anchor Cable. If the Cable bee *Keckell.* well made, we say it is well laid. To keckell or sarve the Cable, as is said, is but to bind some old clouts to keepe it *Splice.* from galling in the Hawse or Ring. Splice a Cable, is to fasten two ends together, that it may be double in length, *A shot of Cable.* to make the Ship ride with more ease, and is called a shot *Quoile.* of Cable. Quoile a Cable, is to lay it up in a round Ring, *A Fake.* or fake one above another. *Pay.* Pay more Cable, is when you carry an Anchor out in the boat to turne over. *Pay cheape.* Pay cheap, is when you over set it, or turnes it over boord faster. *End for end.* Veere more Cable, is when you ride at Anchor. And end for end is when the Cable runneth cleere out of the Hawse, *A Bight.* or any Rope out of his shiver. A Bight is to hold by any *A Bitter.* part of a coile, that is, the upmost fake. A Bitter is but the turne of a Cable about the Bits, and veare it out by *A Bitters end.* little and little. And the Bitters end is that part of the *Gert.* Cable doth stay within boord. Gert, is when the Cable is so taught that upon the turning of a tide, a Ship cannot goe over it.

To bend. To bend the Cable to the Anchor, is to make it fast to *Unbend.* the Ring; unbend the Cable, is but to take it away, which we usually doe when we are at Sea, and to tie two ropes *Bending.* or Cables together is called bending. *Hitch.* Hitch, is to catch hold of any thing with a rope to hold it fast, or with a hooke, as hitch the fish-hooke to the Anchors flooke, or the *Fenders.* Tackles into the Garnets of the Slings. Fenders are *Junkes.* peeces of old Hawsers called Junkes hung over the ships sides to keepe them from brusing. In boats they use poles or boat-hooks to fend off the boat from brusing. A

[P. 31] Brest-fast is a rope which is fastened to some part of the Ship forward on, to hold her head to a wharfe or any thing, and a Sterne-fast is the same in the Sterne. The use for the Hawser is to warp the Ship by, which is laying out an Anchor, and winde her up to it by a Capsterne. Rousing is but pulling the slacknesse of any Cables with mens hands into the Ship. The Shank-painter is a short chaine fastend under the fore masts shrouds with a bolt to the ships sides, and at the other end a rope to make fast the Anchor to the Bow. To stop is when you come to an Anchor, and veares out your Cable, but by degrees till the Ship ride well, then they say stop the Ship. To those Cables and Anchors belongs short peeces of wood called Boyes, or close hooped barrels like Tankards as is said, but much shorter, to shew you the Anchor and helpe to waigh it, there is another sort of Cans called Can Boyes much greater, mored upon shoules to give Marriners warning of the dangers.

Brestfast. *Sternfast.* *Rousing.* *Shank-panter.* *Stop.* *Boyes.* *Can Boyes.*

The maine saile and the fore saile is called the fore course, and the maine course or a paire of courses. Bonits and Drablers are commonly one third part a peece to the saile they belong unto in depth, but their proportion is uncertaine; for some will make the maine saile so deepe, that with a shallow bonet they will cloath all the Mast without a Drabler, but without bonets we call them but courses; we say, lash on the bonet to the course, because it is made fast with Latchets into the eylot holes of the saile, as the Drabler is to it, and used as the wind permits. There is also your maine top-saile, and fore top-saile, with their top-gallant sailes, and in a faire gaile your studding sailes, which are bolts of Canvasse, or any cloth that will hold wind, wee extend alongst the side of the maine saile, and boomes it out with a boome or long pole, which we use also sometimes to the clew of the maine saile, fore saile, and spret saile, when you goe before the wind or quartering, else not. Your Miszen, and Miszen top-saile, your Spret and Spret top-saile, as the rest, take all their names of their yards. A Drift saile is onely used

Sailes. *Maine Saile.* *Fore Saile.* *Maine course.* *Fore course.* *Bonits.* *Drablers.* *Maine top Saile.* *Fore top Saile.* *Top gallant Sailes.* *Studding Sailes.* *Misen.* *Misen top Saile.* *Spret saile.* *Spret saile top-Saile.* *Drift Saile.*

[P. 32] under water, veared out right a head by sheats, to keepe the Ships head right upon the Sea in a storme, or when a ship drives too fast in a current. A Netting saile is onely a saile laid over the Netting, which is small ropes from the top of the fore castle to the Poope, stretched upon the ledges from the Waist-trees to the Roufe-trees, which are onely small Timbers to beare up the Gratings from the halfe Decke to the fore-castle, supported by Stantions that rest upon the halfe Decke; and this Netting or Grating, which is but the like made of wood, you may set up or take downe when you please, and is called the close fights fore and aft. Now the use of those sailes is thus, all head Sailes which are those belonging to the fore Mast and Boltspret, doe keepe the Ship from the wind or to fall off. All after sailes, that is, all the sailes belonging to the maine Mast and Miszen keepes her to wind ward, therefore few ships will steare upon quarter winds with one saile, but must have one after saile, and one head saile. The sailes are cut in proportion as the Masts and Yards are in bredth and length, but the Spret-saile is ¾ parts the depth of the fore saile, and the Miszen by the Leech twise so deepe as the Mast is long from the Decke to the Hounds. The Leech of a saile is the outward side or skirt of the saile from the earing to the clew, the middle betwixt which wee account the Leech. The Clew is the lower corner of a Saile, to which you make fast your Sheates and Tacks, or that which comes goring out from the square of the saile, for a square saile hath no Clew, but the maine saile must bee cut goring, because the Tacks will come closer aboord, and so cause the saile to hold more wind; now when the Saile is large and hath a good Clew, we say she spreds a large Clew, or spreds much Canvas. In making those sailes they use two sorts of seames downe the Sailes, which doth sow the bredth of the Canvas together, the one we call a Munke seame, which is flat, the other a round seame, which is so called because it is round.

Netting Saile. Nettings. Waist-trees. Roufe-trees. Stantions. Gratings. Head Sailes. After Sailes. Leech. The Clew. Goring. A Monke seame. A Round seame.

The Ship being thus provided, there wants yet her

Ordnances, which should be in greatnesse according to her building in strength and burthen, but the greatest commonly lieth lowest, which we call the lower tier, if she bee furnished fore and aft. Likewise the second Tier, and the third, which are the smallest. The fore-Castle and the halfe Decke being also furnished, wee account halfe a Tier. [P. 33]

A Tier. Third. Second. Halfe a Tier.

Stowage or to stow, is to put the goods in Howle in order. The most ponderous next the Ballast, which is next the Keelson to keepe her stiffe in the Sea. Balast is either Gravell, Stones, or Lead, but that which is driest, heaviest, and lies closest is best. To finde a leake, they trench the Ballast, that is, to divide it. The Ballast wil sometimes shoot, that is, run from one side to another, and so will Corne and Salt, if you make not Pouches or Bulk-heads, which when the Ship doth heeld is very dangerous to overset or turne the Keele upwards. For Caske that is so stowed, tier above tier with Ballast, and canting Coines, which are little short peeces of wood or Billets cut with a sharpe ridge or edge to lye betwixt the Caske; and standing Coines are Billets or Pipe-staves, to make them they cannot give way nor stirre. The ship will beare much, that is, carry much Ordnance or goods, or beare much saile; and when you let any thing downe into the Howle, lowering it by degrees, they say, Amaine; and being downe, Strike.

Stowage. To Stow. Ballast. Trench the Ballast. Shout. Canting Coines. Standing Coines. To beare.

[P. 34]

Chap. VIII.

The charge and duty of the Captaine of a ship, and every Office and Officer in a man of Warre.

The Captaines charge.

THe Captaines charge is to command all, and tell the Master to what Port hee will goe, or to what Height; In a fight he is to give direction for the managing thereof, and the Master is to see the cunning of the ship, and trimming of the sailes.

The Master and his Mates.

The Master and his Mates are to direct the course, command all the Sailers, for stearing, trimming, and sailing the ship; his Mates are only his seconds, allowed sometimes for the two mid ships men, that ought to take charge of the first prise.

The Pilot.

The Pilot when they make land doth take the charge of the ship till he bring her to harbour.

The Chirurgion and his Mate.

The Chirurgion is to be exempted from all duty, but to attend the sicke, and cure the wounded: and good care would be had he have a certificate from Barber Chirurgions Hall of his sufficiency, and also that his chest be well furnished both for Physicke and Chirurgery, and so neare as may be proper for that clime you goe for, which neglect hath beene the losse of many a mans life.

The Cape-merchant or Purser.

The Cape-merchant or Purser hath the charge of all the Carragasoune or merchandize, and doth keepe an account of all that is received, or delivered, but a man of Warre hath onely a Purser.

The Gunner with his Mate, and quarter Gunners.

The Master Gunner hath the charge of the ordnance,

and shot, powder, match, ladles, spunges, wormes, cartrages, armes and fire-workes; and the rest of the Gunners, or quarter Gunners to receive their charge from him according to directions, and to give an account of their store. [P. 35]

The Carpenter and his Mate.

The Carpenter and his Mate, is to have the nailes, clinches, roove and clinch nailes, spikes, plates, rudder irons, pumpe nailes, skupper nailes and leather, sawes, files, hatchets and such like, and ever ready for calking, breaming, stopping leakes, fishing, or splicing the masts or yards as occasion requireth, and to give an account of his store.

The Boatswaine and his Mate.

The Boatswaine is to have the charge of all the cordage, tackling, sailes, fids and marling spikes, needles, twine, saile-cloth, and rigging the ship, his Mate the command of the long boat, for the setting forth of anchors, weighing or fetching home an anchor, warping, towing, or moring, and to give an account of his store.

The Trumpeter.

The Trumpeter is alwayes to attend the Captaines command, and to sound either at his going a shore, or comming aboord, at the entertainment of strangers, also when you hale a ship, when you charge, boord, or enter; and the poope is his place to stand or sit upon, if there bee a noise, they are to attend him, if there be not, every one hee doth teach to beare a part, the Captaine is to incourage him, by increasing his shares, or pay, and give the master Trumpeter a reward.

The Marshall.

The Marshall is to punish offenders, and to see justice executed according to directions; as ducking at the yards arme, haling under the keele, bound to the capsterne, or maine mast with a basket of shot about his necke, setting in the bilbowes, and to pay the Cobtie or the Morioune; but the boyes the Boatswaine is to see every Munday at the chest, to say their compasse, and receive their punishment for all their weekes offences, which done, they are to have a quarter can of beere, and a basket of bread, but if the Boatswaine eat or drinke before hee catch them, they are free.

The Corporall. The Corporall is to see the setting and releeving the watch, and see all the souldiers and sailers keepe their armes cleane, neat, and yare and teach them their use. [P. 36]

The Steward & his Mate. The Steward is to deliver out the victuals according to the Captaines directions, and messe them foure, five, or six, as there is occasion.

The quarter Masters. The quarter Masters have the charge of the howle, for stowing, romaging, and trimming the ship in the hold, and of their squadrons for the watch, and for fishing to have a Sayne, a fisgig, a harpin yron, and fish hookes, for Porgos, Bonetos, Dolphins, or Dorados, and rayling lines for Mackrels.

The Cooper and his Mate. The Cooper is to looke to the caske, hoopes and twigs, to stave or repaire the buckets, baricos, cans, steepe tubs, runlets, hogsheads, pipes, buts, &c. for wine, beare, sider, beverage, fresh water, or any liquor.

The Coxswaine and his Mate. The Coxswaine is to have a choise Gang to attend the skiffe to goe to and againe as occasion commandeth.

The Cooke and his Mate. The Cooke is to dresse and deliver out the victuall, hee hath his store of quarter cans, small cans, platters, spoones, lanthornes, &c. and is to give his account of the remainder.

The Swabber. The Swabber is to wash and keepe cleane the ship and maps.

The Lyar. The Liar is to hold his place but for a weeke, and hee that is first taken with a lie, every Munday is so proclaimed at the maine mast by a generall cry, a Liar, a Liar, a Liar, hee is under the Swabber, and onely to keepe cleane the beake head, and chaines.

The Sailers. The Sailers are the ancient men for hoising the sailes, getting the tacks aboord, haling the bowlings, and stearing the ship.

The Younkers. The Younkers are the young men called fore-mast men, to take in the top-sailes, or top and yard, for furling the sailes, or slinging the yards, bousing or trising, and take their turnes at helme.

The Lieutenant his place. The Lieutenant is to associate the Captaine, and in his absence to execute his place, hee is to see the Marshall and Corporall doe their duties, and assist them in instructing the souldiers, and in a fight the fore-castle is his place to [P. 37] make good, as the Captaine doth the halfe decke, and the quarter Masters, or Masters Mate the mid ships, and in a States man of Warre, he is allowed as necessary as a Lieutenant on shore.

[Chap. IX.

Chap. IX.

Proper Sea tearmes for dividing the company at Sea, and stearing, sayling, or moring a Ship in faire weather, or in a storme.

Steep Tubs.

IT is to bee supposed by this the Ship is victualled and manned, the voiage determined, the steepe Tubs in the chains to shift their Beefe, Porke, or Fish in salt water, till the salt be out though not the saltnesse, and all things else ready to set saile; but before wee goe any further, for the better understanding the rest, a few words for stearing and cunning the Ship would not bee amisse.

Starboord. Larboord. Cunning. Stearing. Mid-ships. Port.

Then know, Star-boord is the right hand, Lar-boord the left; Starboord the Helme, is to put the Helme a Starboord, then the ship will goe to the Larboord. Right your Helme, that is, to keepe it in the mid ships, or right up. Port, that is, to put the Helme to Larboord, and the Ship will goe to the Starboord, for the Ship will ever goe contrary to the Helme.

A loofe. Keep your loofe. War no more. No neare. Ease. [P. 38] Steady. Yare.

Now by a quarter wind, they will say aloofe, or keepe your loofe, keepe her to it, have a care, of your Lee-latch. Touch the wind, and warre no more, is no more but to bid him at the Helme to keepe her so neere the wind as may be; no neere, ease the Helme, or beare up, is to let her fall to Lee-ward. Steady, that is, to keepe her right upon that point you steare by; be yare at the Helme, or a fresh man to the Helme. But he that keepes the Ship most from yawing doth commonly use the lest motion with the Helme, and those steare the best.

Geare.

The Master and company being aboord, he commands them to get the sailes to the yards, and about your geare or worke on all hands, stretch forward your maine Halliards, hoise your Sailes halfe mast high. Predy, or make ready to set saile, crosse your yards, bring your Cable to the Capsterne; Boatswaine fetch an Anchor aboord, breake ground or weigh Anchor. Heave a head, men into the Tops, men upon the yards; come, is the Anchor a pike, that is, to heave the Hawse of the ship right over the Anchor, what is the Anchor away? Yea, yea. Let fall your fore-saile. Tally, that is, hale off the Sheats; who is at the Helme there, coile your Cables in small fakes, hale the Cat, a Bitter, belay, loose fast your Anchor with your shank-painter, stow the Boat, set the land, how it beares by the Compasse that we may the better know thereby to keep our account and direct our course, let fall your maine saile, every man say his private prayer for a boone voyage, out with your spret saile, on with your bonits & Drablers, steare steady & keep your course, so, you go wel.

Predy.

A Pike.

Tally.

When this is done, the Captaine or Master commands the Boatswaine to call up the company; the Master being chiefe of the Starboord watch doth call one, and his right hand Mate on the Larboord doth call another, and so forward till they be divided in two parts, then each man is to chuse his Mate, Consort, or Comrade, and then devide them into squadrons according to your number and burthen of your ship as you see occasion; these are to take their turnes at the Helme, trim sailes, pumpe, and doe all duties each halfe, or each squadron for eight Glasses or foure houres which is a watch, but care would bee had that there be not two Comrades upon one watch because they may have the more roome in their Cabbins to rest. And as the Captaine and masters Mates, Gunners, Carpenters, Quartermasters, Trumpeters, &c. are to be abaft the Mast, so the Boatswaine, and all the Yonkers or common Sailers under his command is to be before the Mast. The next is, to messe them foure to a messe, and then give every messe a quarter Can of beere and a basket of bread to stay their stomacks till the Kettle be boiled, that they

How they divide the company at sea, and set, and rule the watch.

[P. 39]

may first goe to prayer, then to supper, and at six à clocke sing a Psalme, say a Prayer, and the Master with his side begins the watch, then all the rest may doe what they will till midnight; and then his Mate with his Larboord men with a Psalme and a Prayer releeves them till foure in the morning, and so from eight to twelve each other, except some flaw of winde come, some storme or gust, or some accident that requires the helpe of all hands, which commonly after such good cheere in most voyages doth happen.

The wind veeres. *Tally.* For now the wind veeres, that is, it doth shift from point to point, get your Starboord tacks aboord, and tally or hale off your Lee-Sheats. The Ship will not wayer, settle your maine Topsaile, veere a fadome of your sheat. The wind comes faire againe and a fresh gale, hale up the slatch of the Lee-boling. By Slatch is meant the middle part of any rope hangs over boord. Veere more *Flowne.* sheat, or a flowne sheat, that is, when they are not haled *Fly.* home to the blocke. But when we say, let fly the sheats, then they let go amaine, which commonly is in some gust, lest they spend their topsailes, or if her quicke side lie *A paire of courses.* in the water, overset the ship. A flowne sheat is when shee goes before the wind, or betwixt a paire of sheats, or all sailes drawing. But the wind shrinkes, that is, when you must take in the Spretsaile, and get the tacks aboord, hale close the maine Boling, that is, when your Tacks are close aboord. If you would saile against the wind or keepe your owne, that is, not to fall to lee-ward or goe backe againe, by halling off close your Bolings, you set your sailes so sharp as you can to lie close by a wind, thwarting it a league or two, or more or lesse, as you see cause, first on the one boord then on the other; this we call boording or beating it up upon a tacke in the [P. 40] winds eye, or bolting to and againe; but the longer your boords are, the more you worke or gather into the wind. If a sudden flaw of wind should surprise you, when you would lower a yard so fast as you can, they call A maine; but a crosse saile cannot come neerer the wind than six points, but a Carvell whose sailes stand like a paire of Tailers sheeres, will goe much neerer.

It over-casts we shall have wind, fowle weather, settell your top sailes, take in the spret-saile, in with your top-sailes, lower the fore-saile, tallow under the parrels, brade up close all them sailes, lash sure the ordnance, strike your top-masts to the cap, make it sure with your sheeps feet. A storme, let us lie at Trie with our maine course, that is, to hale the tacke aboord, the sheat close aft, the boling set up, and the helme tied close aboord. When that will not serve then Try the mizen, if that split, or the storme grow so great she cannot beare it; then hull, which is to beare no saile, but to strike a hull is when they would lie obscurely in the Sea, or stay for some consort, lash sure the helme a lee, and so a good ship will lie at ease under the Sea as wee terme it. If shee will weather coile, and lay her head the other way without loosing a saile, that must bee done by bearing up the Helme, and then she will drive nothing so farre to Leeward. They call it hulling also in a calme swelling Sea, which is commonly before a storme, when they strike their sailes lest she should beat them in peeces against the mast by Rowling. We say a ship doth Labour much when she doth rowle much any way; but if she will neither Try nor Hull, Then Spoone, that is, put her right before the wind, this way although shee will rowle more than the other, yet if she be weake it will not straine her any thing so much in the Trough of the Sea, which is the distance betwixt two waves or Billowes. If none of this will doe well, then she is in danger to founder, if not sinke. Foundering is when she will neither veere nor steare, the Sea will so over rake her, except you free out the water, she will lie like a log, and so consequently sinke. To spend a mast or yard, is when they are broke by fowle weather, and to spring a mast is when it is cracked in any place.

How to handle a ship in a storme. *Try.* *Hull.* *Under the Sea.* *Weather coile.* *Rowling.* *Labour.* *Spoone.* *Trough.* *Founder.* *To spend a mast.* *Spring a mast.*

In this extremity he that doth cun the ship cannot have too much judgement, nor experience to try her drift, or how she capes, which are two tearmes also used in the [P. 41]

A Yoke. trials of the running or setting of currants. A yoke is when the Sea is so rough as that men cannot govern the Helme with their hands, & then they sease a block to the Helme on each side at the end, & reeving two fals thorow them like Gunners Tackles brings them to the ships side, and so some being at the one side of the Tackle, some at the other, they steare her with much more ease than they can with a single rope with a double Turne about the Helme.

When the storme is past, though the wind may alter three or foure points of the compasse, or more, yet the Sea for a good time will goe the same way; then if your course be right against it, you shall meet it right a head, *A head Sea.* so we call it a head Sea. Sometimes when there is but little wind, there will come a contrary Sea, and presently the winde after it, wherby we may judge that from whence it came was much winde, for commonly before any great storme the Sea will come that way. Now if the ship may runne on shore in ose or mud she may escape, or Billage on a rocke, or Ancors flooke, repaire her leake, but if she split or sinke, shee is awracke. But seeing the storme decreaseth, let us trie if she will endure the *Hullocke.* Hullocke of a Saile, which sometimes is a peece of the mizen saile or some other little saile, part opned to keepe her head to the sea, but if yet shee would weather coile, wee will loose a Hullocke of her fore-saile, and put the Helme a weather, and it will bring her head where her sterne is; courage my hearts.

It cleares up, set your fore-saile; Now it is faire weather, *Lardge. Laske.* out with all your sailes, goe lardge or laske, that is, when we have a fresh gale, or faire wind, and all sailes drawing. But for more haste unparrell the mizen yard and lanch it, and the saile over her Lee quarter, and fit Gives at the further end to keepe the yard steady, and with a Boome *Goosewing.* boome it out; this we call a Goose-wing. Who is at Helme there? Sirra you must be amongst the Points; [P. 42] Well Master the Channell is broad enough; Yet you cannot steare betwixt a paire of sheats; Those are words of mockery betwixt the Cunner and the Stearesman. But to proceed,

Get your Larboord Tackes aboord, hale off your starboord sheats, keepe your course upon the point you are directed, Port, he will lay her by the lee; the staies, or backe staies, that is, when all the sailes flutter in the winde, and are not kept full, that is full of wind, they fall upon the masts and shrowds, so that the ship goes a drift upon her broad side, fill the sailes, keepe full, full and by. Make ready to Tacke about, is but for every man to stand to handle the sailes and ropes they must hale; Tacke about is to beare up the helme, and that brings her to stay all her sailes lying flat against the shrowds, then as she turnes wee say shee is payed, then let rise your Lee-tacks and hale off your sheats, and trim all your sailes as they were before, which is cast of that Boling which was the weather boling, and hale up taught the other. So all your Sheats, Brases, and Tackes are trimmed by a winde as before. To belay, is to make fast the ropes in their proper places. Round in, is when the wind larges, let rise the maine *Round in.* tacke and fore tacke, and hale aft the fore sheat to the cats head, and the maine sheat to the cubbridge head, this is Rounding in, or rounding aft the saile; the sheats being *Rounding aft.* there they hale them downe to keepe them firme from flying up with a Pasarado, which is any rope wherewith *Pasarado.* wee hale downe the sheats, blockes of the maine or fore saile, when they are haled aft the clew of the maine saile to the Cubbridge head of the maine mast, and the clew of the fore saile to the Cat head; Doe this when the ship goes large.

Observe the height, that is, at twelve a clocke to take *Observe.* the height of the Sunne, or in the night the North star, or in the forenoone and afternoone, if you misse these by finding the Azimuth and Alnicanter. Dead water is the *Dead water.* Eddie water followes the sterne of the ship, not passing away so quickly as that slides by her sides. The wake *The wake.* of a ship is the smooth water a sterne shewing the way shee hath gone in the sea, by this we judge what way [P. 43]

she doth make, for if the wake be right a sterne, we know
she makes good her way forwards; but if to Lee-ward a
point or two, wee then thinke to the Lee-ward of her
course, but shee is a nimble ship that in turning or tacking
about will not fall to the Lee-ward of her wake when
Disimbogue. shee hath weathered it. Disimbogue is to passe some
narrow strait or currant into the maine Ocean, out of some
A Drift. great Gulfe or Bay. A Drift is any thing floating in the
Rockweed. sea that is of wood. Rockweed doth grow by the shore,
and is a signe of land, yet it is oft found farre in the Sea.
Dipsie line Lay the ship by the Lee to trie the Dipsie line, which is
a small line some hundred and fifty fadome long, with
a long plummet at the end, made hollow, wherein is put
tallow, that will bring up any gravell; which is first marked
at twenty fadome, and after increased by tens to the end;
and those distinguished by so many small knots upon each
little string that is fixed at the marke thorow the strouds
or middest of the line, shewing it is so many times ten
Plummet. fadome deepe, where the plummet doth rest from drawing
the line out of your hand; this is onely used in deepe
water when we thinke we approach the shore, for in the
maine sea at 300. fadomes we finde no bottome. Bring
the ship to rights, that is, againe under saile as she was,
Log line. some use a Log line, and a minute glasse to know what
way shee makes, but that is so uncertaine, it is not worth
the labour to trie it.

Land to. One to the top to looke out for land, the man cries out
Kenning. Land to; which is just so farre as a kenning, or a man
To lay a land. may discover, descrie, or see the land. And to lay a land
Good land fall. is to saile from it just so farre as you can see it. A good
Bad land fall. Land fall is when we fall just with our reckoning, if other-
A head land. wise a bad Land fall; but however how it beares, set it
A Point. by the compasse, and bend your Cables to the Anchors.
Lande marke. A Head land, or a Point of land doth lie further out at
To raise a land. sea than the rest. A Land marke, is any Mountaine,
To make land. Rocke, Church, Windmill or the like, that the Pilot can
A Reach. know by comparing one by another how they beare by
[P. 44] the compasse. A Reach is the distance of two points so

farre as you can see them in a right line, as White Hall and London Bridge, or White Hall and the end of Lambeth towards Chelsey. Fetch the Sounding line, this is bigger than the Dipsie line, and is marked at two fadome next the lead with a peece of blacke leather, at three fadome the like, but slit; at 5. fadome with a peece of white cloth, at 7. fadome with a peece of red in a peece of white leather, at 15. with a white cloth, &c. The sounding lead is six or seven pound weight, and neere a foot long, he that doth heave this lead stands by the horse, or in the chaines, and doth sing fadome by the marke 5. o. and a shaftment lesse, 4. o. this is to finde where the ship may saile by the depth of the water. Fowle water is when she comes into shallow water where shee raises the sand or ose with her way yet not touch the ground, but shee cannot feele her helme so well as in deepe water.

Sounding line. *The Lead.* *Fowle water.*

When a ship sailes with a large wind towards the land, or a faire wind into a harbour, we say she beares in with the land or harbour. And when she would not come neere the land, but goeth more Roome-way than her course, wee say she beares off; but a ship boord, beare off is used to every thing you would thrust from you. Beare up is to bring the ship to goe large or before the wind. To Hold off is when we heave the Cable at the Capsterne, if it be great and stiffe, or slimie with ose, it surges or slips backe unlesse they keep it close to the whelps, and then they either hold it fast with nippers, or brings it to the Jeare Capsterne, and this is called Holding off. As you approach the shore, shorten your sailes, when you are in harbour take in your sailes, and come to an anchor, wherein much judgement is required.

Beare in. *Beare off.* *Beare up.* *Hold off.* *Surges.*

To know well the soundings, if it be Nealed to, that is, deepe water close aboord the shore, or shallow, or if the Lee under the weather shore, or the lee shore be sandy, clay, osie, or fowle and rockie ground, but the Lee shore all men would shun that can avoid it. Or a Roade which is an open place neere the shore. Or the Offing which is the open Sea from the shore, or the middest of any

Neale to. *A Roade.* *Offing.*

[P. 45] great streame is called the Offing. *Land locked.* Land locke, is when the land is round about you.

To Ride. Now the ship is said to Ride, so long as the Anchors doe hold and comes not home. *Ride a great Roade.* To Ride a great roade is when the winde hath much power. They will strike their top masts, and the yards alongst ships, and the deeper *Ride a stresse.* the water is, it requires more Cable; when wee have rid in any distresse wee say wee have rid hawse full, because *Ride betwixt. Wind and tide.* the water broke into the hawses. To ride betwixt wind and tide, is when the wind & tide are contrary & of equall power, which will make her rowle extremely, yet not *Ride thwart tide.* straine much the cable. To Ride thwart is to ride with her side to the tide, and then she never straines it. *Ride a pike.* To ride apike is to pike your yards when you ride amongst *Ride crosse.* many ships. To ride acrosse is to hoise the maine and fore yards to the hounds, and topped alike. When the water is gone and the ship lies dry, we say she is *Sewed.* Sewed; if her head but lie dry, she is Sewed a head; but if she *Sew.* cannot all lie dry, she cannot Sew there. *Water borne.* Water borne is when there is no more water than will just beare her from *Water line.* the ground. The water line is to that Bend or place she should swim in when she is loaded.

To More. Lastly, to More a ship is to lay out her anchors as is most fit for her to ride by, and the wayes are divers; as *More crosse.* first, to More a faire Berth from any annoiance. To More a crosse is to lay one anchor to one side of the streame, and the other to the other right against one another, and *More alongst.* so they beare equally ebbe and flood. To More alongst is to lay an anchor amidst the streame ahead, and another *Water shot.* asterne, when you feare driving a shore. Water shot is to more quartering betwixt both nether crosse, nor alongst the tide. In an open rode they will more that way they thinke the wind will come the most to hurt them. *More Proviso.* To more a Proviso, is to have one anchor in the river, and a hawser a shore, which is mored with her head a shore; otherwise two cables is the least, and foure cables the best to more by.

Chap. X. [P. 46]

Proper tearmes for the Winds, Ebbes, Floods, and Eddies, with their definitions, and an estimate of the depth of the Sea, by the height of the Hils and the largenesse of the Earth.

Hen there is not a breath of wind stirring, it is a calme or a starke calme. A Breze is a wind blowes out of the Sea, and commonly in faire weather beginneth about nine in the morning, and lasteth till neere night; so likewise all the night it is from the shore which is called a Turnado, or a Sea-turne, but this is but upon such coasts where it bloweth thus most certainly, except it be a storme, or very fowle weather, as in Barbaria, Ægypt, and the most of the Levant. We have such Brezes in most hot countreys in Summer, but they are very uncertaine. A fresh Gale is that doth presently blow after a calme, when the wind beginneth to quicken or blow. A faire Loome Gale is the best to saile in, because the Sea goeth not high, and we beare out all our sailes. A stiffe Gale is so much wind as our top-sailes can endure to beare. An Eddie wind is checked by the saile, a mountaine, turning, or any such thing that makes it returne backe againe. It over blowes when we can beare no top-sailes. A flaw of wind is a Gust which is very violent upon a sudden, but quickly endeth. A Spout in the West Indies commonly falleth in those Gusts, which is, as it were, a small river falling entirely from the clouds, like out of our water Spouts, which make the Sea where it falleth rebound in [P. 47] flashes exceeding high. Whirle winds runneth round, and bloweth divers wayes at once. A storme is knowne to

A Calme. *A Breze.* *A fresh gale.* *A Loome gale.* *Eddie wind.* *It over blowes.* *A Gust.* *A Spout.* *A whirle winde.* *A Storme.*

A Tempest. every one not to bee much lesse than a tempest, that will blow downe houses, and trees up by the roots. A *A Mounsoune.* Mounsoune is a constant wind in the East Indies, that bloweth alwayes three moneths together one way, and the *A Hericano.* next three moneths the contrary way. A Hericano is so violent in the West Indies, it will continue three, foure, or five weekes, but they have it not past once in five, six, or seven yeeres; but then it is with such extremity that the Sea flies like raine, and the waves so high, they over flow the low grounds by the Sea, in so much, that ships have been driven over tops of high trees there growing, many leagues into the land, and there left, as was Captaine Francis Nelson an Englishman, and an excellent Sea-man for one.

Becalmed. We say a calme sea, or Becalmed, when it is so smooth the ship moves very little, and the men leap over boord *A Rough Sea.* to swim. A Rough Sea is when the waves grow high. *An overgrowne Sea. Surges.* An overgrowne Sea when the surges and billowes goe *The Rut of the Sea.* highest. The Rut of the sea where it doth dash against *The Roaring of the Sea.* any thing. And the Roaring of the Sea is most commonly observed a shore, a little before a storme or after a storme.

Floods & ebbes. Flood is when the water beginneth to rise, which is young flood as we call it, then quarter flood, halfe flood, full Sea, still water, or high water. So when it Ebbes, quarter ebbe, halfe ebbe, three quarter ebbe, low water, or dead low water every one doth know; and also that as at a spring tide the Sea or water is at the highest, so at a Neape tide it is at the lowest. This word Tide, is *A Tide of ebbe.* common both to Flood and Ebbe; for you say as well *A Tide of flood.* tide of ebbe, as tide of flood, or a windward Tide when *A windward Tide.* the Tide runnes against the streame, as a Lee-warde Tide, *A Lee-ward tide.* that is, when the wind and the Tide goeth both one way, which makes the water as smooth as the other rough. To *To Tide over.* Tide over to a place, is to goe over with the Tide of ebbe or flood, and stop the contrary by anchoring till the next Tide, thus you may worke against the wind if it [P. 48] *A Tide gate.* over blow not. A Tide gate is where the tide runneth *Tide and halfe Tide.* strongest. It flowes Tide and halfe Tide, that is, it will be halfe flood by the shore, before it begin to flow in the channell; for although the Tide of flood run aloft, yet the Tide of ebbe runnes close by the ground. An Eddie tide is where the water doth runne backe contrary to the tide, that is, when some headland or great point in a River hindereth the free passage of the streame, that causeth the water on the other side the point to turne round by the shore as in a circle, till it fall into the tide againe.

Eddie Tide.

As touching the reasons of ebbes and floods, and to know how far it is to the bottome of the deepest place of the Sea, I will not take upon me to discourse of; as knowing the same to be the secrets of God unrevealed to man: only I will set downe a Philosophicall speculation of divers mens opinions touching the depth of the Sea; which I hope will not be thought much impertinent to the subject of this booke by the judicious Reader.

Fabianus in Plinie, and Cleomides conceived the depth of the Sea to be fifteene furlongs, that is, a mile and $\frac{7}{8}$ parts, Plutarch compared it equall to the highest mountaines, Scallinger and others conceited the hils farre surpassed the deepnesse of the Sea, and that in few places it is more than a hundered paces in depth; it may bee hee meant in some narrow Seas; but in the maine Ocean experience hath taught us it is much more than twice so much, for I have sounded 300. fadome, yet found no ground. Eratosthenes in Theon that great Mathematitian writeth the highest mountain perpendicular is but ten furlongs, that is, one mile and a quarter. Also Dicæarcus affirmeth this to be the height of the hill Pelius in Thessalia, but Xenagoras in Plutarch observed the height of Olimpus in the same region to be twenty paces more, which is 1270. paces, but surely all those meane onely those mountaines in or about Greece where they lived and were best acquainted; but how these may compare with the Alps in Asia, Atlas in Africa, Caucasus in India, the Andes in Peru, and divers others hath not yet beene examined.

The height of mountaines perpendicular.

The height of the hils compared with the superficies of the earth and depth of the Sea.

[P. 49]

But whatsoever the hils may be above the superficies of the earth, many hold opinion the Sea is much deeper, who suppose that the earth at the first framing was in the superficies regular and sphericall, as the holy Scriptures directs us to beleeve; because the water covered and compassed all the face of the earth, also that the face of the earth was equall to that of the Sea. Damascen noteth, that the unevennesse and irregularity which now is seene in the earths superficies, was caused by taking some parts out of the upper face of the earth in sundry places to make it more hollow, and lay them in other places to make it more convex, or by raising up some part and depressing others to make roome and receit for the Sea, that mutation being wrought by the power of the word of the Lord, Let the waters be gathered into one place that the dry land may appeare. As for Aquinas, Dionysius, Catharianus, and some Divines that conceited there was no mutation, but a violent accumulation of the waters, or heaping them up on high is unreasonable; because it is against nature, that water being a flexible and a ponderous body, so to consist and stay it selfe, and not fall to the lower parts about it; where in nature there is nothing to hinder it, or, if it be restrained supernaturally by the hand and bridle of Almighty God, lest it should over-whelme and drowne all the land, it must follow, that God even in the very institution of nature imposed a perpetuall violence upon nature. And this with all, that at the Deluge there was no necessity to breake up the springs of the deepe and to open the cattaracts of Heaven, and powre downe water continually so many daies and nights together, seeing the only with-drawing of that hand, or letting goe of that bridle which restraineth the water would presently have overwhelmed all.

How all the hils and dry land above the superficies of the Sea hath made roome for the Sea, therefore they are in equall height & depth.

[P. 50]

But both by Scriptures, the experience of Navigators, and reason in making estimation of the depth of the Sea, reckon not onely the height of the hils above the common superficies of the earth, but the height of all the dry land above the superficies of the Sea, because the whole masse of earth that now appeareth above the waters, being taken as it were out of the places which the waters now possesse, must be equall to the place out of which it was taken; so consequently it seemeth, that the height or elevation of the one should answer the descending or depth of the other; and therefore in estimating the depth of the Sea, wee consider not onely the erection of the hils above the ordinary land, but the advantage of the dry land above the Sea; which latter, I meane the height of the ordinary maine land, excluding the hils, which properly answer the extraordinary deepes and whirle-pooles in the Sea. The rest is held more in large Continents above the Sea, than that of the hils is above the land.

That there is small difference betwixt the springs first rising out of the earth, and their falling into the Sea.

For that the plain face of the dry land is not level, or equally distant from the Center, but hath a great descent towards the Sea, and a rising towards the mid-land parts, although it appeare not plainly to the eye, yet to reason it is most manifest; because we find that part of the earth the Sea covereth descendeth lower and lower towards the Sea. For the Sea, which touching the upper face of it, is knowne by nature to be levell and evenly distant from the center, is observed to wax deeper & deeper the further one saileth from the shore towards the maine Ocean: even so in that part which is uncovered, the streamings of Rivers on all sides from the mid-land parts towards the Sea, sliding from the higher to the lower declareth so much, whose courses are some 1000. or 2000. miles, in which declination, Pliny in his derivation of water requireth one cubit of declining in 240. foot of proceeding. But Columella, Viturnius, Paladius, and others, in their conduction of waters require somewhat lesse; namely, that in the proceeding of 200. foot forward, there should bee allowed one foot of descending downeward, which yet in the course of 1000. miles, as Danubius, Volgha, or Indus, &c. have so much or more, which will make five miles of descent in perpendicular account, and in the course of 2000. or more, as Nilus, Niger, and the River of the Amazons have 10. miles or more of the like descent.

[P. 51]

The determination of these questions.

These are not taken as rules of necessity, as though water could not runne without that advantage, for that respect the conveyers of waters in these times content themselves with one inch in 600. foot, as Philander and Viturnius observed, but is rather under a rule of commodity for expedition and wholsomnesse of water so conveyed, lest resting too long in pipes it should contract some unwholsome condition, or else through the slacknesse of motion, or long closenesse, or banishment from the aire, gather some aptnesse and disposition to putrifie. Although I say, such excesse of advantage as in the artificiall conveyance of waters the forenamed Authors require, be not of necessity exacted in the naturall derivation of them, yet certaine it is, that the descent of rivers being continually and their course long, and in many places swift, and in some places headlong and furious; the differences of height or advantage cannot be great betwixt the springs of the rivers and their out lets, betwixt the first rising out of the earth and their falling into the Sea: unto which declinity of land seeing the deepenesse of the Sea in proportion answer as I before declared, and not onely to the height of the hils: it is concluded, that the deepenesse to bee much more than the Philosophers commonly reputed: and although the deepnesse of the Sardinian Sea, which Aristotle saith, was the deepest of the Mediterranean, recorded by Posidonius in Strabo, to have beene found but 1000. fadome, which is but a mile and a fifth part, and the greatest bredth not past 600. miles: then seeing if in so narrow a Sea it be so deepe, what may we esteeme the maine Ocean to be, that in many places is five times so broad, seeing the broader the Seas are, if they be intire and free from Ilands, they are answerably observed to be the deeper. If you desire any further satisfaction, reade the first part of Purchas his Pilgrimage, where you may reade how to find all those Authors at large. Now because he hath taken neere 100. times as much from me, I have made bold to borrow this from him, seeing he hath sounded such deepe waters for this our Ship to saile in, being a Gentleman whose person I loved, and whose memory and vertues I will ever honour.

Note the difference betwixt the springs of the rivers, and their falling into the Sea is not great.

[P. 52]

Chap. XI.

Proper Sea tearmes belonging to the good or bad condition of Ships, how to finde them and amend them.

A Ship that will try hull, and ride well at Anchor, we call a wholsome Ship. A long Ship that drawes much water will doe all this, but if she draw much water and be short, she may hull well, but neither try nor ride well; if she draw little water and be long, she may try and ride well, but never hull well, which is called an unwholsome ship. The howsing in of a Ship is when shee is past the bredth of her bearing she is brought in narrow to her upper workes: it is certaine this makes her wholsome in the Sea without rowling, because the weight of her Ordnance doth counterpoise her bredth under water, but it is not so good in a man of warre, because it taketh away a great deale of her roome, nor will her tacks ever so well come aboord as if she were laid out aloft and not flaring, which is when she is a little howsing in, neere the water, and then the upper worke doth hang over againe, and is laid out broder aloft, this makes a Ship more roomy aloft for men to use their armes in, but Sir Walter Rawleighs proportion, which is to be proportionally wrought to her other worke is the best, because the counterpoise on each side doth make her swimme perpendicular or straight, and consequently steady, which is the best.

A wholsome ship.

An unwholsome Ship.

Howsing a Ship.

Flaring.

If a ship be narrow, and her bearing either not laid out enough or too low, then you must make her broader and her bearing the higher by ripping off the plankes two or [P. 53]

three strakes under water and as much above, and put
other Timbers upon the first, and then put on the plankes
upon those Timbers, this will make her beare a better
saile, but it is a hindrance to her sailing, this is to be done
Cranke side. when a Ship is cranke-sided and will beare no saile, and
Furring. is called Furring. Note also, that when a Ship hath a
deepe Keele it doth keepe her from rowling. If she be
floty and her keele shallow, put on another keele under
the first to make it deeper, for it will make her hold
A false Keele. more in the water, this wee call a false Keele. Likewise
if her stem be too flat to make her cut water the better,
Gripe. and not gripe, which is when shee will not keepe a winde
A false stem. well; fix another stem before it, and that is called a false
stem, which will make her rid more way and beare a better
The runne. saile. Also the Run of a ship is as much to be regarded,
for if it be too short and too full below, the water comes
but slowly to the Rudder because the force of it is broken
by her bredth, and then to put a false stem post to lengthen
her is the next remedy, but to lengthen her is better; for
when a Ship comes off handsomly by degrees, and her
Tuck doth not lye too low, which will hinder the water
from comming swiftly to the Rudder, makes her she cannot
A good runne. steare well, and they are called as they are, a good runne
A bad runne. or a bad. When a Ship hath lost a peece of her Keele,
and that we cannot come well to mend it, you must patch
A Stirrup. a new peece unto it, and bind it with a stirrop, which is
an iron comes round about it and the Keele up to the
other side of the Ship, whereto it is strongly nailed with
Her Rake. Spikes. Her Rake also may be a defect, which is so
much of the Hull, as by a perpendicular line the end of
the Keele is from the setting on of the stem, so much as
is without that forward on, and in like manner the setting
in of her stem Post. Your French men gives great Rakes
forwards on, which makes her give good way and keepe
a good wind, but if she have not a full bow she will pitch
her head extremely in the Sea. If shee have but a small
[P. 54] Rake, she is so bluffe that the Seas meets her so suddenly
upon the Bowes shee cannot cut the water much, but the

longer a ship is, the fuller should be her Bow, but the meane is the best. The looming of a ship is her prospective, that is, as she doth shew great or little: Her water draught is so many foot as she goes in the water, but the Ships that drawes most water are commonly the most wholsome, but the least draught goes best but rolls most, and we say a Ship doth heeld on Starboord or Larboord, that is, to that side shee doth leane most.

Loome.

Heeld.

To overset or overthrow a ship, is by bearing too much saile you bring her Keele upwards, or on shore overthrow her by grounding her, so that she falls upon one side; and we say a Ship is walt when shee is not stiffe, and hath not Ballast enough in her to keepe her stiffe. And wall reared when she is right built up, after shee comes to her bearing it makes her ill shapen and unseemely, but it gives her within much roome, and she is very wholsome, if her bearing be well laid out. The Masting of a Ship is much to be considered, and will much cause her to saile well or ill, as I have related in the masting a Ship. Iron sicke, is when the Bolts, Spikes, or Nailes are so eaten with rust they stand hollow in the plankes, and so makes her leake, the which to prevent, they use to put lead over all the bolt heads under water. Lastly, the trimming of a ship doth much amend or impaire her sailing, and so alter her condition. To finde her trim, that is, how she will saile best; is by trying her sailing with another Ship so many glasses, trimmed a head and so many a sterne, and so many upon an even Keele; also the easing of her Masts and Shrouds, for some ships will saile much better when they are slacke than when they are taught.

Overset.
Overthrow.

Walt.
Wall reared.

Iron sicke.

Trim.

[Chap. XII.

[P. 55]

Chap. XII.

Considerations for a Sea Captaine in the choise of his Ship, and in placing his Ordnance. In giving Chase, Boording, and entering a man of warre like himselfe, or a defending Merchant man.

How to chuse a Ship fit to make a man of warre.

N Land service we call a man of warre a Souldier either on foot or horse, and at Sea a Ship, which if she be not as well built, conditioned, and provided, as neere fitting such an imploiment as may be, she may prove (either) as a horseman that knoweth not how to hold his raines, keepe his seat in his saddle and stirrops, carry his body, nor how to helpe his horse with leg and spur in a curvet, gallop, or stop; or as an excellent horseman that knoweth all this, mounted upon a Jade that will doe nothing, which were he mounted according to his experience, hee would doe more with that one, than halfe a dozen of the other though as well provided as himselfe. But I confesse, every horseman cannot mount himself alike, neither every Seaman ship himselfe as he would, I meane not for outward ornament, which the better they are, the lesse to be disliked; for there cannot be a braver sight than a ship in her bravery, but of a competent sufficiency as the businesse requireth. But were I to chuse a ship for my self, I would have her saile well, yet strongly built, her decks flush and flat, and so roomy that men might passe with ease; her Bow and chase so Gally-like contrived, should beare as many Ordnances as with conveniency she
[P. 56] could, for that alwaies commeth most to fight, and so stiffe, she should beare a stiffe saile and beare out her lower

tier in any reasonable weather, neither should her Gunroome be unprovided: not manned like a Merchantman, which if they be double manned, that is, to have twise so many men as would saile her, they think it is too many in regard of the charge, yet to speake true, there is few Merchant Ships in the world doth any way exceed ours. And those men they entertaine in good voiages have such good pay, and such acquaintance one with another in shipping themselves, that thirty or forty of them would trouble a man of warre with three or foure times their number manned with prest men, being halfe of them scarce hale Boulings. Yea, and many times a Pirat who are commonly the best manned, but they fight only for wealth, not for honour nor revenge, except they bee extremely constrained. But such a Ship as I have spoken of well manned with rather too many than too few, with all sufficient Officers; Shot, Powder, Victuall, and all their appurtenances, in my opinion might well passe muster for a man of warre.

His reward that first discries a Ship, or enters a prize.

Now being at Sea, the tops are seldome without one or other to looke out for purchase, because hee that first discries a saile, if she prove prize, is to have a good sute of Aparell, or so much money as is set downe by order for his reward, as also he that doth first enter a Ship there is a certaine reward allowed him; when wee see a Ship alter her course, and useth all the meanes she can to fetch you up, you are the chase, and hee the chaser. In giving chase or chasing, or to escape being chased, there is required an infinite judgement and experience, for there is no rule for it; but the shortest way to fetch up your chase is the best. If you bee too lee-ward, get all your Tacks aboord, and shape your course as he doth to meet him at the neerest angle you can, then he must either alter his course and Tacke as you Tacke as neere the wind as he can lye to keepe his owne till night, and then strike a Hull that you may not descry him by his sailes, or doe his best to lose you in the darke; for looke how much he falls to lee-ward, hee falls so much in your way. If he be [P. 57]

How to give chase, and escape the chaser.

right ahead of you, that is called a sterne chase, if you weather him, for every man in chasing doth seeke to get the weather, because you cannot boord him except you weather him, he will laske, or goe large, if you gather on him that way, hee will trie you before the wind, then if your ordnance cannot reach him, if he can out-strip you he is gone: But suppose you are to wind-ward, if hee clap close by a wind, and there goes a head sea, and yours a lee-ward ship, if you doe the like your ship will so bear against the Sea, she will make no way; therefore you must goe a little more large though you chase under his lee till you can run ahead.

Boord & boord. Boord and Boord is when two ships lie together side by side, but hee that knoweth how to defend himselfe, and worke well, will so cun his ship, as force you to enter upon his quarter, which is the highest part of the ship, and but the mizen shrouds to enter by; from whence he may do you much hurt with little danger, except you fire him, which a Pirat will never doe, neither sinke you if he can chuse, except you be able to force him to defend himselfe. But in a Sea fight wee call Boording, in Boording where wee can, the greatest advantage for your Ordnance is to boord him thwart the hawse, because you may use all the ordnance you have on one side, and she onely them in her prow; but the best and safest boording for entring is on the bow, but you must be carefull to cleare the decks with burning granados, fire-pots, poutches of powder, to which give fire by a Gunpowder match, to prevent traines to the powder chest, which are long boards joyned like a triangle with divers broad ledges on either side, wherein lieth as many peeble stones or beatch as can there lie, those being fired will make all cleare before them. Besides in an extremity a man would rather blow up the quarter decke, halfe decke, fore castle, or any thing, than bee taken by him he knowes a mortall enemy, and commonly there is more men lost in entering, if the chase stand to her defence, in an instant, than in a long fight boord and boord, if she be provided of her close fights:

Boording & entering a ship.

Powder chests.

[P. 58]

I confesse, the charging upon trenches, and the entrances of a breach in a rampire are attempts as desperate as a man would thinke could be performed, but he that hath tried himselfe as oft in the entring a resisting ship as I have done both them & the other, he would surely confesse there is no such dangerous service ashore, as a resolved resolute fight at sea. A ships close fights, are smal ledges of wood laid crosse one another like the grates of iron in a prisons window, betwixt the maine mast, and the fore mast, & are called gratings, or nettings as is said, which are made of small ropes, much in like manner covered with a saile, the which to undoe is to heave a kedger, or fix a grapling into them, tied in a rope, but a chaine of iron is better, and shearing off will teare it in peeces if the rope and anchor hold, some have used sheare hookes, which are hookes like sickels fixed in the ends of the yards armes, that if a ship under saile come to boord her, those sheares will cut her shrouds, and spoile her tackling, but they are so subject to breake their owne yards, and cut all the ropes comes from the top-sailes, they are out of request. To conclude, if a ship bee open, presently to boord her is the best way to take her. But if you see your chase strip himselfe into fighting sailes, that is to put out his colours in the poope, his flag in the maine top, his streamers or pendants at the ends of his yards armes, furle his spret-saile, pike his mizen, and sling his maine yard, provide your selfe to fight. Now because I would not bee tedious in describing a fight at Sea, I have troubled you with this short preamble that you may the plainlier understand it.

Evident signes that a chase will fight.

[Chap. XIII.

[P. 59]

Chap. XIII.

How to manage a fight at Sea, with the proper tearmes in a fight largely expressed, and the ordering of a Navy at Sea.

Many bookes of the Art of War for the land, none for the sea.

FOr this master peece of this worke, I confesse I might doe better to leave it to every particular mans conceit as it is, or those of longer practice or more experience; yet because I have seene many bookes of the Art of Warre by land, and never any for the Sea, seeing all men so silent in this most difficult service, and there are so many young Captaines, and others that desire to be Captains, who know very little, or nothing at all to any purpose, for their better understanding I have proceeded thus farre; now for this that followes, what I have seene, done, and conceived by my small experience, I referre me to their friendly constructions, and well advised considerations.

A saile, how beares she or stands shee, to wind-ward or lee-ward, set him by the Compasse; he stands right ahead, or on the weather-Bow, or lee-Bow, let flie your colours if you have a consort, else not. Out with all your sailes, a steady man to the helme, sit close to keepe

To give chase.

her steady, give him chase or fetch him up; hee holds his owne, no, we gather on him. Captaine, out goes his

Wast clothes. Top armings.

flag and pendants, also his waste clothes and top armings, which is a long red cloth about three quarters of a yard broad, edged on each side with Calico or white linnen cloth, that goeth round about the ship on the out sides of all her upper workes fore and aft, and before the cubbridge

[P. 60]

heads, also about the fore and maine tops, as well for the

countenance and grace of the ship, as to cover the men for being seene, hee furles and slings his maine yard, in goes his spret-saile. Thus they use to strip themselves into their short sailes, or fighting sailes, which is onely the fore saile, the maine and fore top sailes, because the rest should not be fired nor spoiled; besides they would be troublesome to handle, hinder our sights and the using our armes; he makes ready his close fights fore and aft.

Fighting sailes.

To hale a ship.

How to begin a fight.

Master how stands the chase? Right on head I say; Well we shall reatch him by and by; What's all ready, Yea, yea, every man to his charge, dowse your top-saile to salute him for the Sea, hale him with a noise of trumpets; Whence is your ship? Of Spaine; Whence is yours? Of England; Are you a Merchant, or a man of War? We are of the Sea; He waves us to lee-ward with his drawne sword, cals amaine for the King of Spaine, and springs his loufe, give him a chase peece with your broad side, and run a good berth ahead of him; Done, done, We have the wind of him, and he tackes about, tacke you about also and keepe your loufe, be yare at the helme, edge in with him, give him a volley of small shot, also your prow and broad side as before, and keepe your loufe; Hee payes us shot for shot; Well, wee shall require him; What are you ready againe, Yea, yea. Try him once more as before, Done, done; Keepe your loufe and loge your ordnance againe; Is all ready? Yea, yea; edge in with him againe, begin with your bow peeces, proceed with your broad side, & let her fall off with the wind, to give her also your full chase, your weather broad side, and bring her round that the sterne may also discharge, and your tackes close aboord againe; Done, done, the wind veeres, the Sea goes too high to boord her, and wee are shot thorow and thorow, and betweene wind and water. Try the pump, beare up the helme, Master let us breathe and refresh a little, and sling a man over boord to stop the leakes; that is, to trusse him up about the middle in a peece of canvas, and a rope to keepe him from sinking, and his armes at liberty, with a

How to fling a man over boord.

[P. 61]

malet in the one hand, & a plug lapped in Okum, and well tarred in a tarpawling clout in the other, which he will quickly beat into the hole or holes the bullets made; What cheere mates, is all well? All well, all well, all well; Then make ready to beare up with him againe, and withall your great and small shot charge him, and in the smoke boord him thwart the hawse, on the bow, mid ships, or rather then faile, on his quarter, or make fast your graplings if you can to his close fights and sheare off. Captaine we are fowle on each other, and the ship is on fire, cut any thing to get cleare, and smother the fire with wet cloathes. In such a case they will presently be such friends, as to help one the other all they can to get cleare, lest they both should burne together and sinke; and if they be generous, the fire quenched, drinke kindely one to another; heave their cans over boord, and then begin againe as before.

A consultation & direction in a sea fight, & how they bury their dead.

Well Master, the day is spent, the night drawes on, let us consult. Chirurgion looke to the wounded, and winde up the slaine, with each a weight or bullet at their heads and feet to make them sinke, and give them three gunnes for their funerals, Swabber make cleane the ship, Purser record their Names, Watch be vigilant to keepe your berth to wind-ward that we lose him not in the night, Gunners spunge your Ordnance, Souldiers scowre your peeces, Carpenters about your leakes, Boatswaine and the rest repaire the sailes and shrouds, and Cooke see you observe your directions against the morning watch, Boy, Holla Master Holla, is the kettle boiled, yea, yea, Boatswaine call up the men to prayer and breake fast.

A preparation for a fresh charge.

Boy fetch my cellar of bottels, a health to you all fore and aft, courage my hearts for a fresh charge, Gunners beat open the ports, and out with your lower tire, and bring me from the weather side to the lee, so many peeces as we have ports to beare upon him, Master lay him aboord loufe for loufe, mid ships men see the tops and yards well manned, with stones, fire pots, and brasse bailes, to throw amongst them before we enter, or if we be put off, charge them with all your great and small shot, in the smoke let us enter them in the shrouds, and every squadron at his [P. 62] best advantage, so sound Drums and Trumpets, and Saint George for England.

How a prise doth yeeld, and how to entertaine him Sea-man like.

They hang out a flag of truce, hale him a maine, a base, or take in his flag, strike their sailes and come aboord with their Captaine, Purser and Gunner, with their commission, cocket, or bils of loading. Out goes the boat, they are lanched from the ship side, entertaine them with a generall cry, God save the Captaine and all the company with the Trumpets sounding, examine them in particular, and then conclude your conditions, with feasting, freedome, or punishment, as you finde occasion; but alwayes have as much care to their wounded as your owne, and if there be either young women or aged men, use them nobly, which is ever the nature of a generous disposition. To conclude, if you surprize him, or enter perforce, you may stow the men, rifle, pillage, or sacke, and cry a prise.

How to call a Counsell of War, and order a Navy at Sea.

To call a Councell of Warre in a Fleet; There is your Councell of Warre to manage all businesses of import, and the common Councell for matters of small moment, when they would have a meeting, where the Admirall doth appoint it; if in the Admirall, they hang out a flag in the maine shrouds; if in the Vice Admirall, in the fore shrouds; if in the Reare Admirall, in the mizen; If there bee many squadrons, the Admirall of each squadron upon sundry occasions doth carry in their maine tops, flags of sundry colours, or else they are distinguished by severall pendants from the yards armes; every night or morning they are to come under the Lee of the Admirall to salute him and know his pleasure, but no Admirall of any squadron is to beare his flag in the maine top, in the presence of the Admirall generall, except the Admirall come aboord of him to Councell, to dinner, or collation, and so any ship else where he so resideth during that time, is to weare his flag in the maine top. They use to martiall or order those squadrons in rankes like Manaples, which is foure square, if the wind and Sea permits, a good

[P. 63] berth or distance from each other, that they becalme not one another, nor come not fowle of each other; the Generall commonly in the middest, his Vice Admirall in the front, and his Reare Admirall in the Reare; or otherwise like a halfe Moone, which is two squadrons like two triangles for the two hornes, and so the rest of the squadrons behinde each other a good distance, and the Generall in the middest of the halfe circle, from whence he seeth all his fleet, and sendeth his directions, as he findes occasion to whom he pleaseth.

Stratagems for Sea-men.

Now betweene two Navies they use often, especially in a harbour or road where they are at anchor, to fill old Barkes with pitch, tar, traine oile, lincet oile, brimstone, rosen, reeds, with dry wood, and such combustible things, sometimes they linke three or foure together in the night, and puts them adrift as they finde occasion. To passe a fort some will make both ship and sailes all black, but if the fort keepe but a fire on the other side, and all the peeces point blanke with the fire, if they discharge what is betwixt them and the fire, the shot will hit if the rule bee truly observed; for when a ship is betwixt the fire and you, shee doth keepe you from seeing it till shee bee past it. To conclude, there is as many stratagems, advantages, and inventions to be used as you finde occasions, and therefore experience must be the best Tutor.

Chap. XIV.

[P. 64]

The names of all sorts of great Ordnance, and their appurteances, with their proper tearmes and expositions, also divers observations concerning their shooting, with a Table of proportion for their weight of metall, weight of powder, weight of shot, and there best at randome and point blanke inlarged.

The Names of great Ordnance. A Canon royal, or double Canon, a Canon, a Canon Serpentine, a bastard Canon, a demy Canon, a Canon Petro, a Culvering, a Basilisco, a demy culvering, a bastard Culvering, a Sacar, a Minion, a Falcon, a Falconet, a Serpentine, a Rabbinet. To all those doe belong carriages whereon *Carriages.* peeces doe lie supported by an axeltree betwixt two wheeles, whereon doth lie the peece upon her trunnions, *Trunnions.* which are two knobs cast with the peece on each of her sides, which doth lie in two halfe holes upon the two cheekes of the carriages, to raise her up or downe as you will, over them are the capsquares, which are two broad *Capsquares.* peeces of iron doth cover them, made fast by a pin with a fore locke to keepe the peece from falling out. That the peece and carriages is drawne along upon wheeles every *Wheeles.* one doth know, if she bee for land service, they have wheeles made with spokes like coach wheeles, and according to their proportion strongly shod with iron, and the [P. 65] pins at the ends of the Axeltree is called Linch pins.

Trucks. If for Sea she have Trucks, which are round intier peeces of wood like wheeles. *To mount a Peece.* To mount a peece is to lay her upon her carriages; *To dismount a Peece.* to dismount her to take her downe. *Beds.* Her Bed is a planke doth lie next the peece, or the peece

Quoines. *Travas.* *Dispert.* *Britch.* *Carnouse.* *Musell.*

upon it upon the carriage, and betwixt the Peece and it they put their quoines, which are great wedges of wood with a little handle at the end to put them forward or backward for levelling the Peece as you please. To travas a Peece is to turne her which way you will upon her Platforme. To dispert a Peece is to finde a difference betwixt the thicknesse of the metall at her mouth and britch or carnouse, which is the greatest circle about her britch, and her mussell Ring is the greatest circle about her mouth thereby to make a just shot, there are divers waies to dispert her, but the most easiest is as good as the best: and that is but by putting a little sticke or a straw that is strait into the toutch hole to the lower part of the Sillinder or Concave, which is the bore of the Peece and cut it off close by the metall, and then apply it in the same manner to the mouth, and it will exactly shew you the difference, which being set upon the mussell of the Peece with a little Clay, Pitch, or Wax, it will bee as the pin of any Peece is to the sight, levell to the carnouse or britch of the Peece, otherwaies you may give her allowance according to your judgement.

Sillender. *Concave.* *Bore.* *How to dispert a Peece.*

Taper boared. *Hony-combe.*

Taper boared, is when a Peece is wider at the mouth then towards the britch, which is dangerous (if the Bullet goe not home) to burst her. Honicombed, is when shee is ill cast or overmuch worne shee will bee rugged within, which is dangerous for a crosse barre shot to catch hold by, or any ragge of her wadding being a fire and sticking there may fire the next charge you put in her; and you may finde if she be Taper boared, either with a crooked wyer at the end of a long staffe, by scratching up and downe to see where you can catch any hold, or a light candle at the end of a staffe thrust up and down to see if you can see any fault. Britchings are the ropes by which you lash your Ordnance fast to the Ships side in foule weather. Chambers is a charge made of brasse or iron which we use to put in at the britch of a sling or Murtherer, containing just so much powder as will drive away the case of stones or shot, or any thing in her. In

How to finde it. *Britchings.* [P. 66] *Chambers.*

a great Peece we call that her Chamber so far as the powder doth reach when she is laded.

A Cartrage is a bagge of Canvasse made upon a frame or a round peece of wood somewhat lesse than the bore of the Peece, they make them also of paper, they have also Cartrages or rather cases for Cartrages made of Lattin to keepe the Cartrages in, which is to have no more powder in them than just the charge of your Peece, and they are closely covered in those cases of Latten, to keepe them dry, and from any mischances by fire, and are farre more ready and safer than your Ladles or Budgbarrels. A Budgbarrell is a little Barrell made of Latten, filled with powder to carry from place to place for feare of fire; in the cover it hath a long necke to fill the Ladles withall without opening. A Ladle is a long staffe with a peece of thin Copper at the end like halfe a Cartrage, in bredth and length so much as will hold no more powder than the due charge for the Peece it belongs to. A Spunge is such another staffe, with a peece of a Lambe skin at the end about it to thrust up and downe the Peece, to take off the dust, moisture, or sparkes of fire if any remaine in her. And a Rammer is a bob of wood at the other end to ramme home the Powder and the Waddings. Waddings is Okum, old clouts, or straw, put after the powder and the Bullet. A Case is made of two peeces of hollow wood joyned together like two halfe Cartrages fit to put into the bore of a Peece, & a case shot is any kinde of small Bullets, Nailes, old iron, or the like to put into the case to shoot out of the Ordnances or Murderers, these will doe much mischiefe when wee lie boord and boord: but for Spunges and Rammers they use now a stiffe Rope a little more than the length of the Peece, which you may turne and wind within boord as you will, with much more ease and safety than the other.

Cartrages. *Cases.* *A Budgbarell.* *A Ladle.* *A Spunge.* *A Rammer.* *Waddings.* *Wood cases.* *Case shot.*

Round Shot is a round Bullet for any Peece: Crosbar-shot is also a round shot, but it hath a long spike of Iron cast with it as if it did goe thorow the middest of it, the

[P. 67] *Round shot.* *Crosse bar shot.*

To Arme a shot. ends whereof are commonly armed for feare of bursting the Peece, which is to binde a little Okum in a little *Trundle shot.* Canvasse at the end of each Pike. Trundle shot is onely a bolt of iron sixteene or eighteene inches in length; at both ends sharpe pointed, and about a handfull from each end a round broad bowle of lead according to the bore *Langrill shot.* of the Peece cast upon it. Langrell shot runnes loose with a shackell, to be shortened when you put it into the Peece, and when it flies out it doth spred it selfe, it hath at the end of either barre a halfe Bullet either of lead *Chaine shot.* or iron. Chaine shot is two bullets with a chaine betwixt them, and some are contrived round as in a ball, yet will spred in flying their full length in bredth; all these are used when you are neere a ship to shoot downe Masts, Yards, Shrouds, teare the sailes, spoile the men, or any *Fire workes.* thing that is above the decks. Fireworkes are divers, *Arrowes of wild fire.* and of many compositions, as Arrowes trimmed with wild fire to sticke in the sailes or ships side shot burning. *Pikes of wild fire.* Pikes of wild fire to strike burning into a ship side to *Granados of divers sorts.* fire her. There is also divers sorts of Granados, some to breake and fly in abundance of peeces every way, as *Brasse Balles.* will your brasse balls & earthen pots which when they are covered with quartered bullets stucke in pitch, and the pots filled with good powder, in a crowd of people will make an incredible slaughter; some will burne under water, and never extinguish till the stuffe bee consumed; some onely will burne and fume out a most stinking poison smoke; some, being but onely an Oile, being nointed on any thing made of dry wood, will take fire by the heat of the Sunne when the Sunne shines hot. There is also a Powder, which being laid in like manner upon any thing subject to burne, will take fire if either any raine or water light upon it; but those inventions are bad on shore, but much worse at Sea, and are naught because so dangerous, and not easie to bee quenched, and [P. 68] their practise worse, because they may doe as much mischiefe to a friend as to an enemy, therefore I will leave them as they are.

There are also divers sorts of Powder, the Serpentine is like dust and weake, and will not keepe at Sea but be moist. The common sort is great corned powder but grosse, and onely used in great Ordnance. Your fine corned Powder for hand Guns is in goodnesse as your Salt Peter is oft refined, and from ten pence a pound to eighteene pence a pound. *Powder. Serpentine powder. Grosse corned Powder. Fine corned Powder.*

A Tomkin is a round peece of wood put into the Peeces mouth and covered with Tallow, and a fid a little Okum made like a naile put in at the toutch hole, and covered with a thin lead bound above it to keepe the Powder dry in the Peece. Shackels are a kinde of Rings but not round, made like them at the hatches cornes (by which we take them up and lay them downe) but bigger, fixed to the middest of the ports within boord, through which wee put a billet to keepe fast the port for flying open in foule weather, which may easily indanger, if not sinke the Ship. To cloy or poison a Peece, is to drive a naile into her toutch hole, then you cannot give fire. And to uncloy her, is to put as much oile as you can about the naile to make it glib, and by a traine give fire to her by her mouth, and so blow it out. *A Tomkin. A Fid. Shackels. To cloy a Peece or poyson her. To uncloy.*

Compasse Callipers belongs to the Gunner, and is like two halfe Circles that hath a handle and joint like a paire of Compasses, but they are blunt at the points to open as you please for to dispert a Peece. A Horne is his touch box, his Primer is a small long peece of iron, sharpe at the small end to pierce the Cartrage thorow the toutch hole. His Lint stock is a handsome carved stick, more than halfe a yard long, with a Cocke at the one end to hold fast his Match, and a sharpe pike in the other to sticke it fast upon the Deck or platforme upright. The Gunners quadrant is to levell a Peece or mount her to any randon. A darke Lanthorne is as well to be used by any body as he. For Morters, or such chambers as are only used for triumphs, there is no use for them in this service; but for Curriours Hargabusacrocks, Muskets, Bastard-muskets, Colivers, Crabuts, Carbins, *Compasse Callipers. Horne. Priming Iron. Lint stocke. Gunners quadrant. Darke Lanthorne. Morters. The names of small Peeces, and their implements.* [P. 69]

Bandilers. Bullet bags. Wormes. Scowrers. Melting Ladles. Lead Molds. Quartered shot.

long Pistols or short Pistols, there belongs to them Bandiliers, bullet Bags, Wormes, Scowrers, melting Ladles, Lead, Molds of al sorts to cast their shot. Quarter Bullets is but any bullet quartered in foure or eight parts, and all those are as usefull a ship-boord as on shore. For the soule, trunke, bore, fortification, the diversity of their metals, and divers other curious Theormes or tearmes used about great Ordnance, there are so many uncertainties as well in her mounting, levelling upon her platforme, as also the accidents that may happen in the powder, the ground, the aire, and differences in proportion, I will not undertake to prescribe any certaine artificiall rule. These proportions following are neere the matter, but for your better satisfaction reade Master Digs Pantrimetria, Master Smith, or Master Burnes art of Gunnery, or Master Robert Nortons Exposition upon Master Digs Stratiaticos, any of those will shew the Theoricke at large. But to bee a good Gunner you must learne it by practise.

[P. 71] Note that seldome in Ships they use any Ordnance greater than Demy Canons, nor have they any certainty either at point blanke or any random.

Note your Serpentine powder in old time was in meale, but now corned and made stronger, and called Canon corne powder.

But that for small Ordnance is called corne Powder fine, and ought to have in strength a quarter more, because those small Peeces are better fortified than the greater.

Now if you have but one sort of Powder for all, abate 1/4 part, and cut off 1/4 of the bredth and length of your Ladle.

But Cartrages are now found the best and most readiest.

Provided alwaies, that all Shot must be a quarter lesse than the height of the Peece.

[P. 70]

A Table of proportion for the weight and shooting of great Ordnance.

		The names of the great Peeces.	The height of the peeces.	The weight of the peeces.	The weight of the shot.	The weight of the powder.	The bredth of the Ladle.	The length of the Ladle.	2400. ll. of powder makes of shot in a	Shot point blanke in	Shot randome in
			Inches.	Pound.	Pound.	Pound.	Inches.	Inches.	Peece.	Paces.	Paces.
These Peeces be most serviceable for battery, being within 80. paces to their marke, which is the chiefe of their forces.	1	A Canon Royall.	8½	8000	66	30	13¼	24⅛	80	16	1930
	2	A Canon.	8	6000	60	27	12	24	85	17	2000
	3	A Canon Sarpentine.	7½	5500	53⅛	25	10½	23⅛	96	20	2000
	4	A Bastard Canon.	7	4500	41¼	20	10	23⅓	120	18	1800
	5	A demy Canon.	6½	4000	30¼	18	9⅛	23¼	133	17	1700
	6	A Canon Petro.	6	3000	24¼	14	9	23	171	16	1600
These Peeces be good and also serviceable to be mixt with the above Ordnance for battery to peeces being crost with the rest, as also fit for Castles, Forts, and Walls to be planted, and for defence.	7	A Culvering.	5½	4500	17⅓	12	8½	22⅓	200	20	2500
	8	A Basilisco.	5	4000	15¼	10	7½	22	240	25	3000
	9	A demy Culvering.	4½	3400	9⅓	8	6⅕	21	300	20	2500
	10	A bastard Culvering.	4	3000	7	6¼	6	20	388	18	1800
	11	A Sacre.	3½	1400	5⅓	5⅛	5½	18	490	17	1700
	12	A Minion.	3¼	1000	4	4	4½	17	600	16	1600
	13	A Faulcon.	2½	660	2¼	2¼	4¼	15	1087	15	1500
	14	A Faulcon.	2⅓	800	3	3	4¼	15	800	15	1500
These Peeces are good and serviceable for the field, and most ready for defence.	15	A Faulconet.	2	500	1¼	1¼	3¼	11¼	1950	14	1400
	16	A Sarpentine.	1½	400	⅓	⅛	2½	10	7200	13	1300
	17	A Rabonet.	1	300	½	½	1½	6	4800	12	1000

[P. 72]

Chap. XV.

How they divide their shares in a man of Warre, what Bookes and Instruments are fit for a Sea-man, with divers advertisements for Sea men, and the use of the petty Tally.

THe ship hath one third part, the victuallar the other third, the other third part is for the Company, and

Shares. this is subdivided thus in shares.

The Captain hath	10	- - -	In some but 9.
The Lieutenant	9	or as he agreeth with the Captaine.	
The Master -	8	- - -	In some but 7.
The Mates -	7	- - - - - -	5.
The Chirurgion	6	- - - - - -	3.
The Gunner -	6	- - - - - -	5.
The Boatswaine	6	- - - - - -	5.
The Carpenter	6	- - - - - -	5.
The Trumpeter	6	- - - - - -	5.
The 4.quarter Mast.	5	apeece, or - - - - -	4.
The Cooper -	5	- - - - - -	4.
The Chirurg. Mate	5	- - - - - -	4.
The Gunners Mate	5	- - - - - -	4.
The Carpent. Mate	5	- - - - - -	4.
The Corporall -	4	- - - - - -	3.
The quarter Gunners	4	- - - - - -	3.
The Trump. Mate	3	- - - - -	3 ½.
The Steward -	4	- - - - - -	3.
The Cooke -	4	- - - - - -	3.
The Coxswaine	4	- - - - - -	3.
The Swabber -	4	- - - - - -	3.

[P. 83] In English ships they seldome use any Marshall, whose shares amongst the French is equall with the Boatswaines, all the rest of the Younkers, or fore-mast-men according to their deserts, some 3. some 2. and ½. some 1. and ½. and the boyes 1. which is a single share, or 1. and ½. or as they doe deserve.

Now the Master, or his right hand Mate, the Gunner, Boatswaine, and foure quarter Masters doe make the shares, not the Captaine, who hath onely this privilege, to take away halfe a share, or a whole share at most, to give from one to another as he best pleaseth.

For to learne to observe the Altitude, Latitude, Longitude, Amplitude, the variation of the Compasse, the Suns Azimuth and Almicanter, to shift the Sunne and Moone, and know the tides, your Roomes, pricke your Card, say your Compasse, and get some of these bookes, but practice is the best.

Master Wrights errours of Navigation.
Master Tapps Sea-mans Kalender.
The Art of Navigation.
The Sea Regiment.
The Sea-mans secret.
Waggoner.
Master Gunters workes.
The Sea-mans glasse for the Scale.
The New Attracter for variation.
Master Wright for use of the Globe.
Master Hewes for the same.

Instruments fitting for a Sea-man.

Compasses so many paire and sorts as you will, an Astrolobe Quadrant, a Crosse staffe, a Backe staffe, an Astrolobe, a Nocturnall. [P. 84]

Advertisments for young Commanders, Captaines, and other Officers.

Young Gentlemen that desires command at Sea, ought well to consider the condition of his ship, victuall, and company, for if there be more learners than sailers how slightly soever many esteeme sailers, all the worke to save, ship, goods, and lives must lie upon them, especially in fowle weather, then their labour, hazzard, wet, and cold, is so incredible I cannot expresse it. It is not then the number of them that here can say at home what I cannot doe I can quickly learne, and what a great matter is it to saile a ship, or goe to Sea; surely those for a good time will doe more trouble than good, I confesse it is most necessary such should goe, but not too many in one ship; for if the labour of threescore should lie upon thirty, (as many times it doth) they are so over-charged with labour, bruises, and overstraining themselves they fall sick of one disease or other, for there is no dallying nor excuses with stormes, gusts, overgrowne Seas, and lee-shores, and when their victuall is putrified it endangers all: Men of all other professions in lightning, thunder, stormes, and tempests with raine and snow may shelter themselves in dry houses by good fires, but those are the chiefe times Sea-men must stand to their tackling, and attend with all diligence their greatest labour upon the deckes. Many suppose any thing is good enough to serve men at sea, and yet nothing sufficient for them ashore, either for their healthes, for their ease, or estates, or state; A Commander at Sea should doe well to thinke the contrary, and provide for himselfe and company in like manner; also seriously to consider what will bee his charge to furnish himselfe at Sea with bedding, linnen, armes, and apparrell, how to keepe his table aboord, and his expences on shore, and provide his petty Tally, which is a competent proportion according to your number of these particulars following.

The petty Tally. Fine wheat flower close and well packed, Rice, Currands, Sugar, Prunes, Cynamon, Ginger, Pepper, Cloves, greene Ginger, Oyle, Butter, Holland cheese, or
[P. 85] old Cheese, Wine vinegar, Canarie sacke, Aqua vitæ, the best Wines, the best waters, the juyce of Limons for the scurvy, white Bisket, Oatmeale, gammons of Bacon, dried Neats tongues, Beefe packed up in vineger, Legs of Mutton minced and stewed, and close packed up, with tried sewet or butter in earthen pots. To entertaine

strangers Marmalad, Suckets, Almonds, Comfits and such like.

The use of the petty Tally.

Some it may be will say I would have men rather to feast than fight; But I say the want of those necessaries occasions the losse of more men than in any English fleet hath beene slaine since 88. For when a man is ill, or at the point of death, I would know whether a dish of buttered Rice with a little Cynamon, Ginger, and Sugar, a little minced meat, or rost Beefe, a few stewed Prunes, a race of greene Ginger, a Flap-jacke, a can of fresh Water brewed with a little Cinamon, Ginger, and Sugar bee not better than a little poore John, or salt fish with oile and mustard, or bisket, butter, cheese, or oatmeale pottage on fish dayes, or on flesh dayes salt Beefe, Porke, and Pease with six shillings beere, this is your ordinary ships allowance, and good for them are well if well conditioned, which is not alwayes as Sea-men can (too well) witnesse. And after a storme, when poore men are all wet, and some have not so much as a cloth to shift him, shaking with cold, few of those but wil tell you a little Sacke or Aqua vitæ is much better to keepe them in health, than a little small beere, or cold water although it be sweet. Now that every one should provide those things for himselfe, few of them have either that providence or meanes, and there is neither Ale-house, Taverne, nor Inne to burne a faggot in, neither Grocer, Poulterer, Apothecary, nor Butchers shop, and therefore the use of this petty Tally is necessary, and thus to be imploied as there is occasion. To entertaine strangers as they are in quality every Commander should shew himselfe as like himselfe as he can, as well for the credit of the ship, and his setters forth, as [P. 86] himselfe; but in that herein every one may moderate themselves according to their owne pleasures, therefore I leave it to their owne discretions, and this briefe discourse, and my selfe to their friendly construction, and good opinion.

FINIS.

Index

This Index has been prepared by Madame Marie Michon, whose care in preparing the Indices of 'Hakluyt's Voyages,' and of 'Purchas His Pilgrimes,' the Publishers have had occasion to acknowledge in other volumes of this Series.

INDEX

INDEX

INDEX

INDEX

INDEX

INDEX

INDEX

INDEX

INDEX

INDEX

19 07
UNIVERSITY·PRESS
GLASGOW

Printed in the United States
80777LV00004B/103-120